Praise for *The Universe Bends Toward Justice*

"Obery Hendricks is one of the last few grand prophetic scholars in these dark and difficult times. This book exemplifies his courageous and visionary vision. Don't miss it."   —**Cornel West,** Princeton University

"Only a scholar with the intellectual versatility and depth of Obery Hendricks could create this provocative and passionate critique of philosophies, policies, and practices that masquerade as Christian and conservative but show no mercy and do great harm to the poor, the elderly, and the very young. Hendricks mounts an innovative and informed analysis that dissects political economy, history, and biblical studies and makes plain the failings of those who profess charity but do not perform it. He calls on all of us to work to 'secure for one's neighbor what one wants for oneself.'"
—**Barbara D. Savage,** author, *Your Spirits Walk Beside Us:
The Politics of Black Religion*

"Obery Hendricks has written a tour de force, exposing the American conservative movement for its ability to use Christian rhetoric to hide the most unchristian behavior. Juxtaposing biblical and historical evidence with the rampant greed and self aggrandizement of the American right, Hendricks demolishes the ideas put forth by both the business community and prominent conservatives that there is even an iota of the teachings of Jesus Christ that could justify what they are doing to their fellow human beings."   —**Gov. Howard Dean,** former chair,
Democratic National Committee

"This is a dense and ambitious exploration of the most politically relevant aspects of the Christian Gospel. Hendricks is unflinching in his criticism of conservative impulses in the church and in the government that prey on the most vulnerable. He applies his keen insight to gospel recording artists, prosperity preachers, and Bible-thumping politicians with the same tenacious insistence on reading history from the bottom up. *The Universe Bends Toward Justice* is an important contribution to the American jeremiad."   —**Melissa Harris-Perry,** Director of
Anna Julia Cooper Project on Gender, Race,
and Politics in the South, Tulane University

D0916406

THE UNIVERSE
BENDS TOWARD
JUSTICE

Radical Reflections
on the Bible, the Church,
and the Body Politic

OBERY M. HENDRICKS, JR.

ORBIS BOOKS
Maryknoll, New York 10545

Founded in 1970, Orbis Books endeavors to publish works that enlighten the mind, nourish the spirit, and challenge the conscience. The publishing arm of the Maryknoll Fathers and Brothers, Orbis seeks to explore the global dimensions of the Christian faith and mission, to invite dialogue with diverse cultures and religious traditions, and to serve the cause of reconciliation and peace. The books published reflect the views of their authors and do not represent the official position of the Maryknoll Society. To learn more about Maryknoll and Orbis Books, please visit our website at *www.maryknollsociety.org*.

Copyright © 2011 by Obery M. Hendricks, Jr.

Published by Orbis Books, Maryknoll, New York 10545-0302.

Queries regarding rights and permissions should be addressed to
Orbis Books, P.O. Box 302, Maryknoll, NY 10545-0302.

Manufactured in the United States of America.

Hendricks, Obery M. (Obery Mack), 1953–
    The universe bends toward justice : radical reflections on the Bible, the church, and the body politic / Obery M. Hendricks, Jr.
        p.   cm.
    Includes bibliographical references and index.
    ISBN 978-1-57075-940-6 (pbk.)
    1. Christianity and politics – United States. 2. Christian sociology – United States.   I. Title.
BR526.H38 2011
261′.1097309051 – dc22   :,   2011014863

For my daughters, Tahirah, Serena, and Nygia
May you always know love, and may you always love justice

When our days become dreary with low-hovering clouds of despair, and when our nights become darker than a thousand midnights, let us remember that there is a creative force in this universe working to pull down the gigantic mountains of evil, a power that is able to make a way out of no way and transform dark yesterdays into bright tomorrows. Let us realize the arc of the moral universe is long, but it bends toward justice.

—MARTIN LUTHER KING, JR.

Contents

Acknowledgments

Many people have helped to bring this project to fruition. Thanks to those who read and offered valuable insights to various chapters, including Robert Jones, CEO of Public Religion Research Institute, on whose board I am honored to sit; Daniel Maguire, professor of ethics at Marquette University; Marc Favreau, editorial director of the New Press; the brilliant and unfailingly gracious literary agent Faith Childs; my friend and former professor Cornel West, for critical insights on the philosophy of John Rawls; and my former New York Theological Seminary student Al Bunis, who, by the way, recently forsook a Wall Street vice-presidency to become a pastor dedicated to building a fair, just, and loving world. Thanks also to the students in my "Politics of Jesus" seminar at New York Theological Seminary for our challenging discussions of theories of justice, which have helped to inform this project. Proud thanks to my stepson, Samson Hearns, for our inspiring dialogues on Baruch Spinoza and Rawlsian egalitarianism. Also many thanks for their encouragement to my colleagues both at New York Theological Seminary and the Department of Religion and the Institute for Research in African American Studies at Columbia University, with special thanks to Josef Sorett, my co-teacher of "The Religions of Harlem" at Columbia, and to our stellar teaching assistant, Joe Blankholm, for having my back while I completed this manuscript. And a special word of appreciation to Robert Ellsberg, publisher of Orbis Books, for his keen professional instincts and passion for justice that helped to shape this book.

There are others who have been important to this project yet have no inkling of it. These include the biblical scholars Richard A. Horsley and Walter Brueggemann, who each in his work has highlighted the crucial interplay of the prophetic and the political in biblical discourse and demonstrated its significance for our contemporary moment; and the economists Jeffrey Sachs and Paul Krugman, for placing the so-called "dismal science" at the service of social justice, economic fairness, and human wholeness.

No matter how great our other influences, in the final analysis it is those we consider family who make the greatest difference in what we do. For me, first among these are my late parents, Willie Beatrice Hendricks and Obery M. Hendricks Sr., neither of whom I remember ever using the term "social justice," yet who through precept and practice imparted to me a sense of what is fair and right that is as profound as the musings of any philosopher. Also, I owe real thanks to my sister, Linda Hendricks-Motley, and my college ensconced daughter, Serena, who both, with good humor, tolerated the frequent lacunae in our communications while I grudgingly bowed to the temporary tyranny of these pages. And much love and appreciation to my daughter Tahirah; my irrepressible granddaughters, Diata and Mariam; and my ageless mother-in-law, Mena Griffin, for their tolerance, understanding, and willingness to share me with my work during our Martha's Vineyard vacations. Finally, I am eternally grateful to my brilliant wife, Dr. Farah Jasmine Griffin, my primary interlocutor and dialogue partner, for her profoundly loving support and her inspiring intellectual companionship. This project, like my life, would be greatly impoverished without her.

OMH
New York City
May 2011

Introduction

We are living in insane times. Like purveyors of a bad Orwellian joke, the religious right and right-wing politicians have hijacked the meanings of justice and equity and cynically perverted them into their very opposites. The Hebrew Bible and the Gospel of Jesus both command all who hold them dear to care for the poor, the weak, and the vulnerable, yet right-wing politicians and "prosperity" preachers shamelessly interpret the Bible in ways that serve America's rich and ignore the suffering of its poor. Right-wingers piously proclaim themselves to be "pro-life Christians," yet their concern for life seems to wane at the womb; their "pro-life" piety cuts funding for childhood care and education, treats undocumented immigrants like lesser forms of life, and hungers after unprovoked wars of domination, while casually speaking in murderous metaphors and loudly advocating homicidal assault weapons and "Second Amendment remedies."

These "Christians" and "people of faith" routinely — and quite publicly — shed tears for love of God and country, yet fight tooth and nail against consumer regulations that would protect the future well-being of their fellow citizens from the devastation that Wall Street has wrought upon them in the past. They give preferential treatment to the very richest Americans, holding corporate interests as sacrosanct, while doing their utmost to dismantle the social safety net that is the last line of aid and succor for the struggling American masses. Although the Hebrew Bible enjoins honesty and truthfulness (*'emet*) in social as well as in personal dealings, right-wing prognosticators cynically purvey untruths and distortions of political realities daily, with whole television networks at their disposal. The hegemonic reach of their influence has become so great that they have convinced untold millions of rank-and-file Americans to support attitudes, measures, and policies that actually militate against their own interests.

As a result of these machinations, the religious right and right-wing politicians now largely control the terms of political and religious discourse in America, with bizarre and unconscionable results. Poor people scream bloody murder against policies that seek to make American economic life more fair and equitable for all, and those enjoying the fruits of trade unionists' sweat, tears, and actual blood now not only demonize unions outright, but also valorize union-busters as heroes. In essence, right-wing religionists have thoroughly domesticated the radical pronouncements of the biblical prophets and Jesus' good news to the poor and woe to the unjustly rich. They have given us instead an ungodly mélange of religious obfuscation and ideological confusion that actually considers "social" and "justice" to be profane words when used together. And their pernicious influence seems to increase daily, spreading throughout the church and society virtually unchecked by truth or reality or even by the Bible they claim as the central adjudicator of their faith.

I must admit that at times the success of the right-wing's purposeful distortions of the biblical witness and their repeated lies in the name of God seem too much to bear. At those moments I despair of my nation ever becoming fully just and equitable. Then I am reminded of the pronouncement of that great Christian apostle of justice and love, Martin Luther King, Jr., that "the arc of the universe is long, but it bends toward justice." And then, in the words of the old Negro spiritual, "I feel like going on." I feel like going on to fight for justice. I feel like going on to challenge forces of reaction, exploitation, and rank obfuscation of scriptural truth. Empowered by the grace of Martin King's reminder, I feel like going on to reclaim the radical witness of the Bible that calls us to "make justice roll down like waters and righteousness like a mighty stream." For the arc of justice contains the promise of a different reality — a reality in which houses of worship really do try to change the world rather than simply changing the way people feel for the moment. A reality in which politicians do not spend the bulk of their time defending corporate greed while every year fewer families are able to make ends meet. A reality in which Christians remember that while Jesus said that the first commandment is to "love the Lord your God with all your heart," they also remember — and act like they remember — that he also said to "love your neighbor as yourself," not just sentimentally, but concretely, that is, actively seeking for our neighbors the same goods, rights, and overall well-being that we want for ourselves and our own loved ones.

This book is yet another attempt on my part to contribute to the reclamation of the radical witness of Jesus and the biblical prophets from their captivity to the forces of political and religious reaction. In my last book, *The Politics of Jesus: Rediscovering the True Revolutionary Nature of Jesus' Teachings and How They Have Been Corrupted,* I wrote of the historical roots and meanings of the radicality of Jesus and his prophetic antecedents, identified the biblical ethics and principles that drove and guided their radical deeds and pronouncements, and explored some of the strategic social and political implications of those principles for us in America today. In *The Universe Bends toward Justice.* I bring the ethical principles I explored in *The Politics of Jesus* to bear upon particular aspects of American public life and cultural practice that have fallen prey to misapplications of biblical meaning, both unintended and strategically inscribed. These include contemporary Gospel music, whose celebratory, performance orientation ideologically domesticates the social radicality of Jesus' message into a politically toothless, emotion-charged entertainment genre, a phenomenon particularly evident in black churches today; traditional modes of biblical interpretation that ignore some of the most significant determinants of Gospel meaning, such as the class character of Jesus' Gospel pronouncements, i.e., the way his words spoke to and out of the particular realities of the social location of his primary audience — and the ways their class location would have allowed them to hear him; and how, in general, religious language has been manipulated by the myriad forces of political conservatism to justify its economic agenda and its obsession with serving the interests of the rich and powerful. In all these cases the emphasis has been placed on the person and the personality of Jesus, rather than on his passion to realize a just world. Jesus has almost been reduced to a cult figure, the obsessive focus of a personality cult. This same process is also at work with the image of Martin Luther King, Jr. King is reduced to a holiday and a few sound bites, while the social, economic, and political radicality of the work for which he gave his life is ignored.

Recovering the political radicality of the message of Jesus and the prophetic witness of the Hebrew Bible from the clutches of those who are devastating our society, our body politic, and our natural environment is not a small thing. Indeed, it is absolutely crucial if we are to save the soul of our society and gather the fullest measure our strength so we may together make a better world.

– 1 –

"I Am the Holy Dope Dealer"

The Problem with Gospel Music Today

People need to get high off something spiritual, and I'm the holy dope dealer. I got this drug, I got this Jesus rock. And you can have a type of high that you've never experienced. — Kirk Franklin.[1]

Ecstatic, euphoric, celebratory worship has always been an important part of the black religious experience. It both predates and lives on in the African American sojourn, as numerous scholars have attested.[2] Those of us who have grown up in the black church not only know Jesus for ourselves, as the old saints said that we must, but we also know for ourselves the centrality of ecstatic worship. We know for ourselves what it means to "make a joyful noise unto the Lord, all ye lands!" We know for ourselves what it means to lift up holy hands in tearful supplication and joyful thanksgiving. We know for ourselves what it means for arms and legs to be carried away by some other spirit, for old and calloused feet to dance unctioned dances of praise, for fire-kissed tongues to speak languages unknown, yet uplifting. Yes, the euphoric, the celebratory, the praise-filled runs in black people as deeply as marrow. Yet it has never been the only blood coursing through our veins; praise and celebration for deliverance, without a concomitant critique of the events and conditions that black people looked to the Lord to deliver us *from,* has never characterized the heart of African American religious expression.

That is, until today. Today we are witnesses to a phenomenon that must turn Nat Turner[3] and Fannie Lou Hamer[4] in their miry graves. Today the prophetic consciousness that, with head and heart, told black people to resist the horrific race-based mistreatment and exploitation that bedeviled their every step no longer informs the music that once inspired them to action. Although vestiges of white skin color preference remains the creed of this nation,[5] today the prophet's call to "let justice roll down like waters, and righteousness like a mighty stream" is seldom voiced in black sacred songs, songs that moved the Fightin' 54th of Massachusetts to brave death for glory;[6] songs that emboldened Fannie Lou to proclaim to the forces of J. Edgar KKK that she was sick and tired of being sick and tired; songs that helped us to brave Bull Connor's vicious beatings with our eyes stayed on freedom, even as our daughters lay bombed in our churches and our sons lay lynched in our yards.

Black sacred music had this power because it took pains to remind us that "Pharaoh's army got drowned-ed"; to remind us that "Didn't my Lord deliver Daniel, so why not everyone?"; to remind us that against all odds, Joshua and his poor band of Hebrew outcasts "fi't the battle of Jericho and the walls came tumblin' down." It gave us songs of the comforting Jesus, yes, but also songs of the defiant, empowering Jesus; songs that helped us to stand boldly and unbowed before the most efficient engine of oppression and dehumanization ever conceived to declare, "Ride on, King Jesus! No man[7] can-a hinder me!" Songs of hope and love and resistance and change. Songs that reminded us, long before Einstein drew breath, that the arc of the universe is long, but it bends toward justice — on earth, as in heaven.

However, despite the empowering nature of the black sacred music of the past, in the dominant mode of black religious music today — contemporary Gospel music — this prophetic voice, this resistance voice, this biblical logic of justice is all but stilled. Gospel music is heard everywhere today, yet, unlike the Spirituals, it does not press our suit for freedom; it does not say, like the Spirituals did, "Moses, way down in Egypt land, tell ole Pharaoh to let my people go."

Once the black songs of Zion were heard only in the hush arbors and sequestered hearth-warmed quarters of clandestine slavery times; then in the soft, spare safety of those humming houses of refuge we called "church"; then in the rented halls and auditoriums where the studiously sweet and mournful voices of church-dressed women and shiny-suited men brought to ultimate rejection the all-American notion that black folk ain't nobody; then as the fruit of paternalistic bemusement, occasionally emerging in the curiously commercial eye-ball venues of Dinah Shore, Arthur Godfrey, Jack Paar and Ted Mack, where many white folks thought our music enjoyably interesting, but too exotic, too raw, and much too jungle-fied for anyone but the downwardly mobile and Aunt Hagar's children to claim as their own.

But the day of limited venues for black religious music is now past. Today Gospel music is featured daily by the most popular entertainment media in the land. The market for Gospel in recent years has grown at an exponential rate! Several Gospel artists are even numbered among the pantheon of international entertainment superstars. Yet despite the ubiquity of Gospel music today, barely a prophet's voice doth grace the chorus; indeed, the biblical prophet's call for justice is nowhere to be found. There is little doubt that Kirk Franklin, arguably the most commercially successful artist in the history of Gospel music, could today utter his deeply problematic 1997 description above of his role as a Gospel artist and cause no uproar or even audible dissent among his Gospel compatriots.

Sadly, in Gospel music today seldom is proclaimed the God of liberation — just the God of escape. Seldom is heralded the God who will deliver the world from evil, just a God who delivers us from reality. Seldom is Moses invoked, or Joshua, or dauntless Hebrew Judges and freedom fighters. And no longer is the Exodus proclaimed, that great event of liberation, that paradigmatic event of our faith, that event that empowered black people through the horrors of slavery and the unrelenting pain of Jim Crow to keep on keeping on, to keep on struggling; that event that assured us, by example and analogy, that Pharaoh in the big house is accursed of God and doomed to fail, while we, the tortured heirs of the chosen Hebrew children, are blessed by heaven and bound to be free.

Gospel music has gained the world, but it has lost the prophetic heart of black sacred music, i.e., the biblical Exodus and its divine mandate of freedom. This divine imperative of liberation is echoed by Jesus in his proclamation of the purpose of his ministry in what the Gospel of Luke presents as the inaugural sermon of his ministry: "The Spirit of the Lord is upon me, because he has anointed me to bring good news to the poor . . . to proclaim release to the captives . . . to let the oppressed go free" (Luke 4:18).

What this means is that at its best, the social orientation of Gospel music today is unmindful of the ongoing social, political, and economic dilemmas that confront black people in America. At worst, Gospel music today actually undermines collective social efforts — especially among African Americans — to address those dilemmas. In this chapter I will examine the reasons for the absence of a politically progressive liberation orientation in Gospel music and the reasons for its divergence from the freedom-seeking social and political emphases of the Spirituals.

I will begin by exploring the shift from the Old Testament liberation motifs and politically prophetic sensibilities that historically permeated the Spirituals to the otherworldly Jesus-centered celebratory proclamations of today's Gospel music that seem to purposefully overlook the social issues and dilemmas that bedevil so much of its black audience. I will examine the relationship of the movement from political liberation in the Spirituals to political apathy in Gospel to the almost simultaneous shift in the predominant mode of black labor from the agrarian fields to the urban assembly line, an evolution that was itself the result of the great urban migration of African Americans in the early part of the twentieth century. Finally I will identify some of the ways the particular emphases of the contemporary Gospel music scene are often harmful to the socio-political interests of African Americans. I will conclude by offering a proposal to address the aesthetic excesses of Gospel that keep it from reaching its potential as a force for holistic political empowerment.

Just a word on my use of terms. I use the term "prophetic" throughout this chapter. By "prophetic" I mean the mode of behavior modeled by the classical biblical prophets, such as Jeremiah, Isaiah, Micah, and Amos, who boldly and publicly critiqued the oppressive and exploitative behaviors of the rulers and ruling classes in their respective settings in life.[8] The term "Spirituals," as I use it here, refers to the body of black sacred songs that evolved as the collective cultural expression of an enslaved people and, to a lesser extent, the later experience of Jim Crow-ed African Americans. This represented a period of creative activity that spanned the seventeenth-century until about the third quarter of the nineteenth century. However, Spirituals remained central to the African American worship experience for decades thereafter and remain so today to various degrees in different black worship traditions. This is a straightforward and, I believe, traditional definition of the term.[9]

My use of the term "early" or "historic," what some call "traditional" Gospel, is self-evident, referring as it does to the first several decades of that genre, roughly from the 1920s to the 1950s and early 1960s. My use of the term "contemporary Gospel music" is less straightforward, however. The roots of contemporary Gospel can be traced to the pioneering works of Andrae Crouch and Edwin Hawkins in the late 1960s and early 1970s.[10] The compositions and performances of these Gospel innovators combined pop riffs and Rhythm and Blues instrumentation and production techniques with traditional Gospel music to create the genre called "contemporary Gospel." As the music critic Horace Boyer explains, "If the sound, devices and accompaniment of the music are distinctly, recognizably 'borrowed' from another already established tradition — that is, jazz, soul or blues, and it is difficult to translate the music into the traditional Gospel sound, it is called contemporary Gospel music."[11]

Crouch was among the first Gospel artists to devote entire songs to praising and worshiping God and Jesus. As the result of this innovation by Crouch and others, claims musicologist Robert Darden, "the emphasis has shifted from detailing humanity's problems and ultimate salvation to focusing instead exclusively on the person of Jesus Christ or "glorifying" an almighty God."[12] Although my use of "contemporary Gospel" includes Crouch and Hawkins in its purview, because of the cultural currency of the Gospel phenomenon today, in this chapter the term should be understood as primarily referring to the most contemporary of African American religious music, that is, to the Gospel music produced since the 1990s.

The Gospel music scene today is not homogenous, yet in terms of popular exposure and acceptance, as well as commercial success, it is dominated by those artists, songs, performances, and sensibilities that focus almost exclusively on "praise-singing," that is, on the ecstatic and the celebratory and on pastoral nurturing and comfort to some extent, to the virtual exclusion of the prophetic. The result is that it not only excludes the explicitly political, it even excludes the coded references to social and political conditions that characterized the Spirituals, as we will see below. The contemporary sector of the Gospel music scene has become so dominant, in fact, as to virtually define the Gospel genre today. Artists that can be understood as typifying the contemporary Gospel music scene by virtue of their commercial success and wide popular acceptance are located along a broad stylistic continuum. They include Kirk Franklin, Fred Hammond, Hezekiah Walker, Yolanda Adams, BeBe and CeCe Winans, Donny McClurkin, Ricky Dolan, Tye Trippett, and Vicki Winans, among others. It is to this stratum of the Gospel music genre that my use of the term "contemporary Gospel music" will refer.

I confess that I write this chapter as a lover of Gospel music. My earliest and fondest memories are tied to Gospel music. My grandmother,
Laura Banks, singing "Precious Lord" (she pronounced it "pry-shush")
and "Glory to His Name," back home in Charlotte Court House, Virginia, as she snapped fresh beans for our supper. My extended family,
with joyful familial anticipation, following my uncle Leon Banks and his
"quartet" as they traveled to myriad tiny venues in rural Virginia to place
their musical gifts at the service of the Lord before handfuls of joyous
believers. Our later home in East Orange, New Jersey, warmed every
Sunday morning by Brother Jonathan Joe Crane and his Gospel Cara-
van on WNJR ("1400 on your radio"), while my father read his Bible,
contentedly drinking his daily Sanka, and my mother readied my sister
and me for Sunday School. As a child of six, my father and I attended
a "Battle of the Quartets" headlined by the Five Blind Boys, at Newark's
Greater Abyssinian Baptist Church.[13] Even today, among the thousands
of recordings in my personal collection, the works of the Soul Stirrers,
Mahalia Jackson, Donny McClurkin, and Richard Smallwood hold pride
of place with Miles Davis, Thelonius Monk, Sonny Rollins, John and
Alice Coltrane, Clifford Brown, Eric Dolphy, Gerri Allen, and Wynton
Marsalis.

As much as I love Gospel music, however, I love even more the prospect
of my grandchildren and all children living lives unhindered by constraints
of race or class or ethnicity or gender. I do not overlook that African
Americans have made great strides in this nation in the last fifty years in
almost every arena including, of course, the election of a black president.
Yet neither can I overlook that African American children continue to die,
on average, more than half a decade younger than their Euro-American
counterparts. Black folks suffer disproportionately higher rates of cancer,
strokes, heart disease, diabetes, and infant and maternal mortality than
the national average, while our access to adequate and timely healthcare
remains shamefully limited; we still receive justice far less fairly from the
criminal justice system, still pay significantly higher interest rates for mortgages and auto loans than other groups, and still have far less access to
higher education and high wage employment. By every significant measure, black people in America still have far less of the good things in life
and far more of the bad than their white counterparts.[14] Yet as the praise
songs of Gospel music thunder across the land, one listens in vain for

lyrics of protest or even explicit acknowledgment of our plight. Because I love both Gospel music *and* cherish the prospect of life with abundance for all people, herein I will engage Gospel as one would a dear beloved friend: honestly, candidly, unflinchingly. Thus in this chapter I offer Gospel music the supreme compliment of taking it seriously by submitting it not to uncritical hagiography, but to the same level of analytical rigor with which thoughtful scholars should engage all subjects they respect. In this I humbly, but sincerely, follow those who have so boldly treaded this ground before me, including W. E. B. DuBois, James Weldon and J. Rosamond Johnson, Amiri Baraka, Wyatt Tee Walker, James H. Cone, Bernice Johnson Reagon, and countless others.[15]

THE SPIRITUALS: THE PRISM OF THE AFRICAN AMERICAN SOCIAL EXPERIENCE

The civil rights figure and musicologist Wyatt Tee Walker has asserted, "The political and social significance of the Spiritual will be obscured if one loses sight of the fact that the Spirituals were born in slavery."[16] The importance of this point cannot be overstated, for it underscores the social setting in which the Spirituals were formed and the social conditions and social relations with which they were invariably in dialogue. The Spirituals' tone of ceaseless hope in the inevitability of their deliverance to justice empowered black people to resist white supremacy's devaluation of their humanity and its definition of their lot as without hope. In this sense the Spirituals are part of what can be called a discursive formation of resistance. A discursive formation is a set of rules determined by the collective needs and aspirations of a particular social group; it arises out of the social and political conditions of that group's particular setting in life, or *Sitz im Leben*.[17] It is the discursive formation that determines "what can and must be said"[18] by the members of that group, and what the terms that are used within that discourse ultimately mean, particularly with regard to the group members' social and political plight. The discursive formation that gave meaning to the terms and images of the Spirituals was the ongoing African American discourse of resistance to systematic legalized institutional white supremacy in America. The term "resistance discourse" denotes terms, phrases, figures of speech, concepts, poetry, and songs that are common to a particular group of subjugated persons, all of which are popularly understood by members of that group as calling them to resist in some way the oppression to which they are subjected.[19] The modes that these discursive forms of resistance may take range from the relatively benign, like feigning inability to understand a command or a directive ("playing the fool to catch the wise," as the folk saying goes), to the outright use of violence.[20]

The great freedom fighter Frederick Douglass contended that the resistance sensibilities of the Spirituals were so pronounced that, "Every tone was a testimony against slavery, and a prayer to God for deliverance from chains."[21] However, to say that Spirituals fit within the spectrum of African American resistance discourse is also to recognize that while not every individual song of the Spiritual genre explicitly refers to freedom from bondage and the eschatological institution of justice, still all Spirituals do in some way hope, counsel, or proclaim resistance to the negation of our forebears' humanity, the negation of their right to have life and that more abundantly, the negation demanded by the very tenets of the system of oppression that weighed upon them. Because of the omnipresence of the oppressor's gaze upon them during the period of their enslavement, African Americans often expressed this resistance in coded language, what Mikhail Bahktin has called "double-voiced" discourse, in which "the word in language is half someone else's. It becomes 'one's own' only when the speaker populates it with his own intention, his own accent, when he appropriates the word, adapting it to his own semantic and expressive intention."[22] Music scholar Gwendolin Warren observes of the double-voiced nature of the Spirituals that "without understanding . . . double meanings it is impossible to get a complete sense of the significance of the Spiritual as a way African Americans resisted enslavement."[23] Booker T. Washington's recollection of his last days in slavery is illustrative of this point:

> Most of the verses of the plantation songs had some reference to freedom. True, they had sung those same verses before, but they had been careful to explain that the "freedom" in these songs referred to the next world, and had no connection with life in this world. Now they gradually threw off the mask, and were not afraid to let it be known that the "freedom" in their songs meant freedom of the body in the world.[24]

The "double-voiced" resistance nature of Spirituals took a number of forms. Some songs explicitly bemoaned the slaves' suffering beneath the white supremacist heel without naming the specifics of their subjugation:

> *Sometimes I feel like a motherless child,*
> *A long, long ways from home.*

Some were songs of perseverance in the struggle for personhood and liberation:

> *I ain't got weary yet,*
> *I ain't got weary yet,*
> *I been in the wilderness a mighty long time,*
> *And I ain't got weary yet.*

Others were outright proclamations of resistance, such as "Marching Up the Heavenly Road," the lyrics of which are possessed of such powerful resistance sensibilities that one could well imagine them being sung by Nat Turner's army or by soldiers in the myriad other slave revolts as they marched to battle:

> *Marching up the heavenly road,*
> *I'm bound to fight until I die.*
> *O fare you well friends, fare you well foes,*
> *Marching up the heavenly road,*
> *I leave you all my eyes to close,*
> *Marching up the heavenly road.*

Also consider "Great Day! Great Day!":

> *This is the day of jubilee . . .*
> *The Lord has set his people free,*
> *God's going to build up Zion's walls!*
> *We want no cowards in our band,*
> *We call for valiant-hearted men,*
> *God's going to build up Zion's walls!*

And, of course:

> *Oh, freedom!*
> *Oh, freedom!*

Oh, freedom over me!
And before I'd be a slave,
I'll be buried in my grave,
And go home to my Lord and be free!

The resistance nature of Spirituals was clear to many slaveholders, as evidenced by their response to the singing of them. Princeton University religious historian Albert Raboteau relates that enslavers in Georgetown, South Carolina, forbade slaves from singing "One of these days I shall be free / When Christ the Lord shall set me free" and jailed blacks for singing certain other Spirituals, such as

We'll soon be free,
We'll soon be free,
We'll soon be free,
When de Lord will call us home.
My brudder, how long,
My brudder, how long,
My brudder, how long,
'Fore we done sufferin' here?
It won't be long [thrice]
'Fore de Lord will call us home....
We'll soon be free [thrice]
When Jesus sets me free.
We'll fight for liberty [thrice]
When de Lord will call us home.[25]

Why have the spirituals played a pivotal role in the articulation of African American resistance discourse? Because by their very nature their public assertions of personhood resist the oppressive definitions of the white supremacist social order, as well as because they occur in a collective medium of expression in which every member of the community can participate. In fact, the collective, communal nature of the Spiritual genre is important for two primary reasons.

First, the very act of collective song — whether in sequestered sites outside the oppressive gaze or in postures of unobtrusive, feigned guilelessness squarely in the oppressors' presence — helped to develop and to

eventually normalize the significance of resistance themes, terms, and figures into a collective and collectively held cultural product. James C. Scott
calls this process "making space for a dissident subculture,"[26] with "dissidence," or rejection of the worldview and definitions promulgated by the
dominant class, being the operative word. After the process of cultural dissidence has repeatedly and systematically discredited status quo claims —
which it must if the process is to be meaningful to the oppressed — the
claims, notions, and definitions that undergird oppression must be redefined, given constructive new meanings, or replaced by terms, concepts,
and figures that serve the liberation interests of the oppressed. What cultural dissidence ultimately seeks is to counter the ideological claims, or
"hegemony," of the oppressive power. Hegemony is the process by which
the lines between the interests of an oppressed group and those of the
class that dominates it become blurred by the systematic efforts of the
oppressor to obscure or hide them, with the result that oppressed people
unwittingly come to give assent to social definitions, even social policies,
that are in opposition to their own interests. The result of this process is
that oppressed people become complicit in their own oppression.[27] In this
sense, the task of cultural dissidence — to counter the confusing effects
of the hegemonic process — can be called "counter-hegemony."

The religion scholar Theophus Smith refers to the particular counter-
hegemonic process by which the African American slaves effectively
redefined biblical events and characters by the term "typological ethno-
genesis."[28] By this he means the process by which enslaved African
Americans "envisioned and revised [their] existence in terms of characters
and events found in the Exodus story."[29] Albert Raboteau explains:

> Slaves prayed for the future day of deliverance to come, and they
> kept hope alive by incorporating as part of *their* mythic past the Old
> Testament exodus of Israel out of slavery. . . . The Christian slaves
> applied the Exodus story, whose end they knew, to their own expe-
> rience of slavery, which had not ended. . . . Exodus functioned as an
> archetypal event for the slaves. The sacred history of God's libera-
> tion of his people would be or was being repeated in the American
> South [emphasis in original].[30]

Because of the affinity the enslaved Africans felt with the enslaved
Hebrews, the Old Testament figures of Moses, Joshua, Daniel, and the

Pharaoh of Egypt became types and characters through which the slaves expressed their hope, their approbation, their derision, and most importantly, their definitions of justice and injustice. What is significant in this process is that the primary biblical figures used typologically in the Spirituals were resistance figures who struggled with and triumphed over *worldly* oppression. They were not mystical, ethereal, or pacific characters, but freedom fighters, servants of God who expressed their faith by struggling for the liberation of their people. Likewise, the litany of biblical liberation events, particularly the Exodus, the vanquishing of the Hebrews' enemies at the battle of Jericho, Daniel's deliverance from annihilation at the hands of his oppressors, and the Hebrews' possession of the land beyond the chilly Jordan, together constituted the most significant and widely invoked motifs of the entire Spiritual genre, with the Exodus primary among them. In this sense, Wendel Whalum's assertion that freedom was the constant theme of the Spirituals is wholly accurate.[31]

Another significance of the Spirituals as collective cultural products is that they reflect the communal, cooperative mode of production in which they were produced, i.e., the agrarian or farming mode of production, which, because it was fully dependent upon cooperative labor, extolled the virtue of, accorded normative status to, and eventually sacralized the ethos of cooperative, communal production as part of its underlying moral economy.[32] Because Spirituals are products of this agrarian-based culture of reciprocity and cooperative action, they are not individual efforts; rather, they are collective expressions of the collective ethos, hopes, dreams, fears, aspirations, angst, and anger of the African American communities that collectively produced them. Nor were Spirituals produced as commodities, that is, for commercial transfer or exchange; they were produced for their producing communities' own collective edification and consumption. Spirituals were not crafted by their producers as personal appeals to the emotions of others but, rather, to express the collective sentiments of the communities that produced them. In other words, in the settings that produced them, the Spirituals were not performance vehicles, but products of collective expression and edification. This is an important point of difference between Spirituals and Gospel songs, as we shall discuss in greater depth shortly.

The agrarian or farming mode of production had a further significance for the formation of the Spirituals. Although the enslaved Africans in the rural South labored for others under the severest compulsion, still the agrarian nature of most slaves' labor and the setting of that labor in rural expanses conspired to offer them a certain sense of empowerment or, at least, possibility. The slaves' agrarian labor was not fully alienated in the Marxist sense, that is, it was not fully devoid of a sense of creation or achievement,[33] for often the slaves literally saw the fruit of their labor grow to full fruition. They raised crops they themselves planted and nurtured, and sometimes lived off the fruits of their own toil. Some slaves were allowed garden plots of their own with which they could augment rations from their enslavers, although they usually could work their own plots only after a full day of exhausting enforced labor or on the Sunday Sabbath day of rest. As a result, despite the compulsory nature of their labor many slaves could still experience a measure, albeit small, of the fulfillment that came from shepherding the span of cultivation from planting to harvest. Therefore, although their labor was forced and often pain filled, it was not always without meaning. Moreover, the rural expanses of most slaves' settings in life offered the omnipresent hope and possibility of escape to new, more humane surroundings in which they would know a greater measure of security, if not justice, in their lives. If nothing else, there always loomed for them the Promised Land of the North and its ideal of freedom. And in the immediate post-Emancipation era in which the later Spirituals were produced, agrarian labor would have been of even greater meaning to those freedmen and freedwomen who had become smallholders working their own soil. Some sense of the meaning labor gave to the lives of black agrarian workers, whether enslaved or experiencing the circumscribed "freedom" of sharecropping or rural proletariat "day work," can be culled from the blues artist B. B. King's recollection of his own boyhood as an agrarian day worker:

> In the Mississippi Delta of my childhood, cotton was a force of nature. . . . It's how I beat back the wolf. Cotton turned me from a boy to a man, testing my energy and giving me what I needed — a means to survive. But I did more than cope with the crop. I actually loved it. It was beautiful to live through the seasons, to break the ground in the chill of winter, plant the seeds against the winds of spring, and pick the blossoms in the heat of summer.[34]

King's recollection of his experience as a fieldworker is clearly idealized, lacking, as it does, any professed memory of the poverty and economic uncertainty, the physical pain and mind-numbing exhaustion that were typically the landless workers' plight. Historian Donald Holley observed that picking cotton was "one of the most backbreaking forms of stoop labor ever known."[35] Isabel Wilkerson describes that labor:

> The hands got cramped from the repetitive motion of picking, the fingers fairly locked in place and callused from the pricks of the barbed, five-pointed cockleburs that cupped each precious boll. The work was not so much hazardous as it is mind-numbing and endless, requiring them to pick from the moment the sun peeked over the tree line to the moment it fell behind the horizon and they could no longer see. After ten or twelve hours, the pickers could barely stand up straight for all the stooping.[36]

Yet somehow the aspects of fieldwork that held meaning for King still remained, even after factoring in the painful aspects that King leaves out. What emerges is a sense of how these small measures of meaning could contribute to the sense of hope in the face of inhumane oppression that is reflected in the Spirituals. That sense of hope found expression on the part of oppressed African Americans as a sense of power, however small, that they could in some way effect changes in their worldly circumstances that might alleviate some measure of their suffering.

This small measure of control of their own destinies that African Americans eked out of the agrarian mode of production, as well as their perception of the possibility that they might one day change their circumstances, is reflected in the eschatological nature of the slaves' hope. Eschatology refers to one's belief or understanding of how the present world order will end. From a perusal of the Spirituals it is clear that the slaves harbored eschatological hopes for the comfort of heaven. Yet it is also clear that they expected justice in this world or, as W. E. B. DuBois put it, they held "a faith in the ultimate justice of things."[37] This eschatological expectation for justice in this world is richly expressed by David Walker's 1829 polemical *Appeal to the Colored Citizens of the World*:

> Remember [white] Americans, that we must and shall be free, and enlightened as you are, will you wait until we shall, under God,

obtain our liberty by the crushing arm of power?...We must and shall be free I say, in spite of you. You may do your best to keep us in wretchedness and misery, to enrich you and your children, but God will deliver us from under you.[38]

Walker uses "shall" and "must," terms that brook no uncertainty. The eschatology of justice that he expresses knew neither the day nor the hour, but it held no doubt of the outcome. This is the same eschatological certainty of deliverance that is expressed by the Spiritual when it proclaims:

> *I ain't got long to stay here.*

THE NORMATIVE ELEMENTS
OF BLACK SACRED MUSIC

The Spirituals grew out of the collective root experience of the political oppression and social exclusion that has always pervaded African American reality and, as a genre, was at every step informed by the contours of that experience. Because the awareness and expression of that root reality is intrinsic to the Spirituals and, as well, because Spirituals are the earliest form of African American music, it is compelling cultural logic that the sensibilities of the Spirituals should be considered to constitute the normative elements of black sacred music. These sensibilities include the prophetic functions of naming the oppressive reality and exhorting resistance to it, as well as the eschatological expectation of justice *in this world*. Moreover, because an important characteristic of Spirituals is that they also offer empathy and comfort for suffering even as they counsel resistance, the empathic nature of the genre should also be included among the normative elements of black sacred song.

Because they constitute the well out of which black sacred music sprang, these normative characteristics must be considered as collectively constituting the primary evaluative criteria by which may be determined the cultural relevance of black sacred music to the ongoing struggle of African Americans for equity and justice. To summarize, these criteria include (1) collective acknowledgment of oppression, (2) prophetic critique of the race-based system and sensibilities that produce and perpetuate that oppression, (3) exhortation to resist the political, social, and

political importunities of that systematic oppression, (4) while simultaneously offering comfort and empathy in its midst. It is my contention that
with the exception of its stress on comfort and empathy, contemporary
Gospel music fails to fulfill these criteria that are so crucial to the quest
of African Americans to have life with the same abundance in American
society as all others. Let us explore this claim.

GOSPEL MUSIC: HEAR NO, SEE NO, SPEAK NO (POLITICAL) EVIL

In many of today's churches, Gospel music has virtually replaced Spirituals, yet Gospel music represents a real shift in consciousness and worldview
from the Spirituals. Despite the very real differences, however, there are
significant points of continuity between the two.

Commonalities with Spirituals: Hope, Immanence, and Deliverance from Burdens

First, both Spirituals and Gospel songs are primarily expressions of
hope and affirmation. Thomas A. Dorsey (1899–1993), who, along with
Charles A. Tindley (1851–1933), was a seminal figure in Gospel music,
said of his role in the origins of the genre during the Great Depression,
"I wrote to give [the people] something to lift them out of that depression."[39] He went on to explain, "We intended Gospel to strike a happy
medium for the downtrodden. This music lifted people out of the muck
and mire of poverty and loneliness, of being broke, and gave them some
kind of hope anyway."[40] Gospel great Mahalia Jackson epitomized the
overall significance of hope to Gospel music in this way: "Gospel songs are
songs of hope. When you sing them you are delivered of your burden."[41]

The unrelenting hopefulness of Gospel songs is seen for instance, in
"I've Got a Feeling (Everything's Gonna Be Alright)" and Dorsey's "The
Lord Will Make a Way Somehow," both of which reflect the certainty of
God's mercy and deliverance from suffering. The Spirituals hold a similar
certainty that despite the pain of the present moment, "There is a Balm
in Gilead," for instance. In addition to the certainty of eventual comfort
and rest, the Spirituals also held the eschatological certainty of justice, as
seen in "Jacob's Ladder":

We are climbing Jacob's ladder . . .
Every round goes higher and higher . . .
We are climbing higher and higher,
Soldiers of the cross.

Both Spirituals and Gospel music attest to the immanence and omni-presence of God as central to their proclamations. While the Spiritual testifies, "God Don't Ever Change," "He's Got the Whole World in His Hands," and "My God Is So High You Can't Get over Him," Gospel music sings "He Has Never Left Me Alone," "His Eye Is on the Sparrow and I Know He Watches Me," and "Hold to God's Unchanging Hand."

Moreover, even as Gospel evolved its own distinctive markings, forms, and accompanying musical culture, in some quarters the early Gospel music retained from its Spiritual roots something of the character of a collective cultural product, at least in the sense that performance of it was not specialized or individualized. This is attested by no less than Sallie Martin, an important associate of Dorsey and a pioneer of Gospel music in her own right, who recalls of those early years, "We didn't have no soloists. We would all sing together."[42]

Differences: Meek Jesus, Absent Moses, Individuation, and the Timetable of Justice

Despite the similarities between the two genres, however, their differences are profound, with worldviews that differ radically. Whereas Old Testa-ment liberation themes and motifs were central for Spirituals, not so with Gospel music. It is not the Hebrew children struggling for freedom that dominate Gospel songs, but Jesus. And not just any Jesus, but specif-ically the pacific, meek, mild, otherworldly Jesus. As Lawrence Levine observes, the figure of Jesus that predominates in the Gospel songs "is not the warrior Jesus of the Spirituals but a benevolent spirit who prom-ised His children rest and peace and justice in the hereafter."[43] This is attested today by Gospel titles such as "Christ is All," "I'd Rather Have Jesus," "Jesus Knows and Will Supply My Every Need," "Jesus, Lover of My Soul" and "Jesus is the Answer to Every Problem," to name just a few.

Moreover, Spirituals generally were the product of anonymous col-lective authorship and, therefore, knew nothing like identification with a particular individual member of the community. Conversely, although the thoughts and emotions expressed in Gospel songs are often universal in scope and emphasis, the songs themselves have, from the beginning, been written, copyrighted, and often widely identified with individuals. Thus, unlike the communal nature of Spirituals, Gospel songs are the stuff of individual authorship and ownership. One commentator observes, "The creation and development of that African American art called Gospel music and its wide acceptance by 1950 can be attributed to fewer than one dozen composers."[44]

Furthermore, whereas the eschatology of the Spirituals ultimately foresees the establishment of God's justice in this world, the eschatology of Gospel songs is apocalyptic and otherworldly in orientation. Apocalyptic as a worldview is an expression of a sense of powerlessness to effect meaningful positive change in an unjust social order, a sense that the odds against victory and vindication in this world are so overwhelming and so insurmountable that there is nothing one can do but "wait on the Lord" for a new day.[45] Although both genres hold hope in common, the Gospel hope is not for justice *in* this world, as is the hope of the Spiritual, but for deliverance *from* this world. The locus of the hope of Gospel songs is "over yonder," as seen in "I'll Fly Away":

> *Just a few more weary days and then,*
> *I'll fly away.*
> *To a land where joys will never end,*
> *I'll fly away.*

Apocalyptic is seen in even bolder relief in the evocation of 1 Thessalonians 4:16–18, one of the foremost examples of New Testament apocalyptic, in "I'll Be Caught Up in the Air to Meet Him":

> *I'll be caught up to meet him,*
> *I'll be caught up to greet him.*
> *Joy and happiness will be mine.*

Also, unlike the Spirituals' general tone of response to and expression of collective, communal woes as they were experienced within the community, Gospel songs generally have a personal, individual tone. Indeed, they are generally written out of specific personal experiences and personal realizations. For instance, "Take My Hand, Precious Lord," the world's best-known Gospel song (it has been translated into some fifty languages), was written by Thomas Dorsey after the death of his young wife and unborn child. Similarly, Lucie Campbell wrote "He Understands; He'll Say Well Done" after her fellow congregants rescinded her beloved local church membership after a bitter church controversy.[46]

Another area of difference between the two genres lies in their respective moral focii. The primary moral focus of Spirituals is horizontal, that is, it focuses on group morality in that it is concerned with effecting right relations with fellow humanity; the practical measure of its ethics and morality is not what one believes or how one worships, but how one functions in community. The Spirituals' focus on collective ethics and morality does not imply that the communities that produced them valued personal moral behavior less highly than collective morality. However, because of the baldness of the systematic white supremacy under which they lived, it was crucial to the survival of the subjugated African Americans that they also judge moral behavior by the person's role in the plight of the black community, as either oppressor (this included collaborators such as loyal "house negroes" and black overseers)[47] or as resistor to oppression, the latter being defined by a person's contribution to the edification and survival of the black community.

Instead of the collective morality of the Spirituals, however, the primary moral focus of Gospel music stresses vertical moral behavior, that is, piety that is mainly concerned with one's own individual relationship to God, with any concern for actively striving to serve one's neighbor as a secondary concern, sometimes very much so — this despite the fact that the only real evidence of one's relationship with God is right treatment of those God created. This difference in moral focus can be seen by considering Jesus' summation of "the greatest Law" in Matthew 22:37–39. While the Spirituals can be understood to stress the horizontal, communal dimension of the pronouncement, "Love your neighbor as yourself" (v. 39), Gospel music stresses its vertical, individual dimension: "Love your Lord your God with all your heart" (v. 37). Even Gospel songs with seeming resistance sensibilities, such as "I Am on the Battlefield for My Lord," ultimately have reference to struggles with personal morality, rather than referring to struggles against the oppressive socio-political forces of the world. This difference in emphasis is rooted in changes in both the social and material conditions of African Americans, as we shall explore shortly.

This emphasis on individual morality was an important emphasis of early Gospel music and is reflected in admirable ways in the lives of its early pioneers who, for the most part, were men and women of great conviction and dramatic personal moral rectitude. This moral emphasis is expressed in songs such as Thomas Dorsey's "Live the Song I Sing About" and his "Highway to Heaven":

> *It's a highway to heaven*
> *None can go up there but the pure in heart.*

In her inimitable way, Sallie Martin reflects the emphasis on personal morality in the early Gospel culture: "There isn't but one thing that I say will keep us back and that is singing one thing and then doing...different when you get out of your service...If we can't live right, then why did Jesus leave it here with us?"[48]

As the result of this emphasis on individual feelings and experiences and personal morality, at its core Gospel music evolved a deeply empathic tone. The empathy of Gospel music, however, differed from the Spirituals' acknowledgment of common suffering under an oppressive social order. Instead, the empathy of Gospel inhered in its acknowledgment of personal angst and suffering, personal doubt, and feelings of unworthiness. It is this dimension of the personal and the empathic that fuels the emotionalism of Gospel music today. This, in turn, informs the highly emotion-charged performance orientation that today underpins the genre.

Eschewing Prophetic Critique

Above I cited the explanation by Thomas Dorsey, universally hailed as the father of Gospel music, that hope lay at the heart of Gospel music. Dorsey's concluding comment in that explanation illustrates the difference between the hope of the Spirituals and the hope of Gospel songs: "Make it anything [other] than good news," he says, and "it ceases to be Gospel."[49] In addition to highlighting the contrasting emphases on hope in the two genres, Professor Dorsey's remark reveals that in its quest to soothe the suffering of the black masses, Gospel music consciously eschews both prophetic critique and activist engagement of the social forces and conditions that underlie much of the suffering Gospel music seeks to assuage. It is understandable that Dorsey sought to lighten the load of a people already inundated daily by more bad news at the hands of systematic racism than any people should be asked to endure. Indeed, lightening their load was necessary for African Americans' pyscho-emotional health. In addition to the great source of comfort Gospel music came to constitute for the beleagured black community, however, the general unwillingness of Gospel artists to cite bad news, to critique or even acknowledge the systemic causes of black folks' pain resulted in an extremely unfortunate consequence: the tone of Gospel music became studiously and conscientiously non-prophetic.

Prophetic Critique and Painful Memory

Prophetic critique can be defined as principled public criticism of and opposition to systemic injustice. An example is this admonition from the prophet Isaiah: "Cease to do evil, learn to do good; seek justice, rescue the oppressed" (1:16–17). Jeremiah 22:17 offers a particularly biting prophetic critique of purveyors of injustice in his setting in life: "your eyes and heart are only on your dishonest gain, for shedding innocent blood, and for practicing oppression and violence." Prophetic discourse is based upon the biblical logic of justice that is reflected, for instance, in Psalm 72:

> *Endow the king with your justice, O God,*
> *the royal son with your righteousness.*
> *He will judge your people in righteousness,*
> *your afflicted ones with justice....*
> *He will defend the afflicted among the people*
> *and save the children of the needy;*
> *he will crush the oppressors.* (1–2, 4)

In the words of a prophet,

> what does the LORD require of you, but to do justice, and to practice steadfast love, and to walk humbly with your God? (Mic. 6:8)

Thus prophetic engagement of social and political issues is grounded in the enduring example of biblical prophets such as Isaiah, Jeremiah, and Amos, who all spoke "thus saith the Lord" against the oppressors in their own socio-historical settings. In fact, one of the most powerful and memorable phrases of the great freedom fighter Martin Luther King, Jr., is from Amos: "Let justice roll down like waters, and righteousness like a mighty stream" (5:24). Close examination of the Spirituals reveals that a considerable number of them embodied this mode of prophetic critique and its concern. Examples of prophetic sensibilities from the Spirituals include "You Shall Reap (What You Sow)," "You Got a Right (to the Tree of Life)," and "Some of These Days (I'm Gonna Tell God How You Treat Me)."

To be sure, similar prophetic critique of the foremost institutional evil of our time, i.e., the intense physical and psychic brutality of systematic white skin color privilege in America, is indispensable to the struggle of African Americans for full social, political, and economic parity in this nation. Despite its importance, however, prophetic critique is yet another reminder for the victims of oppression of the omnipresence of their suffering; it simply is not good news in the sense in which Dorsey speaks. It certainly would not have been good news for Dorsey to have reminded his hearers, for instance, that just a few years before Dorsey wrote, President Woodrow Wilson had refused to sign an anti-lynching law, or that Wilson had tearfully praised the preposterously racist movie *Birth of a Nation* for its "truth," or that one black man, woman, or child was then being lynched every thirty-six hours. The humanity of people of African descent was so devalued in that sad time that Africans had been exhibited as subhuman curiosities in American zoos little more than a decade before Dorsey began his Gospel career. In one of the most infamous of these instances, in 1906 Ota Benga, a Pygmy from southern Africa, was imprisoned and displayed in a monkey cage at New York City's Bronx Zoo.[50] That black folks could once again legally be detained as animals could only have heightened the ongoing sense of insecurity that grew out of living in the overarching context of white supremacy in America; for most, particularly black children, it must have been traumatic and frightening beyond words.

It is understandable, then, that according to Dorsey's stated logic, discussion of or even allusion to the painful social reality of African Americans would have to be off limits if Gospel music was to "strike a happy medium for the downtrodden,"[51] as Dorsey stated as his goal. Unfortunately, the sad result of this unwillingness to explicitly address the bad news of African American oppression is that from its inception, generally the Gospel music genre has self-consciously avoided prophetic critique of the ravages wrought upon black people by white supremacy. In the final analysis, the political quietism of Gospel music, that is, its studied unwillingness to critique the bad news of the injustice and exploitation suffered by black folks, has contributed to the maintenance of the oppressive American social order by domesticating the outrage — that otherwise would have fueled political resistance and activism for the purpose of establishing a more just American society — into an emotion-laden apocalyptic hope.

Residues of the Prophetic

To acknowledge the generally non-prophetic character of Gospel music, however, is not to claim that the genre has been totally devoid of songs exhibiting socio-political sensibilities. To be sure, some of the early Gospel songs seem to stray from Dorsey's definition of the genre. In fact, a number of the early Gospel songs do explicitly acknowledge socio-political and socio-economic realities. Significant examples include "No Segregation in Heaven" and "Stalin Wasn't Stallin,'" both recorded in 1942 by the Golden Gates Quartet, and C. A. Tindley's early yet still popular composition "Leave It There," which begins:

> *If this world from you withhold,*
> *All its silver and its gold*
> *And you have to get along on meager fare.*

Indeed, some of Tindley's songs were exhortations specifically addressed to the poor and downtrodden, as in "I'll Overcome":

> *If in my life I do not yield*
> *I'll overcome some day.*

Socio-political sensibilities are also seen in early Gospel pageants that stressed racial pride. The remarkable Lucie Campbell (1885–1963), who, incidentally, was the first African American woman to publish a Gospel song, was hailed for presenting a number of such events, including "Ethiopia at the Bar of Justice" and "Ethiopia, Stretch Forth Your Hands unto God."[52] And who can listen to Mahalia Jackson's renditions of "How I Got Over" and "My Soul Looks Back and Wonders" without hearing the sting of Jim Crow, the hurt of exclusion, the gnawing pain of unjust enforced impoverishment? Or the Soul Stirrers' "Any Day Now," in which the plaintive tones of the group's lead singer, Sam Cooke, as Michael Dyson observes,

evokes a world teeming with cultural nuances hidden from white
society. ... Though Cook[e] is singing about going to heaven, he
masks a complaint about earthly restrictions on black life by pining
for a day when there's "no sorrow or sadness / Just only complete
gladness. ... " It's the way Cook[e] bends the notes, shaping his
desire for freedom.[53]

Rev. W. Herbert Brewster is probably the most noteworthy example
of a Gospel songwriter whose works reflect socio-political sensibilities.
A political radical for his time, Brewster wrote numerous tracts urging
black liberation. He coined the motto "Out of the amen corner onto
the street corner," by which he both indicted the lack of social action of
his ministerial colleagues and attempted to cajole them to act. Among
his musical compositions was a pageant play with pronounced political
resonances entitled "From Auction Block to Glory," as well as "Deep Dark
Waters," a social commentary about drugs.[54] In a clear act of racial pride,
Brewster even renamed a young choir singer "Q. C. Anderson" in honor
of Queen Candace of Ethiopia.[55]

Brewster's lyrics seemed always to have as a subtext the socio-political-
economic realities facing African Americans. Songs like "How I Got
Over" and "Move On Up a Little Higher" (both later popularized by
Mahalia Jackson), while extolling the "good news" of triumphant deliverance also, in good prophetic fashion, evoked the injustice that the singer —
and the hearer — seeks to triumph over. "The fight for rights here in Memphis was pretty rough on the Black Church," explains Brewster. "The lily
white, the black, and the tan were locking horns; and the idea struck me
and I wrote that song, "Move on Up a Little Higher." That was a protest
idea and inspiration."[56] Also consider "These Are They," Brewster's rich
evocation of images found in the book of Revelation:

> *These are they from every nation*
> *Who have washed their garments white,*
> *Coming up, coming up through great tribulation*
> *To a land of pure delight.*

The line "coming up ... " evokes the image of "they" as the downtrodden who, in the context of Brewster and his African American
audience, would certainly be identified as black folks struggling against

oppression. A student of New Testament Greek, Brewster was probably aware that *thlibo,* the Greek term from which "tribulation" is typically translated in the New Testament, does not simply signify bad luck or random trying circumstances, but literally means "to press down," signifying "oppression," which is political and systemic in nature.

Other songs exhibiting socio-political sensibilities featured applications of biblical passages that exhorted deliverance from subjugation such as "If I Had My Way":

> *Well they tell me God almighty*
> *Rode on the wings of the wind*
> *And he saw old Samson and he called to him*
> *Said he whispered low into Samson's mind*
> *Said "Deliver my children from the Philistines."*

Thus it is clear that some of the early Gospel songs do acknowledge exploitation and social injustice. Yet the consistent solution they prescribe is not the kind of prophetic engagement that is prescribed by the Spirituals; they do not critique the social order that withholds wealth from black folks and relegates them to subsisting on meager fare, to use Tindley's lyrical social description. Rather than prescribing action against the systemic causes of poverty, the Gospel songs seem to counsel *inaction.* An instructive example is seen in Tindley's "Leave It There." Although the song laments the effect of the exploitative American social order, it concludes by advising, in effect, "don't bother to try to change things, simply. . . ."

Take your burdens to the Lord and leave them there.

Despite the existence of a socio-politically conscious stratum in the genre, most early Gospel songs eschewed explicit reference to the ongoing bad news of the socio-political plight of African Americans. Still, because oppression, marginalization, and exploitation represented a large part of the lived experience of African Americans, some early Gospel songs did implicitly reflect that social reality nonetheless, sometimes consciously so, if in the most subtle terms. Unlike early Gospel, however, the Gospel music of today not only seldom reflects recognition of African Americans' plight, but often seems to gloss it over. This can, of course, reflect both the lower level of politicization of African Americans today that is the result of the dismantling of systematic de jure white skin color privilege and the lowering of the most blatant barriers to black advancement. But it probably also reflects an alarming lack of popular awareness of the continuing legacy of de facto white skin color privilege in America, which in turn, is the result of successful hegemonic obfuscation of the racist underpinnings of much of U.S. domestic and foreign policy. Of contemporary Gospel's lack of recognition of socio-political realities, Gospel pioneer Miss Sallie Martin observes, albeit a bit exaggeratedly, "I think the old songs were written out of some kind of burden. . . . Nowadays nobody has no worry or struggles."[57]

The Evolution of Gospel Music

If the Spirituals are normative black sacred music, then why did Gospel music evolve sensibilities that diverged from it? That is, how do we account for the development of the Gospel music genre?

As we saw above, the fundamental theological shifts and perspectival differences between the Spiritual and Gospel musical genres are pronounced and, in some ways, profound. It is my belief that these differences are largely the result of the shift in the mode of production of the masses of African Americans from rural agrarian to urban industrial.

If, as we saw above, the rural agrarian setting of the Spirituals in some ways empowered black folks, the urban industrial settings to which they migrated in the first decades of this century in other ways disempowered them. Whereas the rural settings of the Spirituals afforded some measure of expanse and possibility, the tone of the stifling, overcrowded urban ghettoes was one of constriction and severely limited horizons. And whereas many enslaved Africans and, later, black sharecroppers and smallholders had known the sometimes small, yet often meaningful affirmation that comes from agricultural production, most urban blacks knew only alienated labor, which, as we saw above, is labor that afforded them little sense of the satisfaction of creation and accomplishment.[58]

The majority of black laborers in urban industry, particularly males, worked in factories, most as assembly line workers of some sort. What is significant about this is that assembly line labor, by definition, is mind-numbing and disempowering. Indeed, Frederick Taylor, the father of assembly line production, or "Taylorism," as it first was called, declared, "In our scheme, we do not ask the initiative of our men. We do not want any initiative. All we want of them is to obey orders we give them, do what we say, and do it quick."[59] To assembly workers in general he remarked, "[We] have you for your strength and mechanical ability, and we have other men for thinking."[60] Being confronted by a mode of labor that so discounted their basic humanity could only have compounded the migrants' sense of disempowerment and further dashed their sinking hopes for life abundant.

The Apocalyptic Origins of Gospel Music

Although the de facto chattel status that black migrants found in northern urban industrial settings was in many ways no worse than they were accustomed to in the rural South, because of the stifling working conditions and the alienated nature of the labor they performed, their chattel status in the North was not offset by the psychic satisfaction of being producers and cultivators as it had been offset, to some extent, in the South. The black workers were now simply cogs in a wheel who produced neither crop nor craft nor the fruit of personal ingenuity; as assembly workers they performed tasks that, by themselves, were meaningless and abstract. Under both the slavocracy and Reconstruction the hope of would-be immigrants to the northern cities was on freedom, on leaving behind the white-hot heat of southern oppression. But having followed the drinking gourd to the northern Promised Land that was proclaimed by the Spirituals and still finding themselves counted as chattel, the black migrants' hopes of justice were sorely disappointed. Urban life subjected them to new indignities that were compounded by their alienation from the agrarian lands to which their lives and livelihoods had been tied. Instead of fertile soil and the ubiquitous greenery of nature, they now pondered concrete and asphalt. In the rural South there had been at least the possibility that they might one day own a plot of land free and clear, but in the urban landscape property ownership was a grudgingly, if not bitterly, accepted impossibility for most. Further, limited and grossly inadequate urban living facilities often resulted in the separation of the extended families that had been a mainstay of their lives in the rural South. In short, the world of the black urban migrants offered few of the social support mechanisms they had known in the South. As one commentator put it, "There was no Promised Land to own in the North, just landlords threatening eviction of those who fell behind in their rent. A better name would have been the 'Promises Land.' "[61]

When the harsh realities of their new setting in life became inexorably clear, it must have seemed to the weary migrants that if neither Lincoln's emancipation nor urban migration had brought them relief from oppression, then maybe there simply was no relief to be had in this world. So, like the oppressed and beleagured first-century Christians — who, as the result of their accumulated traumas became unable to envision justice under the Roman Empire and looked instead to "a new heaven and a new earth" (cf. Rev. 21:1) — so too, the black urban migrants succumbed to apocalypticism and began to direct their fading hopes from the here-and-now, which was the locus of defeat and disappointment for them and which did not offer the prospect of justice, to the apocalyptic "new heaven and new earth," a locus that did offer the possibility of justice and victory. Indeed, having left the South for the idealized freedom of the North, where else could these black migrants now hope to run except to a "new heaven and new earth"? In this sense, the hope of Gospel music is a hope born of disappointment, of powerlessness, of conceding the dominion of life on earth to the principalities and powers of earthly domination. It is a hope that says, in effect, "It is clear that there will be no justice for me in this world. Nothing I can do will make a difference, so I'll just wait on the Lord. I'll just leave it all to Jesus." At its core, then, Gospel music embodies the classic apocalyptic feeling of powerlessness to forestall the oppressive forces of this world, accompanied by a sense of resignation to continued social misery at the hands of wielders of unjust power until the apocalyptic "day of the Lord" (cf. 1 Thess. 5:2).

Mode of Production, Mode of Presentation:
Assembly Lines and Trickeration

The influence upon the evolution of Gospel music by both urban industrialism and the assembly line mode of production that emerged in the first quarter of the twentieth century is not only seen in the apocalyticism of the genre, but also in the way Gospel music itself is produced, i.e., in its own mode of production. Just as the restrictive housing patterns and living conditions that were the result of industrialism fractured the extended family form that had characterized the agrarian mode of production, causing both discrete, separate nuclear families and fragmented extended families to eventually predominate, and just as the demands of Taylorism divided manual labor into firmly regimented sets of separate and specialized tasks, Gospel music was also influenced by and succumbed to the specialization demands of the new urban industrial culture in which the new migrants found themselves. In a sense specialization was part of the *zeitgeist* or spirit of the age. Even the highest levels of white collar professions were specializing within their own ranks. For instance, whereas the legal profession had historically been comprised of generalists who handled almost every type of case, the dawn of the twentieth century "saw the emergence of the specialist, first in commercial law as a whole and then in various aspects of it. Soon men devoted their entire careers to real estate or trusts or receiverships or stock issues."[62]

Notwithstanding Sallie Martin's testimony that the early Gospel she witnessed and participated in retained some of the sense of the collective production of the Spirituals,[63] the production of most Gospel music, almost from its beginnings, was caught in the wake of the larger productive forces of the American political economy, becoming widely specialized and individualized. The roots of this process lie with none other than Thomas Dorsey, who in 1926 copyrighted and published his first Gospel tune, "If You See My Savior, Tell Him That You Saw Me." This began the process of Gospel songs being sold as commodities, first as sheet music, then as recordings. Individuals owned copyrights to the songs, which were not identified with locales or the conditions and plights that spawned them, as was the case with the Spirituals, but with particular individual performers, thus effectively removing Gospel songs from their respective contextualizing socio-political referents.

The specialization spawned by the urban industrial mode of production is also reflected in Gospel's mode of presentation, with soloists for the first time becoming the norm in black sacred song. There had often been leaders in the Spirituals' tradition of call-and-response, which was the descendent of the traditional African ring shout, but the role of the solo in Gospel music is much more pronounced. In Gospel music there are two basic types of soloists: individual soloists singing alone and solo leads of quartets. The earliest "quartet"[64] soloists, or lead singers, generally were not emphasized; the accepted practice was that they were given no special position with respect to other group members but simply sang their solos and blended back into the group harmony. This practice changed as the result of the innovations of several Gospel groups, particularly the Soul Stirrers, who not only brought the lead singer physically out in front of the other singers, but also incorporated a second "lead" singer to replace the first lead's role in the quartet harmony. This innovation effectively freed the first lead to take much longer solos without concern for disrupting the group's harmonic flow. This innovation also yielded another development that has become a mainstay in Gospel music: the technique of ad-libbing, or "hard Gospel" style, which was given its first wide exposure, again by the Soul Stirrers and their original lead, Robert H. Harris, on the recording "Shine on Me, Featuring R. H. Harris," which was produced in the mid-1940s.

The Advent of "Clowning"

Initially, for all its ecstatic, emotional quality, the limits of the performance orientation of Gospel music were, for the most part, circumscribed by the emphasis on dignified comportment that most Gospel singers were known to maintain even at the height of ecstatic celebration, or "getting happy," in keeping with Gospel's emphasis on emotional comfort and personal moral and spiritual uplift. For instance, the decorum and dignified bearing of singer/songwriter Miss Lucie E. Campbell was said to be so inspiring that folks came from miles around just to see her walk across stage.[65] However, the freedom to perform and ad-lib that evolved in Gospel music eventually led to a startling new development that transformed Gospel's emphasis on dignified bearing. That development, with its apparent beginnings in the 1940s, was the practice of "clowning," so-called by early Gospel afficionados to denote actions or phrasings undertaken primarily for their entertainment value. In a startlingly candid recognition of the emphasis of this practice on manipulation of the audiences' emotions to maximize the impact of Gospel performances, Ira Tucker, the veteran leader of the Dixie Hummingbirds, called it "trickeration."[66]

Rev. Julius Cheeks of the Sensational Nightingales, a highly popular group in the 1940s and 1950s, claims to have begun the practice of clowning: "I was the first to cut the fool ... [to] do what the people wanted."[67] Ira Tucker made the same claim, asserting that all Gospel singers before him sang "flat-footed." "I started this hip-slapping all the quartets do," Tucker claimed. "I jumped off my first stage in Suffolk, Virginia [in 1944]. . . . Shoot, what James Brown does, I've been doing."[68]

Despite the claims of Cheeks and Tucker, the "clowning" performance orientation in Gospel music was also in evidence as early as the 1940s in the Virginia-based Golden Gate Quartet's performances with swing bands and in the appearances of the guitar-playing Sister Rosetta Tharpe at New York's Cotton Club and Cafe Society Downtown night spots.[69] Although the emphasis on performance orientation does seem to have been heightened, if not originated, by the antics of Ira Tucker, it became much more marked in the 1950s and 1960s with the Clara Ward Singers, who regularly performed their highly stylized and flamboyant act in night clubs, often sporting huge identical wigs and fancy outfits sometimes bordering on the outlandish. It can be argued that it was the Ward Singers who set the stage for the intense commercialism and widespread acceptance of the heightened performance orientation that now characterizes contemporary Gospel music. In this sense, Ward can be seen as the precursor of such developments in Gospel as Kirk Franklin's appearance on the acclaimed R&B, funk, and rap television showcase *Soul Train,* and similar appearances by Gospel artists in other pop music venues.

Like many Gospel performers today, Clara Ward defended her group's behavior by paraphrasing Luke 14:23, the biblical verse often used to justify Gospel performances in secular commercial entertainment venues: "The Lord told us to go into the highways and hedges as well." On one such occasion an angry young man is said to have replied to Ward, "You know folks don't come to clubs to get saved. They want to see Negroes make damn fools of themselves."[70]

The exaggerated "clowning" performance orientation of Gospel music was taken to new heights in the 1960s and 1970s by a number of artists, including the flamboyant Alex Bradford, whom Gospel music scholar Anthony Heilbut calls "Gospel's Little Richard."[71] By this time "wrecking the house," i.e., moving an audience to the heights of emotional pandemonium, had long been the widely accepted goal of Gospel performances and remains so today. In the contemporary era, this performance orientation is seen not only in the vocal gymnastics and the purposefully repetitive arrangements by which Gospel artists routinely attempt to eke every bit of emotion out of songs, but also in the choreography of artists such as Hezekiah Walker and Ricky Dillard, the latter of whom "cut up" as a featured performer in *Leap of Faith,* Steve Martin's motion picture critique of the excesses of the performance-based strain of contemporary evangelical religion.

In response to the pervasive emphasis on the "clowning" and perform-ance orientation of the genre, one of the key-figures in early Gospel, Rev. Claude Jeter, who sang with the Swan Silvertones in the 1940s and 1950s, acknowledges, "we've had too much form and fashion on stage."[72] The venerable Thomas Dorsey was a primary architect of the apolitical apoca-lyptic perspective that came to permeate Gospel, and his business acumen was an important factor in its commercialization. Still, Dorsey professed to be no advocate of "clowning" and excessive performance orientation:

> I find some ... who have too many embellishments that may be mis-taken for spirit. Variations on the piano or organ or swinging a song beyond its beauty is not spirit. Loud vociferous singing, uninspired gesticulations or self-incurred spasms of the body is not spirit. I believe in shouting, running, and crying out if the holy spirit comes upon one, but I don't believe in going to get the spirit before it comes.[73]

The politically astute Rev. Herbert Brewster goes further, characterizing the performance orientation of Gospel music as "all heat and no light."[74] Brewster observed of the early days of Gospel, "We didn't have none of this modern clowning."[75] No less than Aretha Franklin argues passionately that "when it makes you want to dance and pop your fingers, believe me, it isn't Gospel. . . . Gospel is a higher calling; Gospel is about God."[76] In the final analysis, however, although "clowning" initially caused Cheeks and other practitioners of it to be ejected from churches rejecting what they felt to be the trivialization of black sacred music, the practice eventually became an accepted phenomenon, its entertainment value and appeals to emotion winning the day. The triumph of entertainment sensibilities can be witnessed weekly in every broadcast medium. One of the most popular of these venues is *Bobby Jones Gospel,* the fourth longest-running syndicated program on cable television,[77] seen weekly by five million viewers. *Bobby Jones Gospel* presents Gospel performers in a variety show entertainment format in which each performer seems at least as intent on "wrecking the house" as praising the Lord. *Bobby Jones Gospel* is the epitome of the per-formance orientation that has pervaded Gospel. Unfortunately, "Bobby

Jones" and programs like it regularly showcase this performance orientation to America as somehow being normative for black sacred music. This in turn leads to the impression that to criticize the goings on of Bobby Jones Gospel and the like is to criticize the entire Gospel music genre, which is a decidedly politically incorrect position that few seem willing to take, given the genre's popularity. The result is that critical engagement of the excesses of Gospel is effectively silenced.

Commodification and the Evolution of "Audience"

With the development of the specialization and the heightened performance aspects of Gospel, members of the believing community for the first time became auditors of the music; that is, they became "audience" to performances by Gospel soloists or quartets rather than the full participants in collective community expression they had been in the production and performance of the Spirituals. It is the advent of this performer/audience dichotomy that underlies Gospel music's presentation orientation. It is also with the advent of this dichotomy that audience acceptance became a driving force of the genre, causing it to become even more entertainment oriented and geared toward engendering responses that elicited audience approval, having jettisoned the Spirituals' less performance friendly prophetic proclamation of justice on earth as in heaven. This separation of the production of the music from community product into the current phenomenon of writer/performer + audience was of crucial significance because it signaled that Gospel songs were now produced for *exchange,* that is, for remuneration, rather than being primarily produced for the psycho-emotional and socio-political edification of the communities that spawned them, as in the past. The forms this remuneration takes range from public acclaim and deference to financial compensation, although the latter is usually a function of the former. In this sense, the production of Gospel music has become overwhelmingly market driven. By this measure, Gospel songs are now *commodities,* that is, goods produced for sale. Anthony Heilbut observes of this development in the genre, "Instead of looking to the hills [i.e., to God, "from whence comes my help"; cf. Ps. 121:1–2], it looks to the [sales] charts."[78] However, this does not mean that Gospel music does not have the edification of its consumers as its goal. Rather, it means that the forms that edification takes are strongly influenced, if not driven, by market forces. Therefore, the problem with the commodification of Gospel music today is not that it is profitable; it is only fair that if financial compensation is to be realized at all, it should be realized by the creators and performers of Gospel music. No, the problem with the commodification of Gospel music is not that it is profitable, but that it is profit *driven.*

Thus it is the commodification of black sacred music that was begun in earnest by the Gospel genre that accounts for its mode of performance; in response to the demands of the market it has become firmly and patently performance oriented. This is particularly the case with regard to the genre's "clowning" aspects. Replete with highly stylized dress and sometimes dazzlingly choreographed movements, well-staged crescendos of "spontaneous" emotion, and music purposefully arranged to showcase vocal gymnastics and pyrotechnics, Gospel music today appears to be almost totally performance driven into a species of the cathartic vehicle of emotional release Karl Marx apparently had in mind when he bitingly rejected religion and its expressions as "the opiate of the masses."[79] In a 1999 Associated Press article about the growing phenomenon of churches utilizing professional musicians and song stylists as a way to "lure" new members, the president of the Nashville-based Gospel Music Association willingly underscored the importance of the performance and entertainment orientation to Gospel music: "[Churches] recognize this is one of the ways they not only minister to their flock spiritually but *also to their entertainment needs"* [emphasis in the original].[80]

The commodification of Gospel music and the performance orientation it fuels, its reduction of the systemic causes of the collective social, political, and economic struggles of African Americans into individual failings and problems, along with its apocalyptic apoliticality, have all combined to make Gospel music today a force of little consequence in the ongoing struggle of black folks to enjoy the full measure of comfort and security of American society. As a genre, Gospel music lacks most of the normative elements of sacred music that evolved through blacks' sojourn in America. Rather than collective acknowledgment of oppression, Gospel offers individualized expressions of hope and praise. Instead of prophetic critique, it offers political quietism. Gospel songs do not exhort resistance to injustice; they counsel joyful resignation instead. Thus we must conclude that other than its empathic dimension, Gospel music today does not embody the normative features of black sacred music that we have identified.

NO MORE CLOWNING, NO MORE DOPE

Kirk Franklin is the most commercially successfully figure in the history of Gospel music and remains so today. His music reveals him to be sincere in his effort to bring the Gospel of Jesus Christ to the world. He is clearly a young man of great faith and purpose.

To acknowledge that Franklin's music deflects vision and energy from substantive visions of social change and social activism is not to denigrate the significant role of empathy in his music. He shows a deep sensitivity to everyday personal emotional and moral challenges. This dimension of his music is quite powerfully evident in the beautiful "Imagine Me":

> *Imagine me, being free, trusting you totally finally I can....*
> *Imagine me*
> *I admit it was hard to see*
> *You being in love with someone like me*
> *But finally I can....*
> *Imagine me*

In his touchingly revealing autobiography, Franklin writes, "I want to reach nonbelievers in nontraditional ways. I want to see revival come back to this land."[81] And in some of his songs Franklin does reveal social sensibilities. Consider his song "Lean on Me":

> *There's a man standing on the corner with no home*
> *He has no food and his blue skies are gone.*
> *Can't you hear him crying out?*

Consider, as well, his hip hop-influenced "Revolution":

> *Do you want a revolution?*
> *Sick and tired of my brothers*
> *Killing each other...*
> *No more racism...*
> *No pollution.*
> *The solution: a revolution.*

Yet although he speaks of "revolution," the social vision Kirk Franklin's music purveys excludes real revolutionary engagement of the systemic causes of the social ills he decries. As with most of his Gospel contemporaries, Franklin's solutions to socio-political problems are exclusively in the realm of individualized conceptions of salvation. Moreover, in his startling statement in *Vibe* magazine that began this chapter, Franklin inadvertently reveals his estimation of his own music to be consistent with Karl Marx's negative assessment of religion and its modes of expression as "the opiate of the masses": "People need to get high off something spiritual, and I'm the holy dope dealer. I got this drug, I got this Jesus rock. And you can have a type of high that you've never experienced."[82] To be fair, Franklin probably spoke in such shocking terms to capture the attention of *Vibe's* youthful, hip hop-oriented readership. Still, with his use of the term "Jesus 'rock'" (the street name for crack cocaine) Franklin himself characterizes his music as an opiate, a palliative, a drug — a description whose evocation of political quietism could apply as well to most contemporary Gospel music.

In a nutshell, that is the basic problem with Gospel music today. As the result of the "clowning" that has become normative for it; as the result of its pervasive performance orientation, its emphasis on "wrecking the house," and its shameless appeals to emotion, the contemporary Gospel music genre *has* come to function as an opiate for the masses. As with a drug, sensations and emotions have come to be its focus. Like a drug, its primary goal is not to empower its users to change reality, but simply to change the way they feel. Like a drug, it temporarily lifts the people's despair yet, in direct contradistinction to the prophetic mandate of the Spirituals, leaves the causes of that despair virtually unaddressed, unscathed, even unmentioned. Gospel music doesn't attempt to free the people but simply seeks to make them feel good. It doesn't exhort them to political liberation; instead, it lights their emotional fires. Rather than calling for resistance, it rocks the house. And in place of the prophetic mandate, today's Gospel music offers "praise." In fact, since Andrae Crouch and others popularized it in the 1970s "praise," which focuses on extolling God's mercy, grace, and magnificence, has been an important part of the Gospel music equation. Certainly God is worthy of all praise. But unfortunately, the definition of "praise" offered by Gospel music is an attenuated one that begins and ends with singing, clapping hands, speaking in sometimes suspiciously well-timed "unknown" tongues, and "holy" dances that, amazingly, seem never to miss a beat. Sadly, the genre never goes so far as to praise God as a God of justice or to advocate praising God by dismantling the systems of oppression that afflict God's beloved human creation of all colors and creeds. Gospel music hears not, sees not, and speaks not of the evil of the oppression and exploitation of the very people that love it so. The sad reality is that if we follow the lead of Gospel music today, not only will systemic evils never be addressed, they will never even be mentioned! The "holy" dope will continue to tell us to just "leave it to Jesus" while we sing, dance, shout, and overdose on the musical opiates we so gladly consume and purvey. Indeed, if African Americans did everything that Gospel music asks, where would we be? Would we be moved to address the social system that often devalues our humanity and our intelligence, that demonizes and criminalizes our children, that in some ways seems poised to try to turn back the clock on the social progress that we have made? If black folks followed the social vision of Gospel music, would we be inspired or empowered or guided to make a better and more just world for our children?

Put simply, for all its popularity, Gospel music today no longer embodies the best of the black sacred music tradition. Indeed, as basic a constituent of that tradition as the empowering logic of the Exodus liberation typology is almost nowhere to be found in today's Gospel. This absence of liberation sensibilities is reflected in the observation of Cheryl James of the popular 1990s rap group Salt-N-Pepa, who also shared her views on Gospel music within the *Vibe* profile of Kirk Franklin. James, who appears on Franklin's hip-hop–influenced 1997 platinum recording *Stomp,* explains that the appeal of the Gospel music that Franklin and his contemporaries exemplify is precisely that it does *not* evoke liberation motifs or resistance sensibilities. "It's not about slavery and the old ways," she remarks approvingly.[83] This posture of refusing to inform the relative freedom of the present with awareness of the freedom struggles of the past is a basic constituent of the apolitical nature of contemporary Gospel music. What is overlooked by James and those who believe as she does is that the "old ways" they discount are in reality the resistance sensibilities that have brought black people this far. However, in actuality it is not just old-fashioned ways that are discounted by contemporary Gospel music; it also discounts the historical logic of freedom that is still much needed by African Americans if we are to address the social and economic inequities that bedevil black life still. That resistance sensibilities and not simply old-fashioned ways are rejected by contemporary Gospel artists is evidenced by the unwillingness of most Gospel artists to create lyrical resistance strategies that fit their personal or generational sensibilities. The importance of evolving one's own musical resistance strategies is seen in the example of the enslaved African Americans who produced the Spirituals. Not only did they live under the most intense form of systematic domination and dehumanization ever enacted, but also under the most intense campaign of obfuscation and sacralization of oppression ever waged. Yet through the prophetic critique and prophetic consciousness of the Spirituals, they reminded themselves and the generations that followed that although chattel was their status, it was not their identity. Indeed, it was the slaves' willingness to articulate their plight and their refusal to shift responsibility for the resolution of it to somewhere over yonder that gave the Spirituals their power and the slaves their perseverance. That same willingness to articulate and confront African Americans' situation today can afford us that same power—not only to persevere, but to change the world.

As for Kirk Franklin, unfortunately the sensitivity of his music to personal struggles seems to be consistently matched by an insensitivity to social and political struggles. That little has changed in Franklin's perspective in the decade or more since his *Vibe* interview is reflected in his new book, *The Blueprint*.[84]

In it Franklin gives sage advice on personal growth and relational issues, but still gives no attention to issues of political oppression and economic exploitation or how to engage social injustice. As with his music, if his readers were to put into practice his book's every suggestion, the injustices they face daily and from which they need deliverance would continue, unchanged and unchallenged.

FROM SPIRITED SINGING TO SPIRIT-LED ACTION

Gospel music has produced songs possessed of great power and unspeakable beauty. It can move its listeners to emotional and spiritual peaks as no other musical genre can. Who can hear Richard Smallwood's "Total

Praise," or "My Tribute" by Andrae Crouch, or Donny McClurkin's "Stand" without being moved to the heights of reverence? The beauty and power of Gospel music must ever be maintained. Yet it cannot be left unchanged, not as long as so much of its genius and energy is spent on entertainment and emotion rather than on exhorting freedom, justice, and equality for and by its listeners. So let those of us who love Gospel music build upon its strengths and together strengthen its weaknesses. Let us together call upon Gospel artists today to reject the "clowning," the trickeration, the entertainment orientation, the dealing of dope — "holy" or not. We must tell them to stop acquiescing to the popular sensibilities that seductively equate entertainment with evangelism. And we must insist that they end their refusal to engage in prophetic critique of systemic evil. Gospel music must stop reducing the causes of human suffering to weak faith or poor morality on the part of the victim, or to ethereal, disembodied sources for which no one has responsibility. These trivialize the very real struggles of black people, with the dangerous consequence that the actual systemic obstacles to black Americans' full realization of the American dream are not only ignored, but are ultimately relieved of responsibility for the everyday importunities they continue to wreak upon the lives of black people of all ages and all social strata.

But there is a way that Gospel music can become an important constituent of African Americans' struggle for social justice rather than a distraction from it: it can marry the emotional appeal of Gospel music with the prophetic consciousness and resistance sensibilities of the Spirituals to produce a new generation of resistance music, music that moves black people, indeed, *all* people, not just to emotional frenzy, but to that divinely inspired *action* that is the struggle to establish God's kingdom of justice — on earth, as in heaven. Gospel music must move beyond preaching Jesus to preaching what Jesus preached; it must move beyond spirited singing to Spirit-led song that proclaims to all — and moves them to proclaim in turn: "The Spirit of the Lord is upon me, because he has anointed me to bring good news to the poor . . . to proclaim release to the captives . . . to let the oppressed go free." Amen.

- 2 -

The Grapes of Wrath
and the True Vine

Reading from Below Is the Way to Go

*In our usual reconstructions of history, including standard handbooks in
New Testament studies, we seldom devote much attention to the common
people. Those who make history, or so we assume, are the Caesars and the
Herods.* — Richard A. Horsley

Some five centuries before the birth of Christ, a man was born on the
outskirts of Athens who would forever change the way that historical
events are recorded and recounted in the Western world. Born of great
wealth and privilege — "an Athenian aristocrat of the bluest blood," one
scholar called him — in his mid-thirties he was elected as one of the ten top
military and political leaders of Athens. Despite his exalted social status
and his self-description as one of the most influential men of the region,
he was held responsible for a disastrous battle and exiled from Athens,
never to return. Along the way he controlled gold mines and survived a
plague that killed a third of his countrymen. Yet despite his remarkable
life, it is not for any of those experiences that he has been remembered
and lauded for twenty-five hundred years. What distinguishes this man of
antiquity from all who came before him was something much more long
lasting: it is the new and revolutionary way that he recounted the events
of history; the innovative methods that he used and the more stringent
standards that he set to record the collective experiences of humanity.
His name is no household word, yet twenty-five centuries later his legacy
extends to virtually every historical book that we in the Western world
read and to every serious work of history that we write. His influence
extends even to the writing of the New Testament. Accordingly, he is

universally acclaimed as the founder of the scientific approach to Western history. His name? Thucydides.

THUCYDIDES: PUTTING THE "STORY" IN HISTORIOGRAPHY

Before Thucydides, Western history was written in the "epic" form, a form more concerned with the poetic praising of the past than with the accurate reporting of it. The epic is epitomized by two classics of Western literature written eight centuries before the birth of Christ, *The Odyssey* and *The Iliad*. Both were populated with gods and mythological characters, composed in poetic meter, and, it is said, were presented by Homer, their author, as public poetic performances.

It was Thucydides who moved beyond the epic form with its romanticism of the past, and even beyond the *ethnikoi* — reports of the history, culture, and living habits of various ethic groups — compiled by his near contemporary Herodotus,[1] to introduce into the writing of history what he called his *akribeia* treatment of historical events, that is, his conscious emphasis on "accuracy" of fact and detail in the narration of history. Before Thucydides, essentially historians simply reported historical events and personages as they were brought to their attention, with no systematic consideration for gauging accuracy. It was Thucydides who was the first to engage in what is called *historiography,* that is to say, a systematic approach to doing history, replete with practical standards of accuracy to be employed when doing it. He explains his historiographic approach in his masterwork, *The Peloponnesian War:* "But as to the facts of the events of the day, I have thought it right to write them down, not just as they happened to come my way, nor according to my own predispositions, but only after investigating each one with greatest possible *accuracy*" (*akribeia;* 1.22).[2] He somewhat derisively contrasts his more rigorous approach to history with the popular histories of Herodotus before him: "And, perhaps, my account will seem less pleasing to those who hear it because of its lack of fabulous tales, but if it be judged useful by those who seek an exact knowledge of the past as an aid to the interpretation of the future . . . I shall be satisfied. It has been composed, not as an entry to a competition to be heard for the moment, but as a possession forever" (1.23–24).[3] Ouch!

The influence that Thucydides' emphasis on the *akribeia* — accuracy of fact and detail in historical narrative — exerted on the writing of history in the West has been evident for centuries. The weight of his influence is even seen in the New Testament, particularly in the evangelist Luke's pronounced attention to detail in his two contributions to the New Testament canon: the Gospel that bears his name and the book of Acts. Thucydides' influence on Luke's Gospel is reflected in Luke's extensive use of descriptive details to the extent that his critical eye for detail has often been mistakenly explained by portraying him as a physician, according to the logic that as a physician Luke would have been trained to observe details more closely than the average person. Moreover, Luke specifically uses the Thucydidean descriptive term *akribeia* in his description of his own approach to recounting the story of Jesus when he writes, using the term's adverbial form, "having followed all things *akribos* ("accurately" or "in detail")" (Luke 1:3). In addition, Thucydides' literary device of using lengthy speeches to narrate and explain certain events (speeches comprise roughly a quarter of Thucydides' writing) is a major feature of Luke-Acts. Luke's Gospel puts lengthy speeches in the mouths of major figures like Zechariah, Elizabeth, and Mary, and attributes less lengthy but still notable speeches to minor characters like the old holy man Simeon and the elderly prophetess Anna. Luke goes even further in the book of Acts, in which the speeches he attributes to figures such as Peter, Paul, and Stephen comprise some 30 percent of the book's total verses.

The influence of Thucydides' *akribeia* approach to recounting history has been profound and far reaching in the centuries since he took up the pen. But there is another legacy of Thucydides that is no less far-reaching: his emphasis on *klea andron,* the momentous or "great deeds of men," as the focus of his new way of writing history.

The emphasis on *klea andron,* the "great" or "glorious deeds of men," did not originate with Thucydides, for the pre-Thucydidean epic histories also centered on the glorious deeds of men (mortal women were not considered capable of great deeds). Again, Homer's works are prime examples, with their stories told through the actions of gods like Zeus, Apollo, and Poseidon, and warriors like Achilles, Apollo, and Hector. Yet there is a difference between the *klea andron* approach of Thucydides and that of those who came before him: in Thucydides' recounting of the great deeds of men, their lives and deeds were subjected to the rigors of his *akribeia* approach.

In Thucydides' recounting of the Peloponnesian War and its causes, the *klea andron* of the noteworthy political and military figures he writes about are deeds related to conducting wars and engaging in political intrigue — endeavors in which the vast majority of humanity were merely pawns. Thucydides does acknowledge the suffering of the lower classes, the non-elite, rank-and-file humanity situated "below" the upper, dominant classes, from causes such as war, disease, and natural catastrophe (another Thucy-didean innovation; before him, such observations were seldom made). Yet although it is the ordinary frontline soldiers and civilian victims of war whose lives are affected most by military conflicts, in Thucydides' writing they almost never speak for themselves of their plight. Unlike his treatment of major political movers and shakers and despite his proclivity for telling history through speeches, in Thucydides' historiography those in the lower classes seldom speak of their own sufferings or their own truths; instead they almost always are spoken *for*. Despite his professed insistence upon investigation and accurate reporting, Thucydides apparently did not take the same care to seek out the stories of those whose lives were controlled, dominated, and often decimated by "the great deeds of men." This does not necessarily mean that at the times when he did seek out their thoughts and responses that he took less accurate care in recording them, according to his own understanding. What the relative absence of their direct testimony does seem to indicate, however, is that Thucydides, the blue-blooded aristocrat, did not generally see their deeds as qualifying as "great," at least not when it came to shaping the course of human events.

Thucydides' class-based myopia is evident in another of his innovations: analyzing historical events for the purpose of identifying underlying patterns of human behavior. Cicero called this mode of reflection on historical events the *magistra vitae,* the "teacher of life." Or put another way, teaching *about* life. As Lucian explained it, "according to [Thucydides' philosophy of history], it is that if men ever again encounter similar circumstances, they should be able, by paying close attention to what has been recorded of the past, to deal properly with the situation that confronts them."[4] In the *Peloponnesian War* Thucydides gives extensive consideration to mass behavior, yet his primary focus and his *magistra vitae* — his teaching about life — is still the *klea andron,* the deeds of elites and their responses to events and circumstances. Yet both individual and collective responses to actions, events, and pronouncements can be conditioned by and can also vary by class, culture, and certainly by social location. For example, notions of honor and shame can differ greatly according to whether one's purview is shaped in urban or rural locales; or whether one is a peasant smallholder or is instead the principal worker of his own land or a member of the propertied class with slaves and workers in his employ; or whether one is a figure of authority or a person who is subject to the will of authority figures.

One example of this class variance is the difference in class-based attitudes toward something as basic as manual labor. For instance, a fragment from the fourth century B.C.E. Athenian poet Menander indicates that the upper classes saw no honor in honest manual labor, claiming that "farming is slave's work." Instead, "it is deeds of war by which a man ought to prove his superiority," as a preceding line by Menander asserts.[5]

In classical Rome, personally engaging in manual work was seen as dishonorable. Cicero quotes a line from a play by Terence that pronounces digging, plowing, and carrying loads to be *illiberalis labor,* "ungentlemanly toil."[6] For the lower classes, on the other hand, it was not work that was dishonorable, but rather the *unwillingness* to work. Moreover, for the lower classes honor was not a birthright; it had to be earned, *acquired.* And one of the main ways peasants acquired honor was by honest labor; for a peasant, it was wallowing in leisure that was dishonorable. This demonstrates that the respective choices and actions of each of these classes was influenced, if not fully determined, by their differing social locations. This indicates, in turn, that what constitutes a "great deed" is class based and culturally based. That is why any attempt to predict either individual or collective behavior through a projected one-size-fits-all social location is problematic, for it simply cannot anticipate the crucial differences in their responses.

Further, Thucydides' approach to history reflects a strong belief in the ability of individuals to change the course of history by the force of their personal character alone. Thus for Thucydides a military leader named Themistocles was "the wisest in foreseeing what would happen in the distant future" and "surpassed all others in the faculty of intuitively meeting an emergency."[7] The implication is that without Themistocles, emergencies that arose in Athens during his lifetime would have had less satisfying ends. Similarly, it was primarily, if not singularly, the unwavering honesty and foresight of Pericles, the Athenian head of state, that made Athens great: "For so long a time as he was at the head of state during the peace...its greatness was at its height" (2.65.5). Yet those Thucydides cites as possessing the personal character to change history are all men of power in one arena of society or another. Apparently there is no provision in Thucydides' mode of analysis for observing — either accurately or inaccurately — strong character and leadership traits among members of the ordinary populace. He does seem to take an admiring view of the sailors in Part 8 of the *Peloponnesian War.* However, it is mostly their collective behavior that he lauds and his discussion of them is not typical of him. Moreover, the sailors are nameless with no acknowledged leader among them. Otherwise, the subjects that get Thucydides' most significant attention are social and political elites.

According to Thucydides' *klea andron* approach to history, small-time figures hardly merit a mention. This certainly is the case with Jesus. Although he himself is one of the most renowned figures in human history, the peasant Jesus of Nazareth hails from the ignored, overlooked, devalued masses of history. Poor, of questionable parentage, low of social station, and bereft of political connections, he was raised in a backwater so insignificant that it is mentioned nowhere in the literature of the first century other than in the New Testament. In Jesus' day Nazareth was such a non-entity outside its immediate confines[8] that the Gospel of John tells us that some in Israel questioned whether it could possibly be a source of "anything good" (cf. John 1:46).

For these reasons Jesus was certainly not a fitting subject of *klea andron* history from above. That is why he merits only a few terse, unsympathetic mentions in the writings of the Thucydides-influenced historians of the Early Common Era — Tacitus, Suetonius, Pliny the Younger, and Josephus — and then not in acknowledgment of his own personhood or accomplishments or character or beliefs but rather only about how his presence registered in the concerns of elites.[9] Even then he is mentioned only as one would mention a nuisance, a gnat easily brushed from the elitist cuff. Outside the New Testament writings, the three or four first-century mentions of him say nothing of his character or beliefs.

Thus, for Thucydides the vantage points and experiences of those below were not of the same order of significance as the perspectives of those in positions of power, control, and social authority. For Thucydides *akribeia* — detailed reporting — seems not to have fully extended to the sentiments of folks beyond a certain remove from the centers of power.

TELLING THE FAMILY'S HISTORY, NOT THE ODD UNCLE'S

As influential as Thucydides' historiography continues to be in the West, there have been significant developments since the Enlightenment that have taken the purview of historiography beyond the focus on the great deeds of men. In *The Eighteenth Brumaire of Louis Napoleon* (1852), Karl Marx analyzed the events surrounding Napoleon Bonaparte's 1851 coup d'état in France by going beyond *klea andron* and looking at the material forces and conditions that led to it. Marc Bloch and Lucien Febvre, the founders of the Annales School of historiography in France in the 1920s, broke radically with traditional historiography by insisting on the importance of taking all levels of society into consideration and treating events as less important than the mental framework that shaped decisions. What has come to be called the "new" social history emerged in the United States in the 1960s in the works of such historians as Natalie Zemon Davis, Eugene Genovese, Herbert Gutman, and Lawrence Levine, and E. P. Thompson in Great Britain. These historians reoriented the study of American history (British history in the case of Thompson, although he has been very influential in the United States) along the lines of the behavioral sciences (economics, political science, and sociology) and shifted the emphasis of reading history from the top down to the bottom up — in effect, the very opposite of the Thucydidean *klea andron* gaze. Under the influence of the Italian Marxist activist intellectual Antonio Gramsci, in the 1980s Asian historians Ranajit Guha and Gayatri Spivak spearheaded the Subaltern Studies Group, whose central subject of study was "subalterns," i.e., those who are socially, economically, and politically "of inferior rank," specifically peasants and the working class, including the working poor. The stated purpose of the Subaltern Study Group is "help[ing] to rectify the elitist bias characteristic of much research and academic work in these particular areas."[10]

These developments began to filter into biblical studies in the 1980s in the works of anthropologist Bruce Malina,[11] Marxist biblical scholars like Fernando Belo[12] and Michel Clevenot,[13] Ched Myers's socio-literary reading of Mark's Gospel,[14] and Itumeleng Mosala's insightful treatment of "the word of God" ideology and his materialist reading of the book of Micah.[15] Richard A. Horsley's savvy critique of the structural function-alist sociology of Emil Durkheim and August Comte that underpinned the work of major New Testament scholars like Gerd Theissen[16] demon-strated how the traditional modes of biblical study had underestimated the political radicality of the Jesus movement.[17] In 1991 there appeared more mainstream works like John Dominic Crossan's *The Historical Jesus: The Life of a Mediterranean Peasant*[18] and John P. Meier's *A Marginal Jew: Rethinking the Historical Jesus*,[19] that attempted to take seriously Jesus' class and cultural origins. Biblical scholar Kenneth E. Bailey's literary-critical studies explored the meaning of Gospel parables through the prism of Middle Eastern peasant culture.[20] The 1993 edited volume *The Bible and Liberation: Political and Social Hermeneutics*,[21] explored the advances made in the area of sociological and political approaches to the Bible in the previous decade, particularly noting the rising influence of feminist, third world, and other liberationist perspectives. *Mark and Method: New Approaches in Biblical Studies* explores a number of nontraditional meth-ods of biblical reading including cultural critical readings and postcolonial readings based on the insights of the Subaltern Study Group.[22]

Despite the contributions of these and other works to understanding the meaning of the Gospels and the ministry of Jesus in their settings in life, the historiographic insights that have gained wide acceptance in aca-demic historical and cultural studies have yet to enter the mainstream of biblical studies. Today works by biblical scholars that incorporate recent developments in doing history are growing in number yet are rela-tively few compared to the huge number of Bible-related titles published annually. Indeed, their influence is virtually non-existent in the major mainstream reference works and biblical commentary series. By most mea-sures it is still traditional ways of doing history that hold sway over the biblical studies profession, particularly works by evangelical and funda-mentalist academic and lay scholars, whose works comprise the largest number of titles published and books sold.

This is unfortunate, for in terms of methodology, writing history without a full accounting of the socio-economic locations of the persons involved and the socio-political concerns that confronted them is like telling the story of an extended family in all its diversity of age, gender, geographic location, individual personality, and social and economic accomplishment by focusing on the deeds, the thoughts, and the actions of the one family member who is the richest or the most powerful or the most accomplished in one way or another — in other words, a family member whose experiences, social stature, and economic mobility are not representative of the family at large. In actuality, this person might be estranged from the rest of the family, with huge gaps in his or her knowledge of family history and shared experiences. Yet if the criterion for being the definitive representative of the family's history is wealth or social accomplishment rather than proximity to the most commonly held family attitudes, experiences, and social locations, such skewed and unrepresentative representation can occur. This can especially be the case if the chosen spokesperson is more literate, more articulate, and possessed of greater social capital than other family members. In such a scenario, not only is just a mere sliver of the family's history revealed; most of the thoughts and instructive experiences of its members are overlooked as *if they never existed*. And so it is with the historiographic obsession with *klea andron,* the great deeds of men: in its bias toward social elites, most of the family of humanity are ignored as if they never existed.

This mode of retelling history through the deeds of those in positions of domination and control that Thucydides has bequeathed to us has often had tragic consequences. It has caused the concerns and contributions of great swaths of humanity — entire cultural and ethnic groups and socio-economic strata — to be overlooked and ignored. In Western historiography the little folk, the non-elite peoples, have virtually never been the *subjects* of history, almost never the focus of its gaze, instead only *objects,* mere props on history's broad stage. Think of it. Their hopes, ignored. Fears, ignored. Dreams, ignored. Love for their children, ignored. Love for their elders and spouses, ignored. Deeply felt needs, laudable ethics and morality, human trials, tribulations, and tears — all ignored. Intelligence devalued, integrity doubted, humanity negated. If you were not rich, if you were not an important social, political, or military presence, if you were not a political mover and shaker or related in some significant fashion to those who were, then who you were and what you thought counted only to the extent that it impacted the lives and perquisites of elites. Otherwise, you simply were considered unworthy of detailed or even specific historical mention. It brings to mind the 1960s hit song by the R&B vocal group the Whispers: "Seems Like I Got to Do Wrong (Before They Notice Me").

The Gospels and "Everyman"

That is why the New Testament Gospels are so significant. In his seminal text of literary criticism, *Mimesis: The Representation of Reality in Western Literature,* Erich Auerbach points out that prior to the Gospels, the only time that little folks were treated as subjects in the literature of antiquity was in comedies and then usually as objects of fun and ridicule.[23] The concerns, interests, and perspectives of poor folk, and certainly of peasants, were simply not thought to be worthy of serious consideration. In contrast, in the Gospels the most important actions, images, examples, and models are not the deeds and conventions and images of rulers and cities, but are those related to farm work, to peasant images of the *chora,* the "countryside." There are vineyards, vineyard workers, and landless rural laborers. There are vines and sprouting seeds and lilies of the field. There is planting and harvesting, plowing and reaping, gathering of fruit and shepherding of livestock.

But most importantly, Auerbach points out that what is especially distinctive about the Gospel genre is that it was written, in Auerbach's words, "directly for everyman," that is, for ordinary, everyday people.[24] That is, the Gospels were not written about the great deeds of elites, and they certainly were not written with dominant social or political movers and shakers in mind. They were written for everyday people.

The Gospel of Luke can be forgiven if it in some way contradicts this, for at the outset Luke tells us that the careful Thucydidean *akribeia* approach will be integral to the Gospel he is writing (cf. 1:3). Luke also tells us that he writes his Gospel for the benefit of a certain "most excellent Theophilus," whose honorific could indicate that the purpose of Luke's writing is to inform or persuade to his cause a member of the ruling elite. However, the literal meaning of Theophilus — Greek for "God lover" — could instead indicate that Luke writes to all lovers of God, which at the least would signify Christian believers in general. But whether or not Luke dedicates his work to a member of the social or political elite, to his credit Luke's subjects remain mostly "little folks," those at the bottom of Israel's social ladder — beggars and tax collectors, women and working poor — most of whom he actually calls by name. For instance, it is Lazarus the beggar, not the callous rich man that he calls by name (Luke 16:19–31). Indeed, it is Luke who even makes subjects out of shepherds, who, as an occupational class, languished near the very bottom of first-century Israel's social ladder.[25]

Thus, as Auerbach observes, we have in the Gospel the first time "everyman" and every woman — that is, ordinary human beings — are not portrayed just as props and backdrops to stories of elites or incidental objects to help flesh out the stories of big shots, but are themselves *subjects* of the story. Beleaguered Galilean peasant farmers, threadbare day laborers, struggling fishermen, desperate sharecroppers, sick lame folks forced to beg to eat, bleeding women alienated and ostracized for years on end by purity laws — now, in the Gospels' telling, all somebody at last. This is one of the most compelling reasons why Jesus' message and the model of his compassionate, respectful social relationships with society's discarded, discredited, and disregarded was extolled as "good news" by his overwhelmingly poor and peasant hearers: because in Jesus' ministry and the evangelists' recounting of it, the devalued *objects* of humanity all became valued *subjects*. Rather than insult and condescension, they now heard acceptance and affirmation: "Blessed are you poor.... You are the light of the world... As you have not done it to the least of these you have not done it to me."[26]

As for the social locations of the Gospel writers themselves, most scholars acknowledge that other than Luke, the evangelists' literary skills and the quality of their Greek were not the most polished, which indicates that although they were literate at a time when the vast majority of their countrymen were not, apparently none of them hailed from their societies' upper social echelons in which they would be expected to write Greek of higher quality. This seems especially so in the case of Mark, whose rudimentary Greek so often uses the connectives *kai* ("and") and *kai euthus* ("and immediately" or "and then") that one can almost hear in his recounting the breathless, unadorned vernacular of campfire reportage: "and then... and then... and then." Considering that Mark's Gospel is acknowledged by most scholars as the first Gospel to have been written, it is likely no exaggeration to say that if a relative nobody (or a few rel-ative nobodies) in the larger socio-political scheme of first-century Israel and its environs had not taken it upon themselves to tell the story of Jesus from the social location they held in common — beneath the heel of power and authority — our knowledge of Jesus' teachings would be greatly impoverished. Yet no matter the social station or origins of Luke and the evangelists, rather than telling the story of those in power and authority, they all chose to look at the lives of those who were victimized by the choices and actions of those who held power and authority.

From the Great to the Little

Some scholars have characterized reading and interpreting texts "from above" (from the vantage points of those with social and political author-ity and power), as distinct from the act of reading "from below" (from the perspective of those who are subject to — and sometimes resistant to — the power and authority of the dominant elites). This mode of reading from above is called the "great tradition," while reading from below is called the "little tradition." Historian Robert Redfield explains, "The great tradition is cultivated in schools and temples; the little tradi-tion works itself out and keeps itself going in the lives of the unlettered in their village communities."[27] The purpose of the great tradition is to sup-port the status quo, which it accomplishes by portraying it as normative and fully legitimate, if not God ordained.

The little tradition is the polar opposite of the great tradition. Rather than supporting the status quo, it opposes and resists it. "The little tra-dition does not merely represent some parochial version of the great tradition," political scientist James C. Scott explains. "Rather, the little tra-dition often constitutes . . . normative opposition to the politico-religious tradition of ruling elites."[28] Richard A. Horsley notes more specifically that "for the ancient Jewish peasantry, life's fundamental values were artic-ulated in the covenantal Torah, *which attempted to protect the Israelite/Jewish peasant against undue exploitation by others* (cf. Exod. 21–23 and the stories and oracles of the prophets, who protested against ruling-class abuses)."[29]

In Judaism, the great tradition of the Jerusalem priestly aristocracy emphasized biblical texts that supported the interests, legitimacy, and social and political ascendency of the status quo. One such text is 1 Samuel 7:8–16, which bestows divine sanction on the Jerusalem Temple and declares that the throne of David will retain God's love and support no matter what transgressions David and his descendants commit. The Temple of which the priestly aristocracy were caretakers in Jesus' day was actually the Second Temple, the successor to the Temple that David and Solomon built (which was destroyed by the Babylonians in the sixth century B.C.E.). Despite the historical distance, the authority and prestige of the first-century priestly aristocracy was legitimated and reified by its association with the Davidic legacy.

Yet the great tradition was constituted by more than just the act of privileging texts that supported the interests of the status quo. Even more significantly, it interpreted every text, no matter its original intent or class origin, in ways that supported the interests of the priestly aristocracy and ruling elites, including texts that were originally written to oppose them. Thus, in the reading of the great tradition, not even the books of Amos, which decried the luxurious excesses of the ruling class and its lack of concern for justice, or Malachi, which criticized the moral and ethical corruption of the Jerusalem priestly aristocracy, or even Jeremiah 7:1–15, which excoriated the temple priesthood for cheating widows and orphans, brought into significant question the practices and the legitimacy of successive generations of aristocratic priests and other ruling elites who committed similar transgressions.

For example, the book of Micah, written by an eighth-century B.C.E. prophet of clear non-elite, possibly peasant origins,[30] expresses the outrage of those on the lower rungs of Israel's socio-economic ladder toward the unjust and exploitive practices of the priestly ruling class: "Hear this, you rulers of the house of Jacob and chiefs of the house of Israel, who abhor justice and pervert all equity; who build Zion with blood, and Jerusalem with wrong!.... yet they lean upon the LORD and say, 'Surely the LORD is with us!'" (Mic. 3:9–11). The legacy of the great tradition's reading of Micah is that the significance of Micah's identity as a peasant and the class nature of Micah's critique have slipped from view. This erasure of Micah's class identity and class concerns effectively gives the impression that Micah's excoriation of the ruling class for its oppression and exploitation of Israel's rank-and-file is not an expression of class conflict, but a complaint by an individual prophet with no class identity or commitments, about oppressive acts by individuals and groups of individuals — but not an oppressive class! — who, at any rate, lived in the distant past.

This misreading deflects attention from the fact that the exploitive behaviors against which Micah railed remained structurally embedded in the practices of Israel's ruling class until that class effectively ceased to exist with the destruction of the Jerusalem Temple in 70 C.E. The continuity of the exploitive nature of the Jerusalem ruling class's behavior is indicated by Jesus' indictments of the priestly aristocracy in the Gospels, including his ire at retainers who were aligned with it, like scribes and Pharisees, for the same types of abuses as those decried by Micah many centuries before, such as unjustly seizing family farms and using their positions for exploitive purposes (e.g., compare Mic. 3:1–4 and Matt. 23:23–33; Mic. 2:2 and Mark 12:40). This continuity of corrupt and exploitive practices by the priestly class can be seen in a first-century legal arrangement of the Jerusalem priesthood called the *prosbul*.

Leviticus 25 specified that all loans were to be canceled every seventh, or sabbatical, year to protect borrowers and their families from being enslaved by debt for perpetuity. However, this biblical measure had an unintended consequence: it caused loans to dry up in the last several years of a sabbatical cycle because lenders feared the remaining term would be too short to recoup the full balances of their loans. To address the situation the Temple authorities created the *prosbul* (Greek for "before the court"), which entailed a public declaration before a Temple court by anyone seeking a loan that he was accepting a legally enforceable duty to repay the loan even after the start of the sabbatical year rendered the debt void.[31] The short-term effect of the institution of the *prosbul* was positive, in that it kept much-needed loans available at all points in the sabbatical cycle. But the long-term effect was disastrous, because it resulted in the long-term enslavement to debt that the Bible instituted the sabbatical year to guard against. In that most of those who had pools of capital available for lending were priests (from their share of Temple dues), it was they who benefited from a legal measure of their own contrivance that hurt, even impoverished many of those they were supposed to serve. Thus the *prosbul* effectively kept large numbers of Israel's people indebted to priestly and ruling-class lenders, who were now effectively freed from having to recognize the sabbatical year prescribed in the same Torah that their lives were supposed to be guided by. That the *prosbul* and the heightened levels of indebtedness that it in part engendered was seen as a major source of oppression by the lower classes is evinced in Josephus's report that one of the first acts of the rebels at the start of the Jewish War in 66 C.E. was to destroy the Temple's debt archives.[32]

This continuity of ruling-class abuses into the first century is also reflected in the resistance activities directed toward the ruling class and its abuses that were mounted by later groups, such as the Sicarii and the Zealots, who went further than simply critiquing the priests' ruling class abuses; they effectively waged guerrilla warfare against them.[33]

Thus the great tradition's disconnection of Micah's indictment from its class origins and the legacy of ruling class abuses effectively shielded generations of Israel's ruling elites from the full measure of the opposition their actions rightfully deserved by disassociating their practices from the types of practices that Micah decries. In this way the great tradition of biblical interpretation has continued at every point in history to shield ruling classes in societies that claim the Bible as sacred text from Micah's critiques of their behavior. So rather than being rightly read as a biting critique of those in power, a searing expression of class conflict, instead the critique of the powers-that-be offered by Micah the peasant prophet is treated as no more than a quaint complaint from years gone by. Yet little tradition readers of Micah generally were not fooled by the great tradition's readings because the little tradition shared the same general class location as Micah, as well as his *signified* adversarial relationship to ruling class practices.[34]

The lesson to be drawn from our consideration of the great and little traditions of biblical interpretation is that if we read the Gospels through the lenses of the great tradition or the *klea andron* perspective or from any social location or vantage point other than from the general perspectives of the Gospel writers and their subjects themselves — that is, from "below" — our hearing of the full-bodied richness of Jesus' "good news" story will be distorted and historically incomplete. Moreover, we will miss the majesty of the struggles of both Jesus and the little folk he loved, the marvelous measure of their hopes, the magnificence of their spirits of resistance and perseverance. In addition, we would never fully understand the nature of the bad news that made Jesus' "good news" so compelling that ordinary people were willing to leave all that they knew to follow it and even die for it.

READING AND THE ASSERTION
OF "SOMEBODINESS"

Thus we are faced with a monumental contradiction in biblical interpretation today: because the traditional way of writing history is "from above" while the Gospels are written "from below," we are faced with the methodological equivalent of telling the life story of Fannie Lou Hamer from the social location of a dyed-in-the-wool WASP, or assessing the legitimacy of the concerns of a struggling peasant from the vantage point of a feudal lord or a Roman imperial official, if not Caesar himself. These examples are not exaggerated; they well represent the essence of our dilemma, which is this: *in the traditional study of the Gospels we have an incompatibility of historical method and historical subject.*

The Gospels were written from beneath the heel of dominationist might, by dominated folk, with other dominated folk in mind. Virtually everyone mentioned in the Gospels was a poor colonized subject of Rome, with all of the violence, exploitation, fear, insecurity, and psychoemotional debilitation that attended that status. A sense of the toll that the brutality of colonial occupation can take upon a subject people can be gauged by the catalogue of psychotic reactions suffered by the people of Algeria in the 1940s under the brutal French colonial occupation. The catalogue was compiled by Frantz Fanon, a psychiatrist who worked there in the employ of the French regime. These "reactionary psychoses," mental disorders that found expression in physical symptoms, include severe disruptions of women's menstrual cycles, hysterical lameness, and repeated masochistic episodes, all of which are reflected in the Gospels.[35]

Yet few today teach or are taught to read the Gospels with these crucial realities in mind. Those who do consider these realities when publicly interpreting the Bible are often marginalized and dismissed as some species of political radical, such as "Marxist theologian" or "liberation theologian," the latter of which, despite its respectability in many quarters of academia, has nonetheless become a damning media charge in the wake of its association with the scandalous political demonization of Rev. Jeremiah Wright.[36] I am not a theologian, yet I am personally demonized in this way in a silly book with the wild-eyed subtitle *Barack Obama's Ties to Communists, Socialists, and Other Anti-American Extremists.*[37]

The irony is that without taking into account the observations of so-called biblical radicals, the full meaning of many crucial teachings and proclamations of Jesus simply cannot be known. For instance, consider the prayerful phrase in the Lord's Prayer, "forgive us our debts." From the perspective of a rich first-century urban merchant with no worries about economic indebtedness, or from that of most contemporary Westerners who, no matter their financial status, do not face the possibility of torture and imprisonment for inability to discharge legitimate debts, this verse can be easily seen as a simple prayer for forgiveness of personal sins. However, when it is considered that *opheilamata,* the Greek word for "debts" in the Lord's Prayer, specifically denotes financial debts, and that *aphiemi,* the word rendered "forgive" in the prayer also means "release," as in "Our father . . . release our financial debts," it becomes clear that it would take no leap at all for a peasant farmer or sharecropper in first-century Israel to primarily understand this prayerful phrase as a desperate entreaty for deliverance from a terrible fate: as expressing the raw fear of being sold into debt slavery or tortured and imprisoned, which were true and abiding possibilities for peasants in first-century Israel, as indicated by Jesus' matter-of-fact reference to it in Matthew 18:34.

Likewise, to be the recipient of the affirmation "blessed are you poor ones" might have little meaning for one possessed of comfortable financial means. But it could change the entire self-perception and sense of self-worth of those on the socio-economic underbelly of society, especially those used to being treated as having questionable worth, as unworthy of the best things in life, like the beggars that emerge from the pages of the New Testament, for instance. Can you imagine the tears in the eyes of an old man after hearing Jesus intone that blessing? Can you hear him say to his grandchildren in his unlettered way, in a voice choked with joy and pride, "Did you hear what Jesus said? He said we's somebody. He said God has not forsaken us, that we's blessed. We's poor, but we's blessed." Crying out like Simeon in the Temple: "Thank you, O God, for letting me live long enough to see this, Galilean poor folk standing up like somebody!" (cf. Luke 2:29–32).

But if we read the Gospels only from above, from the perspective of the privileged with our gaze only on the *klea andron* — the politically and militarily great deeds of humanity — we will miss the revelatory, life-changing nature of pronouncements like "Blessed are you poor ones." We will remain deaf to the small and silenced voices that the Gospels were written to give voice to.

Actual examples of reading the Gospels from below were compiled by Ernesto Cardenal, a Catholic priest who in the 1960s and 1970s served a peasant community in Solentiname, a remote lake archipelago in Nicaragua. Father Cardenal held regular Bible studies for the Solentiname peasants and encouraged them to share their interpretations and related thoughts on numerous biblical passages. Weekly he recorded the peasants' interpretations, eventually compiling them into the four volumes of *The Gospel of Solentiname*.[38] Because the interpretations recounted are the responses of peasants with social locations that are generally similar to those to whom Jesus spoke and those whom the four evangelists envisioned when they wrote, the responses and interpretations of the Solentiname peasants can be instructive. Like peasants in Jesus' setting in life, they were also subsistence farmers on the lower rungs of the social, economic, and political ladders. Like those in Jesus' setting, most of the Solentiname peasants were not readers of the Gospel message, but illiterate "hearers" of it. It is fascinating to see how the shared social location of Solentiname peasants with first-century peasants of Israel allowed them to elicit understandings from Gospel passages that modern scholars have only recently come to realize. After years of recording the peasants' interpretations of the Gospel narratives Father Cardenal concluded, "The commentaries of the *campesinos* [peasants] are usually of greater profundity than those of many theologians, but of a simplicity like that of the Gospel itself. This is not surprising: the *Gospel* or 'Good News' (to the poor) was written for them, and by people like them."[39]

An important factor in understanding the social location of the Gospels is that as a matter of material survival, all peasantries throughout history share the common denominator of basic shared moral and ethical principles, what cultural anthropologists call the "moral economy of the peasant."[40] These basic principles — the right of subsistence and the norm of reciprocity — are the definitive ethics through which peasants order their work, their lives, and their relationships, and which they use to assess the morality of their own actions and the actions of others.

And so, if the meanings of the Gospels and the sentiments of the voices therein are to be heard as the evangelists wanted and expected them to be heard, and if those voices that speak from "below" are actually to be heard by the rest of the world, then scholars and serious students of the Bible must provide the clear class and culturally sensitive interpretive lenses and angles of vision that will allow the fullness of the events and occurrences, thoughts, and sentiments the evangelists recounted to be fully appreciated. This includes the responses the Gospel writers hoped to evoke in their implied or envisioned readers who, excluded from the ranks of wealth and power, languished on the lower rungs of the socio-economic ladder. By the implied readers of the Gospel writers I mean those whom they expected to understand everything in their Gospel texts because of a common investment in the Gospel story and because of their generally similar social locations.

It is crucial to keep the Gospels' implied or envisioned readers in mind because what is recognized in some quarters as irony, humor, and even sarcasm, in other quarters can have very different meanings and purposes, depending on whether it is read from above or from below. These varying meanings and intentions can include entertainment, affirmation, embarrassment, or bitter denunciation, among others. Consider something as basic as Nathaniel's question in John 1:45, uttered in response to Phillip's pronouncement that the Messiah has been found in the person of Jesus of Nazareth: "Can anything good come out of Nazareth?" When viewed from above, this can be seen as a rhetorical question reflecting local notions of Nazareth as a place that was, as my grandmother would say, "evil, no 'count and no good."[41] But when this same passage is read from a social location farther down the social ladder, it can be seen to have a very different meaning, that of a sarcastic restatement — and implicit rejection — of elitist estimations of the residents of Nazareth in particular and of all rural backwaters in general. This elitist attitude was so great a chafing point for Nathaniel and his Galilean compatriots that it was always just beneath the surface of their consciousness and so asserted itself at diverse junctures. As an African American, a member of a portion of humanity that has been and in some quarters continues to be questioned as the source of anything good, I can attest to similar sensibilities and resentments ever lurking beneath the surface of consciousness. The well-worn phrase "If you're white, you're right; if you're black, get back" is precisely such a sentiment. To socially privileged outsiders, this statement might sound like black self-hatred or self-indictment, but when spoken by African Americans, even in a tone of resignation, it always contains at least an implicit indictment of the American social order that for centuries enforced that sentiment in law and too often still expresses it in practice. Only with a clear picture of the specificities of the speakers' social location do the meanings of their utterances begin to become clear.

READING FROM BELOW
IS THE WAY TO GO(D?)

What determines whether one will recognize the ironic, the sarcastic, the class-coded and class-nuanced subtexts in the Gospel narratives? It will largely be determined by whether or not one discards the *klea andron* approach that overlooks the perspectives and personal sense of agency of shepherds and peasants and instead reads the Gospels from the vantage point that fully values them, from the vantage point of the beleaguered poor, the hopeless expendables, the oppressed colonial subjects. That is, "from below," according to the resistance sensibilities of the little tradition.

How does one do this? The first step is to become what we might call a consciously "resisting" reader.[42] In the context of interpreting the Gospels this has a number of meanings. It means resisting readings of the lives of disempowered Galilean peasants from the self-authorized upper-class perspective of the religious establishment or any dominant establishment. It means resisting the temptation to ignore the fact that a major purpose of Jesus' earthly ministry was to empower his beleaguered countrymen to resist the depredations of the religious, social, economic, and political status quos. It means resisting the temptation to forget that Jesus was persecuted by the Jerusalem priestly aristocracy for challenging their sacerdotal legitimacy and that he was executed by the Roman Empire for challenging the legitimacy of the power of the state. And it means resisting the temptation to engage the utterances of Jesus and the Gospel characters as if they come from the mouths of upper-class Brits from Elizabethan England (ever notice that in movie depictions biblical characters never have lower-class cockney accents?). It means resisting these and many other factors that have resulted in countless Christians throughout the ages imagining the New Testament as having a cultural setting that neither Jesus nor the Gospel writers would recognize. The truly resistant reader refuses to engage in or to in any way honor these erroneous and self-serving readings.

This mode of reading is not as radical as it may sound. The Gospels themselves engage in a similar process. For instance, John 1:12–13 resists the traditional reading of the legitimacy of the hereditary Jerusalem priesthood by declaring that class and heredity have no standing in the divine economy: "But to all who received him, who believed in his name, he gave power to become children of God; who were born, not of blood nor of the will of the flesh nor of the will of man, but of God." When read from below, this text, which is traditionally believed to be a christological reference, is also recognized as a radical rejection of the claims of the Jerusalem priesthood to a privileged hereditary standing in the household of God. Indeed, it is a rejection of claims to privileged social and economic status that priests and ministers today would well to take seriously. That is another discussion, yet it gives a sense of just how much can be learned by reading the Gospels from below.

Moreover, the Gospels themselves tell us that Jesus was a resistant reader. His sayings depict him as resisting traditional and status quo readings of reality that were promulgated in a number of types of texts of his day: not only written texts, but also spoken texts of conventional wisdom and official texts of pronouncements by those in power. A prime example is the Lord's Prayer. In that prayer Jesus resisted official readings of the divinely sanctioned legitimacy and infallibility of Roman sovereignty by calling for it to be replaced by the sovereignty of the God of Israel: "Our father . . . *your* kingdom come, *your* will be done." Elsewhere Jesus repeatedly resisted the self-estimation of the religious establishment, personified by its close retainers the scribes and Pharisees, that they were righteous men, as in this representative instance: "Woe to you, scribes and Pharisees, hypocrites! for you tithe mint and dill and cumin, and have neglected the weightier matters of the law, justice and mercy and faith" (Matt. 23:23). He also resisted the implicit texts of the conventional wisdom of the rich and urbane that devalued the worth of his peasant compatriots with pronouncements to peasants like "you are the salt of the earth" and "you are the light of the world."

Thus being a resistant reader is not a marginal act; it is part of the Gospel tradition itself.

Yet our task is not only to resist readings from above that miss the character of writings that hail from below. We must also explicitly embrace ways of reading the Gospels that are methodologically sensitive to the plights and circumstances, concerns, interests, and worldviews of those "below": the subjects and implied readers of the Gospel writers. In this chapter I have repeatedly asserted the importance of reading "from below," but what does that actually mean? What were the specific factors that characterized what it meant to be "below" in Jesus' setting in life?

THE SALT OF THE EARTH

When unadorned by romanticized evocations of Jesus' setting in life such as "Silent Night, Holy Night" ("all is calm, all is bright"), the historical picture that emerges of the overarching context of Jesus and the Gospels is this: Israel in the first century was a colony of the Roman Empire. Israel and everyone and everything in it were totally subject to the control of Rome and the whim and whimsy of the various officials Rome dispatched there. In that context, other than their imperial Roman overlords, the Jerusalem hereditary priestly aristocracy and those aligned with it effectively comprised the upper-class elites, which was a privileged economic and political status in relation to their non-priestly countrymen that was of long standing. Because of the biblical sanction that was accorded to their priestly status, the hereditary priests of Jerusalem exercised a great deal of authority over Israel, which, by all historical indications, they too often abused to enrich themselves.

On the other hand, the social location of Jesus and most of those he encountered in the Gospels was situated decidedly beneath the upper-class elites: they were members of the peasant class, the lowest class on Israel's socio-economic ladder. The primary characteristics of peasants are: (1) that either they work the land for their sustenance and livelihood, or that their livelihood is directly dependent upon those who work the land; and (2) that they are politically dominated, economically exploited, and treated as social inferiors by urban elites, in whose hands most of their society's wealth and power are concentrated.

If rural settings and lack of access to centers of power and influence are features of peasant life and culture, this means that peasants as a class comprise not only farmers and sharecroppers, but also those whose livelihoods depend on economic intercourse with peasants and other workers of the land. Those dependent upon peasants for their livelihoods include fishermen, village-based small merchants, carpenters, craftsmen, and artisans, all of whom share the same rural settings and the same general social, economic, and political status in the body politic. In Teodore Shanin's description, they are all "analytically marginal groups" that share the same "hard core" of social and material existence.[43] Moreover, in the estimation of urban dwellers, especially urban elites, all of them — peasant, sharecropper, village carpenters, fishermen — all are simply *choritai* ("country folk"); all are essentially the same in the estimation of the citified folk, a point we will return to shortly.

Although this is a crucial point, readings of Jesus' setting in life from above often miss it. For instance, because some commentators view Jesus' New Testament occupation of *tekton*, "carpenter," through the lens of today's high-wage unionized professional, they make the mistaken claim that Jesus was "middle class." However, they seem to be unaware of the fact that *tekton* can also be translated as "manual laborer," which in no historical setting has ever been a high-wage occupation. Yet even if we do understand Jesus as a highly skilled carpenter rather than as a simple manual laborer, because he was fully integrated into peasant life and peasant culture his socio-economic status was essentially no different from that of his peasant clients. As subsistence producers subject to the vicissitudes and uncertainties of farming, even in the best of times peasants could have paid little for carpentry services. In hard times they could pay even less, if anything. With only the most rudimentary technology with which to construct the farm implements, furniture, tools, and other goods that were the primary commercial tasks of village workers of wood, there was no way a carpenter could achieve economies of scale to boost his production and, thus, his income. And because rural carpenters were fully embedded in peasant life and culture, in the estimation of urbanites they held the same social status as peasants and, therefore, were subjected by those in power to the same attitudes and treatment as peasants. Thus in first-century Israel carpenters were essentially peasants in that they shared the same social status as peasants, and carpenters' fortunes were tied to theirs.

Yet some readers of the Gospels from above still hew to the erroneous presentation of Jesus as "middle class." This is particularly true of proponents of the patently ahistorical "prosperity gospel," whose money-centered interests are served by this historical distortion.[44] This, despite Jesus' dependence on peasants for his livelihood, his itinerant lifestyle, and his admissions of personal poverty (e.g., "the son of man has nowhere to lay his head," Matt. 8:20), and, as well, despite the overwhelming evidence of every relevant sort that there were only two classes in late antiquity: the rich and the poor.[45] Indeed, there was nothing that could be likened to a middle class in first-century Israel, or anywhere else in late antiquity. In fact, the term "middle class" or any description that could conceivably fit that term does not appear until the mid-eighteenth century, when it was used by Queen Caroline of Denmark, ironically to deny — quite accurately at the time — that such a class existed in her country. What can properly be considered a "middle class" did not appear until the rise of the bourgeoisie in nineteenth-century Europe. Apparently those reading from above, mired in modernist views of political economy and economic life, continue this misreading of Jesus' social location because they find it difficult to imagine *their* Jesus as threadbare and lacking in the manners and decorum of the upper classes. *Klea andron* bias strikes again.

JESUS' SETTING IN LIFE

In reality, among the most significant factors in the shared plight and social location of Jesus and his peasant compatriots was widespread hunger and poverty. That hunger was widespread in first-century Israel is reflected in the Gospel sayings of Jesus himself. An example is the Lukan Beatitudes, in which he speaks about hunger, not in the abstract, but in the present tense: "Blessed are you who hunger now," he says (Luke 6:21). Indeed, in the Gospels Jesus speaks about poor people and the effects of poverty on their lives more often than any single subject except God. These pronouncements range from his efforts in the Beatitudes to salve the psycho-emotional wounds of poverty ("Blessed are you poor," Luke 6:20), to his parable about impoverished landless workers desperately seeking a day's employment (Matt. 20: 1–16),[46] to his anger that a widow was led to think it more important to give her last penny to the Temple treasury than to feed herself (Mark 12:41–44),[47] to his instruction to his disciples to pray that they will have sufficient daily food to eat (Matt. 6:11).[48] Through rigorous quantitative analysis of crop yields and the caloric content of the most common constituents of a Mediterranean peasant's diet, scholar Douglas Oakman has demonstrated that despite the demands of daily manual labor peasants in first-century Israel had an average daily intake of 2,000–2,500 calories.[49] A. Ben-David claims that the peasants' average daily intake was a meager 1,400 calories, barely enough to maintain their strength.[50] Even these levels of caloric intake could be drastically reduced in times of drought or bad harvests. In the estimation of some scholars the peasants' plight in first-century Israel was so precarious that it has been likened to R. H. Tawney's description of the plight of twentieth-century Chinese peasants: "the position of the rural population is that of a man standing permanently up to the neck in water, so that even a ripple is sufficient to drown him."[51]

The plight of every peasant class, no matter its time and place, has always been precarious because of the normal agricultural vagaries of disease, drought, and soil exhaustion. But in addition to its typical natural causes, the poverty and hunger of peasants in Jesus' setting in life had several major artificial, man-made causes. Probably the major such cause was the combination of imperial and religious taxation.

Taxation

That taxation was a major issue in first-century Israel is indicated by the Pharisees' use of it in Matthew 22:17 in their attempt to trap Jesus into committing the potentially fatal political crime of publicly opposing the Roman imperial regime: "Is it lawful to pay taxes to Caesar or not?" The Jewish scholar Salo Baron indicates that Roman taxation imposed an onerous burden on the peasants' subsistence: "even according to Caesar's most friendly decree, the Romans levied a tax as high as one-fourth of the crop... every other year."[52] In addition to Roman tax levies, which could be collected by the most violent means, the peasants were also expected to pay religious dues for the upkeep of the Temple and the priestly aristocracy. As New Testament scholar E. P. Sanders notes, "every year farmers had officials of their religion knocking on the door and asking for tithes."[53] In addition to the biblically mandated 10 percent tithe of all produce, there were special offerings. The Bible itself prescribes seven classes of sacrificial offerings that, in effect, were enacted for the financial benefit of the priests alone. All told, there were twelve different classes of tithes and offerings that were expected of first-century Jews in Israel.[54] It has been estimated that the combination of secular and religious taxes consumed up to 40 percent of the peasants' subsistence income.[55]

Debt

A consequence of the heavy burden taxation placed upon the peasantry was the development of an onerous debt structure and widespread peasant indebtedness. By definition, peasant farming is subsistence production that rarely produces a surplus of any significance. Lacking a surplus with which to meet the demands of the imperial and religious authorities, many peasant farmers were forced to borrow funds to pay their taxes and religious dues. As we saw above, the lenders of these funds were often the priests.

The consequences for defaulting on repayment of borrowed funds could be severe, ranging from confiscation of all land and belongings, to much worse. As we saw above, Jesus' parable of the unforgiving servant in Matthew 18:34 tells us that one of the consequences for peasants who defaulted on debts is that they could be handed over to the "jailers" (*basanistais,* literally, "torturers," from the Greek) to be imprisoned. In other cases, defaulted debtors were sold into slavery. Many debtors were forced to sell their own children into slavery so they could stay behind to attempt to keep the remaining children from succumbing to creeping starvation. Others were themselves sold with their spouses, children, and all belongings. Still others committed suicide to avoid slavery and its tortures. In cases involving very large debts the authorities sometimes enslaved extended family members down to the most distant — cousins, aunts, uncles. If after their sale the debt still was not fully paid, the debtors' neighbors could be enslaved to cover it. In this way sometimes whole villages and towns were deserted,[56] because everyone was either sold into slavery or had escaped into the hills, where many were forced to become thieves and robbers in order to survive.[57] Because Galilee was the largest and most fertile agricultural region in Israel, taxation and tithing requirements and their attendant pressures fell most heavily upon the Galilean peasants in Jesus' setting in life.

Social Marginalization

It was not only their economic plight that bedeviled peasants in first-century Israel, however. In addition to their economic exploitation and political oppression, they were also socially marginalized and oppressed as well. Their marginalization meant that in significant ways they were excluded from Jewish religious life and social consideration. One primary cause of their social marginalization was the phenomenon of the urban/rural dichotomy that existed in human societies for as much as a millennium before the birth of Jesus.

Since early antiquity urban dwellers have seemed to regard themselves as superior to peasants and rural dwellers. We see this in Greek classical literature, which regularly referred to rural dwellers as *choritai,* that is, country bumpkins. The Greeks even projected the notion of the superiority of the urban dweller over the rural dweller into the divine sphere. One of the fables attributed to Aesop relates that the simple-minded among the gods live in the countryside, while the superior gods, who live in the city, are infallible and rightly run the cosmos.[58] James C. Scott explains that this notion of urban superiority and rural inferiority develops, in part, because "the existing cultural hierarchy holds out a model of behavior for civilized man that the peasantry lacks the cultural and material resources to emulate. Whether it is a matter of knowing the sacred texts, of speaking and dressing properly... peasants are asked, in effect, to worship a standard that is impossible for them to achieve."[59]

This notion of urban superiority was no less present in first-century Jerusalem, particularly in the notion of the superiority of the priestly aristocracy. Although, as scholar Roland de Vaux observes, "there is not a single text which suggests that the Temple itself ever had cosmic significance,"[60] the priestly elites compounded the notion of the superiority of Jerusalem by promulgating the notion that the earth was divided into ten concentric circles of holiness, of which fully nine were within Jerusalem, with the Holy of Holies at the center, followed by the various precincts of the Temple and finally all of Jerusalem.[61] In addition to the religious preeminence accorded it, Jerusalem was also the center of trade and commerce in Israel. Indeed, the Jerusalem Temple was the central bank to which all Jews by divine edict were to make at least a yearly deposit. In their role as caretakers of the Temple, which they taught encompassed virtually the entire geography of holiness on earth, it must have seemed that the superiority of the Jerusalem priestly elites was indeed divinely sanctioned and their social and economic privilege a divinely bestowed entitlement.

GALILEANS: TWICE MARGINALIZED

Acknowledging Jesus' social location as a peasant is fundamentally important to understanding who he was, but that is not enough. We must
also factor into his identity equation that he was also a *Galilean* peasant from the northern province of Galilee. In addition to the poverty,
economic exploitation, and the social cleavage between city and country
to which peasants in general were subjected, there were two factors that
exposed Galileans in particular to additional derision and marginalization
at the hands of their urban countrymen, especially the Jerusalemites: their
"country" Galilean accents and the estimation of Galilean peasants as *am
ha aretz.*

In Mark 14:70 and its parallel passage, Matthew 26:73, Peter was identified as a Galilean follower of Jesus solely by his *lalia,* his distinctive
Galilean accent. That was because Galileans' pronunciation of Hebrew
and Aramaic, the common spoken languages of Israel, had a distinctive
slur (it appears that Aramaic was most commonly spoken). According
to Geza Vermes, "The distinction between the various gutturals almost
completely disappeared in Galilean Aramaic; the weaker guttural sounds,
in fact, cease even to be audible."[62] An example of the slurred Galilean
pronunciation is seen in the proper name, "Lazarus," which appears in
the Gospels of Luke and John. Lazarus is the slurred Galilean pronunciation of the proper Hebrew name, "Eleazar."[63] Similar to the way the
country accent of the popular stereotype of the countrified "hick" has
made it the object of ridicule and humor in popular American culture,
the Galileans' distinctively accented speech also made them subjects of
ridicule and humor. The phrase *Galili shota,* "Galilean fool," apparently
was a common term of derision in Israel. It seems that the simple act
of speaking subjected Galileans to ridicule at the hands of the Jerusalem-
centered Judeans and relegated them to marginal status in the mainstream
of life in first-century Israel.[64] Later Jewish texts testify that Jerusalemites
and others in the southern province of Judea found the northernmost
Galileans' mispronunciations so objectionable that they did not allow them
to publicly read the Bible at synagogues outside their home districts. Some
thought the Galileans' speech was so defective that it should preclude them
from studying the Bible altogether.[65]

Am ha aretz

There was one further factor that contributed to the marginalization of Galileans: as a regional group they were derogated, if not despised, as *am ha aretz.* Initially this Hebrew designation, which literally translates as "people of the land," meant simply a peasant or rural dweller as distinct from Israel ruling elites, as in Jeremiah 1:18. It evolved into a term of reference to the entire nation of Israel, as reflected in 2 Kings 15:5 and Ezekiel 46:3. The term took on derogatory overtones in the post-exilic period, describing those who had not been taken into exile and were derided by the returned exiles as not having remained fully observant of the rites of Israel in their absence (e.g., Ezra 6:21 and Neh. 10:31). By the first century, however, *am ha aretz* had come to designate specifically those considered to be lax in their observance of tithing prescriptions. This is reflected in a rhetorical question in the rabbinic writings: "Who is an am ha aretz? . . . 'Anyone who does not tithe his property properly.'"[66]

It was not only the lack of observance of tithing prescriptions that underlay the *am ha aretz* designation, however. There were two additional factors as well. First was their sometimes less than complete observance of the Sabbath. The daily requirements of peasant work and living made it nearly impossible for peasants to fully observe the Sabbath. For instance, if a cow or a sheep died during the Sabbath night they couldn't be left to rot all day until sundown. Or if a foal was having difficulty calving, intervention was the only humane option, not to mention the only economically feasible one, given the importance of livestock for peasant farmers. In these and other necessary interventions the demands of the farmer's livelihood gave him no choice but to violate biblical prohibitions against working on the Sabbath and sometimes to violate prohibitions against touching dead animals on the Sabbath. Second, because of their geographic distance from the Temple the Galileans had less exposure to, and therefore less knowledge of, the *mitzvot* (biblical laws), not to mention the various additional rituals and theological nuances promulgated by the priests that are not found in the Hebrew Bible. This distinction seems to have resulted in a distinctly Galilean outlook on the ritual and doctrinal demands of their faith that differed from the orthodoxy represented by the Jerusalem priests. Some scholars believe that as a result of this geographical and theological distance, the average Galilean Jew gave little consideration to biblical strictures like the Levitical rules of purity. Although offered half a century ago, the observation of British scholar L. E. Elliott-Binns is representative of this stance: "The Galileans, partly owing to their distance from Jerusalem . . . were in general lax in their attitude towards strict orthodoxy and its demands. Such matters seemed too petty."[67] Although this articulates a distinctly minority position on the matter, the existence of such a Galilean theological "attitude" is not necessarily far-fetched. It seems that John 15 reflects just such a theological attitude or outlook, as we will see below.

Of these several modes of non-observance, however, it was the failure to diligently tithe that was the major sin in the eyes of the religious establishment, not only because it violated biblical prescriptions, but also because the withholding of tithes cut into the priests' income, which principally derived from tithes and offerings and the priests' investment of those funds. To what extent Galileans were not fully scrupulous in their rendering of tithing dues is not clear. Yet it is fairly certain that there is at least some truth to the charge that Galileans were not completely observant of tithing laws because, as we saw above, after paying Roman taxes many peasants had barely enough resources left to feed their families. Also surely many Galileans resented having to support the distant Jerusalem economy with the fruit of their labor when urban dwellers, who had no agricultural production and thus no responsibility to tithe, were exempt from agricultural tithing demands. Because Galilee was the most distant province from Jerusalem, the priests had little control over Galileans' tithes, and the distance may well have made the Galileans feel even less accountable to them. Josephus tells us that elsewhere priests were so intent on pocketing their priestly dues that they were known to send their servants directly to threshing floors to take tithes by force (*Antiquities of the Jews;* 20:181). Yet the Galileans were generally too geographically distant for that, which might have further fueled the priests' resentment. Moreover, going to Jerusalem to fulfill tithe and offering responsibilities required a journey of at least three days, plus a stay of several days in or on the outskirts of Jerusalem in order to fulfill Temple obligations amid thousands of fellow pilgrims. With daily farming responsibilities at home, it is not likely that large numbers of Galilean peasants regularly made that journey.[68]

These factors caused many Jerusalem priests to paint Galileans in general as *am ha aretz la torah:* non-observant of the laws of Moses. For this reason Galilean peasants were special targets of the Jerusalem priests' ire, as reflected in the complaint attributed to the most prominent first-century rabbi, Yochannon ben Zakkai: "Galilee, Galilee, you hate the Torah!"[69]

Because withholding of tithes by those they considered *am ha aretz* was considered stealing both from God and from the priestly aristocracy (the latter of which the priests themselves might have considered equally as heinous as the first), they did not consider it possible for the *am ha aretz* to have good character or sound intelligence. It is recounted in the Mishnah, the second-century codification of Jewish laws, that even a liberal-minded religious leader like the rabbi Hillel (c. 70 B.C. to 10 C.E.) could say, "An uneducated man is not slow to sin, and no *am ha aretz* is righteous."[70] The humanity of the *am ha aretz* was even questioned, as reflected in strident sayings like this: "A man . . . should not marry the daughter of an *am ha aretz*, because they are detestable and their wives vermin, and of their daughters it is said, 'Cursed be he who lies with any kind of beast.'"[71] The transgressions of the *am ha aretz* were thought to be so great as to make them deserving of violent abuse: "One may tear an *am ha aretz* like a fish. . . . And [this means] along his back."[72] The rhetorical estimation of members of the religious establishment was that the lives of the *am ha aretz* were of such little value that it was permissible to kill them on the holiest possible day in all of Judaism: "An *am ha aretz* may be stabbed even on a Day of Atonement which falls on a Sabbath."[73] These sayings were codified in texts dated after the destruction of the Temple in 70 C.E., yet the available historical evidence indicates that the sentiments they express had essentially already developed by the time of Jesus' ministry.[74] Biblical scholar Sean Freyne summarizes the Galileans' plight: "Thus the Galilean peasant found himself in the rather strange position that those very people to whom he felt bound by ties of national and religious loyalty, the priestly aristocracy, were in fact his social oppressors."[75]

These were the factors that characterized the plight and life circumstances of the social location of Jesus and his Galilean compatriots: on the one hand beneath the oppressive, exploitive heel of the Roman empire and, on the other, beneath the never-ending demands by a Jerusalem priestly aristocracy that showed no inclination to serve their needs, or to treat them as equals or to acknowledge them as full-fledged members of the house of Israel. Thus by virtually every measure Galilean peasants were a subjugated, socially and politically inferior class in their own land.

ASSERTING A NEW SUBJECTIVITY: THE CASE OF JOHN 15:1-5

How might exploring the plight and circumstances of those "below" rather than employing the pervasive *klea andron* focus on those "above" actually help us to arrive at a more authentic understanding of the Gospels? Let us consider this question by looking at a Gospel passage that appears to have no relationship to social, political, or economic exigencies for its meaning.

John 15:1-5 appears to be simply an affirmation of Jesus' claims of sonship and preeminence in the household of God and a declaration of the consequence of rejecting Jesus' preeminence. Yet if we read this passage from below, both within the little tradition of challenge to priestly status claims and in the overarching context of the Galilean peasants' ongoing experience of abuse by, or at least alienation from, priestly power, this seemingly innocuous proclamation can be seen to have a much more radical meaning.

> I am the true vine, and my Father is the gardener. He cuts off every branch in me that bears no fruit, while every branch that does bear fruit he prunes so that it will be even more fruitful. You are already clean because of the word I have spoken to you. Remain in me, and I will remain in you. No branch can bear fruit by itself; it must remain in the vine. Neither can you bear fruit unless you remain in me. I am the vine; you are the branches. If a man remains in me and I in him, he will bear much fruit; apart from me you can do nothing.

Neither this nor any other passage in the Gospel of John *directly* refers to the economic and political conditions of first-century Israel. This is partly because many of the indications and details of these conditions in the New Testament are embedded in parables, beatitudes, and model prayers, none of which are included in John's Gospel, owing either to John's unfamiliarity with them or to their unsuitability to his theological purpose. But another possible reason that these conditions were not cited by John is that they were known and experienced every day by John's readers and thus were part of what the French sociologist Pierre Bourdieu calls a "discourse of familiarity," which "leaves unsaid all that goes without saying."[76] That is to say that the experiences of everyday life were so commonly held that they didn't need to be articulated; they could be left unsaid and still understood, because they were everyone's experience in that setting.

What is clear in John's Gospel at any rate is that he writes from below. In John, as in the Synoptics, especially Mark, it is always the rural perspective that is offered and given privileged position. As in the Synoptic Gospels, the images of John's Gospel are rural and agrarian:

- harvesting, reaping, and gathering of fruit (4:35–38)

- sprouting grain (12:2)

- sheep, a sheepfold, and a "good shepherd" (10:1–18)

- the vine, the branches, and the vinedresser of 15:1–6

- a peasant, Nathaniel (Hebrew for "gift of God"), upon whom the Johannine Jesus bestows his highest accolade ("Israelite without guile") without Nathaniel having done anything to warrant it (1:47).

Additionally, it is Nathaniel the peasant whom John's Gospel identifies as the first to recognize Jesus as the Son of God (1:49). Also for John, cities in general and Jerusalem in particular are not where one *is,* but places one *goes,* generally only to fulfill the demands of religion — pilgrimage and tithing — and they are generally inhospitable places at that.

The central claim of the John 15 passage is that Jesus is the "true vine." In numerous passages in the Hebrew Bible Israel is symbolically represented as a vine. Among them are Hosea 10:1, 14:7; Jeremiah 6:9; Ezekiel 15:1–7, 17:5–10, 19:10–14; and especially Psalm 80:8, which, in its plea to God clearly signifies Israel as a vine: "You brought a vine out of Egypt." In addition to identifying Israel in general with the vine imagery, portions of these passages can also be understood as specifically identifying the Jerusalem priestly aristocracy with the vine. For instance, the Ezekiel 15:1–7 passage identifies the vine, specifically the wood of the vine, with "inhabitants of Jerusalem." The most powerful and influential of those inhabitants, of course, was the priestly caste. And Ezekiel 17:12 likens the vine and its branches to the ruling elites of Jerusalem, the most prominent of whom were, again, the priests.

By the time of Jesus, the great tradition had effectively combined the priests' role as caretakers of the Temple with their role as intercessors with God—and with the Bible's occasional conflation of the priestly class and Israel as well—to successfully equate the priestly aristocracy's class interests with the interests of everyone in Israel, regardless of class or social location. As a result, the priests were able to use their biblically sanctioned servant's *role* as the basis for arrogating to themselves the biblically sanctioned privileged *status* with which they enriched themselves from Israel's tithes and offerings. Their riches came not only from their role as Temple functionaries receiving their due portion of Temple proceeds, but also from their status as owners of land purchased with their Temple remuneration, which they compounded by renting those lands to tenant farmers whose tithes and offerings, ironically, were in large part the source of the priests' wealth in the first place. The priests also enriched themselves as lenders of their wealth at interest, mostly to peasants to enable them to pay their full complement of imperial taxes and religious dues.[77] In this way they became rich beyond anything that all but a relative handful of their countrymen could imagine. Josephus, our major correspondent from first-century Israel, who was also a member of the priestly aristocracy, tells us of priestly colleagues who amassed "a large amount of property from the tithes which they accepted as their due."[78] He also tells us that Ananias, a high priest who reigned from 47 C.E. until 58 or 59 C.E., was not only "a great procurer of money," but also that Ananias's behavior was representative of the behavior of all high priests: "the other high priests acted in like manner."[79]

Thus the priests used the legitimacy accorded them by the great tradition not only to dominate religious life in Israel, but to dominate economic, political, and social life as well. They guarded their privileged status quite jealously, to the point of great violence at times. A report by Josephus illustrates this point. He tells us that in 66 C.E. Yeshua ben Hananiah, a "simple peasant," walked the streets of Jerusalem pronouncing imminent judgment upon "Jerusalem and this holy house." This challenge to their power caused such consternation among the aristocratic priests that they had Yeshua ben Hananiah scourged until his bones could be seen.[80] Their apparent justification for these and other self-serving policies was their assertion that they were divinely entitled to do whatever protected their interests, for as the intercessors between God and Israel, they believed that among the chosen people of Israel, they themselves were most chosen.

In John 15 Jesus stands in radical opposition to the priests' "great tradition" reading of Israel's social structure, which portrays their uniquely privileged social and economic status in Israel as their legitimate right. He does this by emphatically declaring that it is not the priests who embody the salvific leadership that God had once expected of Israel's priests, but Jesus himself: "*I* am the true vine," he declares. The Greek construction here is both emphatic and contrastive, that is, while emphasizing what Jesus is ("*I* am the true vine") it also contrasts him with those who are not that: if Jesus is the "true" vine, then the priests are not.[81]

Further, it is often overlooked that when Jesus declared in verse 3, "You are already made clean by the word that I have spoken to you," this is not just a simple declaration that faith in Jesus has cleansed his hearers of their previous sins. It is also a subversion of the very foundations of the legitimacy of the religious establishment; indeed, it is a repudiation of the legitimacy of the Temple itself. Why? Because *kathos,* the word translated as "clean" here, can just as well be translated as "pure," i.e., signifying purity in the ritual, sacramental sense. What makes Jesus' statement more radical and even more threatening to the priests is that the purity Jesus signified was the purity that is supposed to come only as the result of priestly sacrificial intercession. Thus Jesus' declaration that the rank-and-file of Israel are already ritually clean meant, in effect, that in order to be declared clean they no longer needed to journey to the Jerusalem Temple to proffer tithes and offerings or to make sacrifices there. More to the point, it meant that they did not need to seek the intercession of anyone, not even the high priest, in order to be declared clean in God's sight. In other words, Jesus declares that because of his presence and his pronouncements, the priestly vocation and, indeed, the very purpose of the Temple itself are now null and void, no longer necessary, and thus no longer worthy of the people's loyalty or financial support. This, of course, was a disaster in the making for the lifestyles of the priestly aristocracy. In other words, without explanation or apology, Jesus publicly appropriated the intercessory roles of priest and Temple for himself! As with his declarations of the blessed status of the poor in the household of God, one can only imagine the electrifying effect caused by Jesus' subversion of the legitimacy of the Jerusalem Temple and its aristocratic priesthood had on his peasant hearers.

But Jesus did not arrive at this subversive point alone. Long before he appeared on the scene his economically exploited and socially marginalized hearers would have longed for good news of deliverance from their plight. It would have been their shared need for good news in their common social experience that moved him to counter the great tradition narrative by declaring that the authority of those who looked down upon him and his peasant compatriots and enriched themselves at their common expense no longer had to be obeyed or considered. In other words, Jesus' reading was a resistant reading, a reading in the little tradition of resisting the great tradition's grand hegemonic narrative of unstinting affirmation of the priests' entitlement to social privileges and wealth.

The fuller meaning of John 15 that our act of reading from below has given to us is proof not only of the viability of such readings, but also of their necessity, for they give us crucial insight into the situational circumstance that made the proclamation of John 15 so compelling to the envisioned readers and hearers of the Gospel. Through our consideration of this passage I have tried to show that because the traditional Western *klea andron* approach to writing (and reading) history could not and would not have given us the Gospels, there is no way to fully understand the Gospels or to plumb the depths of Gospel meaning except by attempting to read them from below — from as close as we can postulate what the perspective of a typical first-century peasant in Israel would have been.

It is my hope that I have also shown that reading from below as informed by the little tradition of biblical interpretation yields fuller and more authentic Gospel meaning. Yet to get a picture of the day-to-day pain and struggles of Jesus' peasant hearers, we cannot stop there. The next step is to try to model how such Gospel passages can be brought to life for modern-day readers. How can we go beyond our understanding of Jesus' setting in life to bring this passage to life for readers of the Gospels today?

THE GRAPES OF WRATH
AND THE TRUE VINE

One way of bringing the meaning of Gospel narratives to life is to view them through the lenses of situations roughly contemporaneous to our day that have significantly analogous social, economic, and political characteristics and whose greater currency and familiarity to readers will make the biblical narratives' meanings more accessible, if not more compelling. Although the obvious candidate for this process would be roughly contemporaneous historical accounts, I would argue that fictional narratives could be much more informative and revealing for our purposes. Why use fiction for such an endeavor? Because the best of fiction reveals the complexities of human character, relationships, motivations, and responses in ways that writing that strictly hews to the details of historically verifiable evidence often cannot, at least according to traditional methodologies and standards. And because of the freedom of plot that fiction affords, it can take its time in the exploration of subtle psychological details and the emotional effects of occurrences in order to bring larger emotional and relational truths to the fore. An instructive example is Fyodor Dostoevsky's meticulous exploration of the murderous psyche of his character Raskolnikov in his classic of Western fiction *Crime and Punishment,* which brings to life the pathos, the desperation, the pathological moral inversions of certain kinds of murderous acts and their aftermath in ways no straightforward historical account can. Although not specifically advocating the use of fiction, classical historians like the scholar Ramsay MacMullen similarly suggest that modern scholars should consider data from more recent peasant societies to understand phenomena they hold in common in order to "humanize" ancient subjects.[82]

But is it methodologically sound to use a work of fiction, no matter how attentive it might be to *akribeia,* the accuracy of detail of background information, to explain and bring to life the details of a Gospel story? My answer is resoundingly in the affirmative: yes, it is methodologically sound because the Gospels themselves are literary works. That doesn't mean that the Gospel narratives are fictional, of course, but neither are they straightforward historical narratives. The Gospels are literary accounts of history in the sense that they use literary devices to convey the truths of the narratives they recount.[83]

A marked example of the literary nature of the Gospels in general can be seen in the different ways Matthew, Luke, and John narrate Jesus' origins. None of their treatments are simply straightforward accounts of events. And not only does each tell of Jesus' origins from a different angle of approach, each also tells his story with marked differences. In his account of Jesus' birth and infancy, Luke, in good Thucydidean fashion, uses a number of speeches, in addition to numerous individual and collective characters, and even a hymn (the Magnificat; 1:46–55) to tell his story, the longest Gospel version of Jesus' origins. Matthew's shorter account of Jesus' beginnings opens with "begats," which clearly are intentionally reminiscent of Hebrew Bible genealogies; uses biblical proof texts to bolster his plot; and features only a few characters who each say little. The account of Jesus' origins in John's Gospel, the briefest of all, evokes Hellenistic philosophy with its introduction of the abstract *logos*, while at the same time evoking the Genesis creation story with, "In the beginning" (1:1). In sum, the diversity of the strategies used to convey Jesus' origins attests to the literary nature of the Gospels.

Because the Gospels are themselves literary productions, the use of fictional works that feature analogous, roughly contemporary situations for elucidating the meaning of certain Gospel narratives can be a useful and methodologically sound way of bringing to life certain aspects of Gospel stories. One work that might be helpful in this regard is *The Grapes of Wrath*, John Steinbeck's dramatic portrayal of the plight of the Oklahoma peasants during the Great Depression.

The Grapes of Wrath

The Grapes of Wrath is considered one of the premier English works of the twentieth century and one of a handful of books that have changed America. Why? Because, like *The Jungle*, Upton Sinclair's 1906 fictional exposé of the meatpacking industry, which inspired numerous reforms, including the establishment of the U.S. Department of Agriculture, *The Grapes of Wrath* brought to the nation's public consciousness the desperate plight of a large number of its fellow citizens of which most Americans were completely unaware. Perhaps even more importantly, it recounted that plight from its victims' own perspective and social location: that is, from below. As a result, the unjust laws and inhuman conditions that stunted the lives and life chances of the beleaguered Americans that Steinbeck wrote about were dramatically transformed so they could enjoy more of the liberty and pursuit of happiness vouchsafed by the laws of the land. As testament to the power of its portrayal, *The Grapes of Wrath* has sold more than fifteen million copies and continues to sell some 150,000 copies every year.

The Grapes of Wrath is formally a work of fiction, but it is more like fictionalized history or, rather, history recounted through the medium of fiction. Indeed, the book began as a respected seven-part investigative series on the plight of migrants in California in the *San Francisco News* in October 1936. Due to popular demand, the series was reprinted verbatim in 1938 as a pamphlet entitled *Their Blood Is Strong*. The power and pathos of those investigative reports solidified Steinbeck's bona fides as a serious commentator on the subject. That Steinbeck's research for *The Grapes of Wrath* was in-depth and prodigious is reflected in its interspersed chapters that offer anthropological "thick descriptions"[84] of the migrants' circumstances, the natural causes of their plight, the machinations of agribusiness that exacerbated their plight, and detailed narrations of the migrants' struggle to survive with their families, health, sanity, and self-respect intact.

In 1936–38 Steinbeck made several grueling trips to Oklahoma to immerse himself in the field conditions of his subject. He interviewed numerous migrant families, reporting that he "sat in the ditches with migrant workers, lived and ate with them."[85] He wrote to his agent of the suffering he witnessed close up at one Oklahoma camp: "There are about five thousand families starving to death over there, not just hungry but actually starving. . . . In one tent there are twenty people quarantined for smallpox and two of the women are to have babies this week."[86] At one point he worked night and day for two weeks in a California camp serving the migrant workers' desperate needs alongside Farm Security Administration personnel, exerting himself to the point that several times he collapsed, exhausted, in the mud.

The research that informed the accuracy of Steinbeck's portrayal of the Oklahoma migrant peasants' plight included voluminous documents describing migrants' diets, their daily activities, sayings, observations, even their entertainments. Many of the documents were given to him by Thomas Collins, the manager of a Farm Security Administration camp in California. Representative of Steinbeck's attention to detail, he specifically used Collins as the prototype for Jim Rawley, the manager of the Weedpatch government migrant camp in *The Grapes of Wrath*. Steinbeck also immersed himself in film documentaries about the unfolding Dust Bowl tragedy from President Franklin D. Roosevelt's Resettlement Administration and contemplated Dorothea Lange's heart-wrenching photographs of

Dust Bowl Oklahoma. As a result he was familiar not only with the events and conditions that constituted the peasants' plight; his close proximity also helped him to understand how they felt. It was this understanding of the Oklahoma peasants' internal struggles that is so useful to our efforts.

Thucydides would have approved of Steinbeck's careful investigation and his efforts to achieve *akribeia* accuracy with firsthand observations and eyewitness testimony. Yet Thucydides is likely to have frowned on Steinbeck's choice of primary subjects, for like the Gospel writers, Steinbeck's understanding of the struggles of the people was from below, through the prism of the "little tradition" of those who are the lowest on the socio-economic totem pole. Thus, ironically, it is precisely because John Steinbeck did not use Thucydides' *klea andron* approach that he was able to successfully chronicle the migrants' plight. If Steinbeck had used Thucydides' approach, the focus of his research would not have been the Oklahoma peasant; it would have been the policy actions and machinations of government officials and corporate chieftains of agribusiness during that period rather than the experiences of the peasants and migrant workers who were forced to live under their policies and machinations.

Because we will utilize *The Grapes of Wrath* in our effort to bring the John 15 passage to life, it is appropriate to question Steinbeck's objectivity and the historical veracity of the situational picture he paints, that is, to inquire whether Steinbeck's proximity to his subjects tainted the objectivity of his observations, in that he'd long been a passionate advocate for workers' rights. In a 1937 statement for a League of American Writers booklet he wrote, "I believe in the despotism of human life and happiness against the liberty of money and possessions."[87] That Steinbeck shared the migrants' concerns and privileged their vantage point on their mistreatment is evidenced by another remark in the letter to his agent: "I've tied into the thing from the first and I must get down there and see . . . if I can't do something to help knock these murderers [major agricultural corporations] on the heads."[88] In fact, nowhere does Steinbeck portray in any detail the perspectives or struggles of anyone who is not in the lower class. No less than Woody Guthrie, folksinger and writer of the populist anthem "This Land Is Your Land, This Land is My Land," writing of the movie version of *Grapes* in "Woody Sez," his column in *People's World* magazine, affirmed that Steinbeck accurately recounted the

Oklahoma migrants' story from below: "You [the people] was the star in that picture."

Yet by itself, Steinbeck's admittedly biased advocacy for workers' rights does not disqualify him as a chronicler of historical events and conditions, for it is a myth that any reteller of human events in any medium can be truly objective. Indeed, the accuracy of Steinbeck's portrayal of the situation of the Oklahoma peasants in *Grapes* has been vindicated in numerous ways, including the official findings of Senator Robert M. La Follette's 1939–40 federal investigations of farm labor conditions, and *Factories in the Field,* the highly respected 1939 sociological study of the farm workers' plight by Carey McWilliams, the attorney, former head of the California State Division of Immigration and Housing, and former editor of *Nation* magazine. In addition, the accuracy and integrity of Steinbeck's portrayal of the migrant workers' plight were repeatedly defended by two Americans whose own investigations put them in a position to know: President and Mrs. Franklin D. Roosevelt. After inspecting California migrant camps in 1940, Mrs. Roosevelt again affirmed Steinbeck's accuracy as she had on a number of previous occasions, "I never thought *The Grapes of Wrath* was exaggerated," she declared.[89]

So what did John Steinbeck have in common with John the Evangelist? Although they wrote two thousand years apart, both rejected the *klea andron* approach to writing history from "above." That is to say, they both defied convention and chose to write about the socially disinherited and economically dispossessed from "below," specifically from the peasants' own vantage point of exploitation and social marginalization and social derision. Just as John did not write the story of Jesus and his nascent movement through the eyes of Caesar or the chief priests of Jerusalem, Steinbeck did not narrate the story of the Great Depression through the eyes of Herbert Hoover or J. P. Morgan, nor through the class perspectives of bankers or corporate chieftains. As did the Gospel writers, Steinbeck chose to relate his historically based account of the Depression from the perspective of those "below."[90]

Bringing the Gospel Story to Life

The Grapes of Wrath tells the story of the economic dispossession, exploitation, and social alienation of Oklahoma peasant farmers during the great drought in the Oklahoma Dust Bowl of the 1930s. It recounts their mistreatment at the hands of rich elites — banks and large agricultural corporations — as well as their mistreatment at the hands of everyday city folk. The book's main characters are the Joad family, an extended clan of failed peasants and smallholders turned sharecroppers who, like scores of other Oklahoma tenant farmers and peasant families, were ejected from their family farms either because they defaulted on mortgages and other debts, or because the banks and corporations that rented farmland to ten-ant farmers and sharecroppers chose to end those arrangements in order to pursue more profitable uses of the land. As a result, the Joads were forced to emigrate to California to seek work as migrant laborers. The bulk of the tale is about the struggle of the Joad family and, by exten-sion, the struggle of all peasants in that circumstance to survive materially, physically, and psycho-emotionally in a society that devalued, abandoned, and often despised them.

The full range of analogous correspondences between the material plight and the social marginalization of the first-century Galilean peas-ants and that of the Oklahoma peasants as portrayed in *The Grapes of Wrath* is too great to consider here. However, I will offer a few examples to demonstrate how this approach can bring Gospel narratives to life for contemporary readers in a way that hopefully is both informational and inspirational.

We have seen that among the defining circumstances in the setting in life of Jesus and his hearers, including those in John 15, are widespread poverty and hunger. But simply knowing this does not by itself give us a real sense of the desperate *effects* of the hunger that was a world-shaping background factor to the John 15 passage. The descriptions in *The Grapes of Wrath* of hunger and its effects help to bring this background factor to life.

References to hunger, poverty, and scarcity pervade *The Grapes of Wrath*. In chapter 17, a "ragged man" tearfully relates the starvation deaths of his children: "I can't tell ya about them little fellas layin' in the tent with their bellies puffed out an' jus' skin on their bones, an' shiverin' an' whinin' like pups, an' me runnin' aroun' tryin' to get work — not for money, not for wages! . . . jus' for a cup of flour an' a spoon a lard."[91]

An even more moving portrayal of the effects of hunger and poverty in *The Grapes of Wrath* occurs in the book's final scene. There a man is near death from starvation after having fed his young son every scrap of food he had been able to forage for the past six days. When Ma Joad and her daughter Rose of Sharon come upon the man and his son, they realize he is dying, but they have no food either. But after an exchange of knowing looks, Ma Joad places a comforter around Rose of Sharon, who beneath the modesty it provides, feeds the starving man the breastmilk her child, stillborn just hours earlier, will never taste.

Despite the ubiquity of the Gospels' mentions of hunger, they never directly describe hunger's effects. The closest the Gospels come to a comparably touching description of the effects of hunger and poverty is Luke's narration of the dogs licking the beggar Lazarus's sores (Luke 16:21). The depictions of the effects of hunger and poverty in *The Grapes of Wrath* move beyond hunger as a concept or description of one's general state to bring to life the horror and desperation that accompanies hunger and poverty and the real ways they can wreak havoc in people's lives.

There is another effect of poverty that is central to understanding the impact of the True Vine pronouncement on Jesus' hearers that a simple reading of John 15 cannot convey, even with some knowledge of its background setting in life: the psycho-emotional assault of poverty on poor people's pride and dignity. Chapter 15 of *The Grapes of Wrath* portrays a man's humiliation and shame at having to repeatedly ask a waitress to sell him a partial loaf of bread at a roadside diner because he can afford no more. The waitress repeatedly responds that the diner sells bread only in sandwiches. The man tells her that he badly needs the bread because he and his family are hungry: "Whyn't you buy a san'widge?" she asks. The man responds, "We'd sure admire to do that, ma'am. But we can't. We got to make a dime do all of us . . . We ain't got but a little."

When the waitress tells the man the loaf costs fifteen cents, he has no choice but to virtually beg, "Won't you — can't you see your way to cut off ten cents' worth?"

Jesus' True Vine pronouncement is made in the context of a similar legacy of shame in peasant culture of fathers who cannot consistently provide for their families and cannot shield them from the derision of haughty priests and heartless Roman soldiers, not to mention being unable fulfill other aspects of a father's honor, such as providing a decent wedding dowry for his daughters, as one example. *The Grapes of Wrath*'s portrayals of hat-in-hand humility and humiliation bring to life a sense of the humiliation that was part of the lived experience of Jesus' Galilean hearers.

For instance John 7:49 gives a sense of the Jerusalem priestly aristocracy's haughty dismissal of pilgrims it has denigrated as *am ha aretz la
torah:* "this crowd that does not know the Law is accursed." As we saw
above, peasants in general were called *choritai,* "country." We also saw that
Galileans in particular were called by the pejorative *am ha aretz* and subjected to all types of hateful invective, even having their daughters likened
to beasts. Similarly, the westward moving migrants from Oklahoma that
Steinbeck wrote about were called "Okies," a derisive term that signified
that they not only were countrified, but also poor, dirty, ignorant, and
backward. In fact, a 1935 sign outside a diner in the Central Valley of California encapsulated the hostility and devaluation of their humanity that
the Oklahoma peasants faced: "OKIES AND DOGS NOT ALLOWED
INSIDE."[92]

The analogy between the devaluation of those called *am ha aretz* and
those called "Okies" is brought to life in *The Grapes of Wrath*'s portrayal
of the condescension and hostility to which the so-called Okies were
subjected. In the instance below this comes not from urban elites, as in
John 7:49, but from an average town worker. This imparts an even more
poignant sense of the derision visited upon Galilean peasants, not only by
urban elites like the aristocratic priests but also at the hands of the average city dweller, particularly Jerusalemites: "you and me got sense. Them
goddamn Okies got no sense and no feeling. They ain't human. A human
being wouldn't live like they do. A human being couldn't stand it to be so
dirty and miserable. They ain't a hell of a lot better than gorillas."[93]

From this passage comes a sense of the similar hostility and condescension the Galilean peasants often had to endure, as when they arrived
in Jerusalem dusty and disheveled after their days-long pilgrimage to the
Temple. It is something no one should have to experience, especially from
those they have been taught to trust as intercessors with God. It is appropriate to restate the observation of Sean Freyne here: "Thus the Galilean
peasant found himself in the rather strange position that those very people
to whom he felt bound by ties of national and religious loyalty, the priestly
aristocracy, were in fact his social oppressors."[94] Yet with one declaration
Jesus offered his peasant compatriots a powerful measure of counter-
hegemonic psycho-emotional freedom from the tyranny of the religious
establishment and their psychic assaults on the Galileans' dignity: "You are
already made clean by the word I have spoken to you."

John 15:1–5 narrates no response to Jesus' monumental declaration that his hearers are now pure in the sight of God and thus must no longer have to seek the intercession of the haughty priests. Yet for those who took his words seriously, for those who had hungered for the slightest bit of affirmation, for even the smallest measure of permission to push back against priestly hegemony, how could their response have been anything but a sense of relief and release from centuries of feeling like they did not measure up? At the least it planted seeds of the liberation from internalization of the estimation of them as second-class citizens in the household of God. A sense of their relief and vindication can be seen in Ma Joad's response to the realization that in her encounters with the management and her fellow residents at the Farm Security Administration camp that her humanity is finally fully being acknowledged: "Praise God, we come home to our own people. . . . We was farm people till the debt. And then — them people. They done somepin to us. Ever' time they come seemed like they was a-whippin me — all of us. . . . Made me feel ashamed. An' now I ain't ashamed. . . . Why, I feel like people again."[95]

Similar sentiments can be discerned in Tom Joad's muted response when he learns that all residents of the camp, despite their poverty and country ways, will be treated respectfully there: "Ma's gonna like this place. She ain't been treated decent for a long time."[96]

In Jesus' day, despite the Jerusalem religious establishment's implications to the contrary, the reason the Galilean peasants were considered *am ha aretz* was not because they did not value a relationship with God. Nor was it only because the great difficulty of observing tithing prescriptions made it impractical, if not impossible to comply with them. As was hinted in our discussion of the *am ha aretz,* perhaps an additional reason for the Temple priests' apparent contempt for Galilean peasants was that their distance from the Temple and its obsession with pomp and routinized religiosity caused them to place less value on the rituals and outer trappings of their faith and more on its inner relational core. This would certainly be consistent with peasant culture, which as we saw above is based, to the point of sacralizing it, upon the relational ethics of *general reciprocity* (caring for others in need without having to be asked because of the cultural assurance that in the same circumstance one will receive the same) and *the right of subsistence* (the culturally recognized right of everyone to an adequate subsistence according to community norms and capacities).[97] If the name of Jesus is replaced by the name of a biblical prophet like Elijah (as would have been the case during Jesus' lifetime; obviously the resurrection that bestowed exalted status upon him had not yet occurred), the soliloquy by Jim Casy, the lapsed "Okie" preacher, gives an illustrative sense of what the faith of some of the peasants who were called *am ha aretz* might well have held:

> I been in the hills, thinkin', almost you might say like Jesus went into the wilderness to think His way out of a mess of troubles.... Nighttime I'd lay on my back an' look up at the stars; morning I'd set an' watch the sun come up; midday I'd look out from a hill at the rollin' dry country; evenin' I'd foller the sun down. Sometimes I'd pray like I always done. On'y I couldn' figure what I was prayin' to or for. There was the hills, an' there was me, an' we wasn't separate no more. We was one thing. An' that one thing was holy.... An' I got thinkin', on'y it wasn't thinkin', it was deeper down than thinkin'. I got thinkin' how we was holy when we was one thing, an' mankin' was holy when it was one thing. An' it on'y got unholy when one mis'able little fella got the bit in his teeth an' run off his own way, kickin' an' draggin' an' fightin'. Fella like that bust the holiness. But when they're all workin' together, not one fella for another fella, but one fella kind of harnessed to the whole shebang — that's right, that's holy.[98]

Jim Casy's holistic understanding of holiness as oneness with humanity and all the created world raises another dimension of the meaning that Jesus' pronouncement must have held for his Galilean peasant hearers. It would have validated the Galilean's self-estimation that their less than scrupulous observance of the Torah's tithe and offering strictures did not estrange them from God's favor. It would have affirmed to them that they were more important in the sight of God than all the agricultural produce and ritually slaughtered flesh they could offer; that tithing was not the measure of their value to God or their relationship with God; that they were indeed righteous as long as they endeavored to love God with all their hearts and minds and to love their neighbors as themselves.

There are other analogous factors between the plights of the first-century Galilean peasants and the so-called Okies in the settings of *The Grapes of Wrath*, including the betrayal of both by their co-religionists;

the economic exploitation of both peasantries by upper-class elites; the repression both experienced when they resisted the domination of ruling elites, particularly in the case of Jim Casy's sacrificial death while trying to help the peasants' cause; and the fact that the poverty of both had significant structural causes in addition to the typical cyclical and meteorological causes. These and other analogous factors can be explored in the effort to bring Gospel stories to life. One obvious candidate is the narrative of the workers in the vineyard in Matthew 20:1–16, in which landless peasants congregate in the marketplace, so desperate for a day's wage that two separate groups of workers jump at the chance to work without even asking what their wages will be. The similarity in relations of production between the two is obvious.[99]

Acknowledging the similarities between the plight of the so-called Okies and the first-century Galilean peasants helps us better understand what Jesus meant in his True Vine pronouncement, why he might have said it, and how it would have been heard. In a general sense, *The Grapes of Wrath* has helped us to better understand what John the evangelist apparently hoped to convey to his readers and hearers. It also has helped us to envision the depth of the response Jesus' declaration would have received from his immediate hearers, the depth of its meaning for them, the pain it would have assuaged for them, the ways it would have validated, empowered, and liberated them — liberated them from shame and from the tyranny of the smothering, exploitive religious obligations and the jaundiced eye of oppressive orthodoxy. As Jesus put it, they were already clean. Or, to paraphrase Ma Joad, they could feel like people again.

PARTAKING OF THE FRUIT OF THE TRUE VINE

New Testament studies must give much more consideration to the importance of bringing Gospel narratives to life today in a way that helps readers of the Gospels better feel what the hearers of Jesus and the evangelists' envisioned hearers and readers felt. This is important for the general enhancement of the understanding and knowledge base of contemporary biblical readers and believers.

Specifically, reading the Gospels "from below" can offer important instruction about how to conduct certain affairs and actions in the public square. For example, if it becomes clear that those Jesus meant to affirm and inspire in John 15 were not just devalued *individuals* but included an entire devalued *class,* then those who take the Gospel message seriously must work to become sensitized to *class issues;* they must affirm and actively support measures that seek to address the plights of the working poor and impoverished in our communities, our nation, and our world. If from the Gospel message we indeed ascertain that Jesus was affirming the ostracized, the maligned, and the marginalized, then those who profess to follow him must actively affirm the worth of all people by working to dismantle social structures and definitions that erect barriers that deny even one person the God-granted right of full social fellowship. If we take seriously Jesus' pronouncement that his "word" has "made clean" or nullified judgments of religion and class that ostracize and devalue some as impure and unacceptable because in some way that they do not conform to the status quo, then it is a biblical duty to struggle against any social stigma that places anyone's worth in question. Most importantly, taking Jesus seriously demands that we interrogate the role of centralized religious hierarchies and doctrinal orthodoxies in general that, like the Jerusalem priestly aristocracy, develop litmus tests and doctrinal requirements that must be satisfied before one can be recognized as "clean" and deemed worthy of full membership in the household of God. And if we find that they contradict the witness of Jesus in the Gospels, we must reject them.

- 3 -

A Camel through
the Eye of a Needle (Part I)

Class, Political Conservatism,
and Anti-Christian Economics

*The real test of a man of faith is that he sees to it that those who have too
little get enough.*   —Hubert Humphrey

THE CONUNDRUM
OF POLITICAL CONSERVATISM

In recent years conservative politicians have met with great success in their
quest to identify their brand of political conservatism with Christianity
itself. Indeed, a number of conservative politicians have either explicitly
claimed or strongly implied — with no apparent fear of contradiction —
that their policies and political rhetoric are the direct result of divine guidance, if not divine intervention. For instance, Stephen Mansfield reports
that in the early days of his campaign for the Oval Office George W. Bush
repeatedly declared, "I believe God wants me to run for president . . . God
wants me to do it."[1] The Jerusalem daily *Haaretz* reported that Bush said
to Palestinian prime minister Mahmoud Abbas after the 2003 U.S. inva-
sion of Iraq, "God told me to strike at al Qaida and I struck them, and then
he instructed me to strike at Saddam, which I did."[2] Bush went so far as
tell a 2004 gathering in Pennsylvania, "I trust God speaks through me."[3]

Terry Schiavo was a severely brain-damaged woman whose husband
successfully petitioned the Supreme Court to have her feeding tube
removed in 2005 — which made her death imminent — after her doc-
tors deemed it medically certain that she would never emerge from the
coma in which she had lain for fourteen years. Yet in a March 2005 speech

to the conservative Family Research Council, then House Majority Whip Tom DeLay claimed Schiavo's tragic plight was a divine sacralization of his party's national political agenda. "One thing God has brought us," DeLay declared, "is Terry Schiavo, to help elevate the visibility of what is going on in America."[4]

More recently, at an April 2010 convention of Christian women in Louisville, Kentucky, conservative former vice presidential candidate and Tea Party doyenne Sarah Palin thanked her "prayer warriors" for the "prayer shield" they built around her, quoted from Proverbs 3 ("Trust in the Lord with all your heart . . . and he will make straight your paths"), and then recounted a conversation with her nine-year-old daughter about the Jewish Queen Esther, the retelling of which was clearly intended to compare Palin herself to that biblical heroine: "[Esther] was out there on the stage, wondering if she'd have the opportunity to be chosen to really help change the world."[5] More recently still, Representative Steve King (R-IA) actually invoked the divine imprimatur upon Republicans' efforts to repeal the 2010 Health Care Act. King declared, "We will carry on this struggle until in God's good time, with all his power and might, he steps forth to the rescue and liberation of our God-given American liberty." This divine deliverance, one supposes, includes in its purview something as arcane as the Health Care Act repeal.

Statements like these, as well as the oft-repeated public confessions of Christian faith by conservative politicians that today seem to constitute a veritable conservative political litmus test, are clearly meant to equate the focus and thrust of their politics and policies with biblical faith itself. This is the face conservative politicians have presented to the American public for some time now. Among the ways they legitimate themselves is with hugely influential, unabashedly Christian political gatherings such as the Family Research Council's Values Voter Summit, which is held annually in Washington, D.C., with thousands in attendance, including numerous powerful public figures and elected officials. With workshop topics like "Activism and Conservatism: Fit to a Tea (Party)," "Obamacare: Rationing Your Life Away," "Indivisible: Social and Economic Foundations of American Liberty," "American Apocalypse — When Christians Do Nothing, Secularists Do Everything — The Case for Christian Activism," "Indivisible: Social and Economic Foundations of American Liberty," "Who Are Tea Party and Christian Voters and What Do They Believe?" "Establishing a Culture Impact Team in Your Church," and "Thugocracy: Fighting the Vast Left Wing Conspiracy," it seems that political conservatives have all but anointed themselves and the candidates and policies they support as the actual party of Christ.

Yet is this really the case? Are the precepts and policies of political conservatism as consistent with the biblical tradition and the teachings of Jesus as conservative politicians would have us believe? It is tempting to quickly answer yea or nay according to one's personal political biases. Yet it is a query that should not be treated lightly. Why? Because religion and religious commitments loom high and large on today's political stage; much of today's political rhetoric is shaped by the desire to garner the support of "values voters," to borrow the Family Research Council's description of its politically conservative "Judeo-Christian" constituency. It is also important because many current-day conservative politicians articulate their views and legitimate their actions in religious terms, be they explicit, implicit, or transparently coded with easily recognizable biblical references and hymn wordings, what the scholar Bruce Lincoln calls, "double-coding."[6] Moreover, many political conservatives purport to base their political policies and legislative proposals not on political interests or worldly considerations, but on the dictates of the Bible alone, and then with only minor adjustments. But not only do major aspects of their policies have no firm basis in the biblical tradition, but when they are closely considered, many of those policies are actually revealed to be in direct opposition to the most foundational biblical principles.

Nowhere is this more evident than with the economic principles of political conservatism. Rather than attending equally to the interests of all persons regardless of wealth or class as the Bible quite specifically commands from the Exodus account forward, instead conservative economic principles consistently skew toward the interests of the rich.[7] This can be seen in the political conservatives' perennial push to minimize capital gains and estate taxes, which benefits the wealthiest Americans in vast disproportion; their demonizing of the poor and dismissal of their needs; and their hands-off, laissez-faire approach to regulatory protections that, if fully realized, would allow businesses to pursue profits with virtually no restraints or oversight of their actions. (The French term, laissez faire, literally means "let do." Those who apply the term to economic markets mean by it that markets should be left alone to function without regulatory intervention of any kind.[8]) Conservative economic principles do not seem even to condemn such obvious transgressions of biblical precepts as engaging in monopolistic practices.

There is little question that business monopolies violate basic biblical ethics because, on the one hand, they unfairly and unequally benefit those who contrive to monopolize products and markets; as we will see later in this chapter, the biblical prophets railed against such abuses with unalloyed outrage. On the other hand, business monopolies harm the public interest because their owners are free to manipulate consumer prices at will, particularly in the absence of market regulations, as well as to use the advantage of their size to weaken or even destroy smaller competitors. Yet, political conservatives have found ways to legitimate and even give moral standing to such practices. For instance, in the *Journal of Markets and Morality*, a publication of the Acton Institute, a well-respected conservative think tank whose motto is "Integrating Judeo-Christian Truths with Free Market Principles," Jeffrey Tucker, an Acton faculty member, asks, "Are antitrust laws immoral?" This is a strange query, given the inequalities and barriers to honest competition in markets that antitrust laws seek to combat. But Tucker's assessment of the motivating factors behind legal challenges to monopolistic practices is nothing short of Orwellian: "Envy," he concludes, "is the moral subtext to nearly every antitrust case brought under American law since the signing of the Sherman Antitrust Act."[9] According to this view, then, it is not opposition to exclusionary practices or the exercise of unfair, even extortionate advantage that are the motivating factors behind antitrust regulations and lawsuits. In fact, in this view objections to monopolistic practices are not even primarily economic. For Tucker and the kind of political conservatism he represents, antitrust suits are the result of a *moral* lapse, specifically the *moral* failing of complainants against exploitive monopolistic practices. Tucker's essay and its conclusions are representative of the skewed ethical compass underlying the economics of political conservatism that quite consistently favors the interests of big business and wealthy individuals.

However, where politically conservative commentators like Tucker employ selective (mis)readings of biblical morality both to justify their conservative economic principles and consequently to discredit — implicitly or explicitly — those who question or oppose them, others choose instead to sacralize conservative economic principles by presenting them as synonymous with the Bible itself.

In the modern U.S. political era this approach began in earnest in the 1930s in opposition to Franklin Roosevelt and the New Deal. One of its earliest purveyors was Spiritual Mobilization, an organization founded by the Rev. James Fifield, a Los Angeles minister. By most accounts, Spiritual Mobilization, which was active from the 1930s into the early 1960s, engaged in no spiritual or evangelizing activities; its only apparent purpose was to defend laissez-faire economic policies by developing and propagating theological justifications for the unbridled and unregulated capitalistic pursuit of wealth. In his 1957 book, *The Single Path,* Fifield wrote, "The blessings of capitalism come from God. A system that provides so much for the common good and happiness must flourish under the force of the Almighty."[10] Fifield's implication is clear: America's economy is guided by God, so there is no need to protect the interests of rank-and-file Americans from market abuses by enacting protective legislation and market regulations. Just leave that to God and the largesse of capitalists.

This strategy was resurrected in the late 1970s and 1980s by the Rev. Jerry Falwell, among others, in conjunction with the presidency of Ronald Reagan and the rise of supply-side economics.[11] In the periodical Falwell founded, the *Journal-Champion,* which later became the *Moral Majority Report,* he defended laissez-faire capitalism and attacked efforts to impose even minimal protections on unbridled markets: "The greatest threat to the average American's liberty does not come from Communistic aggression," he wrote. "It comes from the growing encroachments of government bureaucrats as they limit the freedom of Americans through distribution of rules and regulations, many times called guidelines."[12] More recently Wayne Grudem, a respected scholar in conservative circles, has given biblical sanction to laissez-faire economics and its attendant policies in a lengthy survey of contemporary political issues and public policies that has garnered the effusive praise of leading political conservatives. Grudem's text is unambiguously entitled *Politics According to the Bible.*[13]

This strategic bestowal of religious sanction upon conservative economic principles, whether explicit or implicit, has been continually employed by political conservatives ever since. It remains an important component of conservative political discourse today. This can be seen in the rhetoric of the Tea Party movement, which in equal measure bases its calls for both deregulation of markets (particularly financial markets) and the dismantling of the modern welfare state (both fundamental components of conservative economic philosophy) upon a selective reading of the Founding Fathers, which is then valorized to near biblical heights,[14] and a *mis*reading of actual biblical writings about social and economic issues that is devoid of the level of knowledge of the social and economic contexts that is so crucial to understanding their meaning.

I hope it is clear, then, that we are treading serious ground. So here I restate the question, albeit a bit more sharply: Are the precepts and policies of political conservatism — specifically its economic philosophy — as consistent with the biblical tradition and the teachings of Jesus as conservative politicians would have us believe? I am convinced that the answer is an emphatic No! It is my intention to make this demonstrably clear by the end of this chapter and the one that follows.

Before we proceed, however, there are several clarifications that I must offer. First, in this chapter I use the terms "political conservatism" and "political liberalism," both of which describe political perspectives on the role of government in the distribution of power, authority, and resources in society. I use these terms to distinguish them from *moral* conservatism and *moral* liberality, both of which have more to do with matters of personal piety and moral conduct than with public policy matters.

Second, although I am aware, of course, that most political conservatives self-identify with the Republican Party, when I speak of "political conservatism" and "political liberalism" I do not refer to any particular political party; I specifically refer to those whose actions, specifically with regard to economic matters, are consistent with conservative or liberal political principles. However, it is the case that since the early twentieth century, the period this study will focus on, Republicans have typically championed the economic principles of political conservatism in America. This remains the case today. If there is any doubt just witness the secret White House meetings convened with the heads of America's top energy corporations by Vice-President Dick Cheney, the former CEO of the energy giant Halliburton Corporation, to formulate the very governmental policies that were supposed to regulate their activities. Following that meeting the industry went on to post record earnings.[15] Or note the 2010 meeting of Republican House Minority Leader John Boehner (now Speaker of the House) with over a hundred Wall Street executives and financial industry lobbyists to plan his strategy to oppose the financial oversight reforms contained in the 2010 federal financial reforms bill.[16] Or see the letter from chairman of the House Oversight and Government Affairs Committee, Republican Darrell Issa, to a comparable number of lobbyists, actually asking them to identify the workplace safety laws they wanted repealed.[17]

However, it is not only members of the Republican Party who champion conservative economic principles. Democratic senator Charles Schumer is proof of that. Schumer has so consistently advocated for financial industry interests that political commentator David Callahan describes him as "one of Wall Street's biggest defenders on Capitol Hill."[18] Schumer has championed favorable tax treatment for hedge funds, tried to block stricter oversight of Wall Street credit rating agencies, and attempted to cut the fees the Securities and Exchange Commission assesses on Wall Street firms. According to John Bogle, the head of the colossal Vanguard mutual funds group, Schumer "serv[es] the parochial interest of a very small group of financial people, bankers, investment bankers, fund managers, private equity firms, rather than the general public."[19] To be fair, Wall Street and many of the nation's largest financial institutions are among New York Schumer's senatorial constituents. Collectively these organizations pay millions of dollars in real estate, payroll, income, and other taxes and fees into New York's state and local coffers, in addition to employing thousands of New Yorkers. So in an important sense, Schumer's support of Wall Street can simply be seen as Schumer appropriately representing his constituents' interests. However, that does not mitigate the service his actions provide to the economic interests of political conservatism. Therefore, when I speak of political conservatives in this chapter, I am not employing a euphemism for members of the Republican Party; I am referring to all those who serve the ends of conservative political principles.

Finally, as regards my appeals to the biblical witness, both the pronouncements of the Hebrew Bible, or Old Testament, and the Gospel sayings of Jesus regarding political and economic ethics are relatively straightforward when considered in the cultural contexts in which they were respectively written. I shall make every effort to offer intellectually honest and critically informed readings of the Bible that take seriously the historical and cultural implications of every passage I cite. I will also resist the popular temptation to spiritualize every biblical pronouncement, as seems to be so commonly done these days, especially with respect to the sayings of Jesus, including even those of his pronouncements that clearly are economic in nature.

THE TENETS OF CONSERVATISM

In 2002 the award-winning political commentator Kevin Phillips published *Wealth and Democracy*.[20] In his "political history of the American rich" Phillips explores three centuries of economic policies and politics in America. Thankfully, our task here calls for an effort much less ambitious. Unlike Phillips, in order to answer the question facing us — whether the economic principles of political conservatism are consistent with biblical principles — we do not have to consider Tories and Whigs or Jeffersonian versus Madisonian conceptions of the appropriate balance of interaction between government oversight, economic enterprise, and public finance. We have only to go back to the dawn of modern conservatism, that is, to the first three decades of the twentieth century.

With the decisive victory of Franklin D. Roosevelt's New Deal, which gave America such important social safety net legislation as social security and unemployment insurance, by the end of the 1940s observers like the social and literary critic Lionel Trilling were claiming that political liberalism was not only the dominant intellectual tradition in America, but the sole intellectual tradition, which was another way of saying that conservatism as a political force in America was dormant, if not dead. But what is political liberalism? How do its goals and emphases differ from those of political conservatism? And why have political conservatives consistently and so furiously opposed the goals of political liberalism?

Political conservatives today spend much energy portraying political liberalism as a godless mélange of immorality, irreligiosity, and social irresponsibility that is in love with bloated government and huge, inefficient bureaucracies.[21] Yet the basic meaning and moral impetus behind political liberalism is offered by no less than George Washington: "As mankind become more liberal, they will be more apt to allow that all those who conduct themselves as worthy members of our community are equally entitled to the protections of the civil government. I hope ever to see America among the foremost nations in examples of justice and liberality."[22] In essence, what Washington's hopeful vision enumerates is a concise version of the core principles that comprise political liberalism: (1) equal status and freedom under the law for all and (2) the crucial role of governmental protection of the poor from the rich, the weak from the strong.

Yet many political conservatives claim that the major difference between political conservatism and political liberalism is that political conservatives place greater value on the importance of freedom. Case in point: in the short statement of political conservative Congressman Steve King cited in the preface above, in just one sentence he used "liberty" and "liberation," and managed to imply that those who agreed with his political party's policy stance stood for freedom while those who disagreed did not stand for freedom. Yet as economist Robert Kuttner offers, "Liberals and conservatives agree, in principle, about the value of liberty. But where liberals differ," Kuttner explains, "is their insistence that liberty requires greater equality than our society now generates."[23] That is to say that in principle, at least, both political conservatives and political liberals value real opportunities for unfettered upward mobility and a decent standard of living *for* everyone, regardless of class, creed, or color, while expecting *from* everyone basic levels of responsibility for their own lives. The crucial difference is that political liberals believe that when those rights and opportunities are threatened or denied, it is the duty of the government of the people, by the people, and for the people to take appropriate measures to provide and protect people's rights and opportunities — political, social, and economic — through lawful policies and legislation designed for those purposes. In contrast, political conservatives have historically advocated the laissez-faire, non-interventionist approach that relegates the adjudication of economic rights, at least, to the vagaries of the free marketplace — free, that is, from legal controls and oversights that seek to ensure open equality of economic opportunity and economic mobility to all Americans. With regard to the New Deal, then, in a real sense, the policy prescriptions that the political conservatives offered in the wake of the New Deal were simply negations: *no* market regulations, *no* governmental interventions, *no* governmental oversight, *no* measures to provide equality of economic opportunity.[24]

Thus in 1950 Trilling could write, "For it is the plain fact that there are no conservative or reactionary ideas in general circulation," but only "irritable mental gestures that resemble ideas." That last phrase became a popular, if tongue-in-cheek, description of political conservatism. Yet Trilling was not ready to gloat. "When we say that a movement is 'bankrupt of ideas' we are likely to suppose that it is at the end of its powers. But that is not so, and it is dangerous for us to suppose that it is so."[25]

It is debatable whether Trilling was right on the first count — that there were no politically conservative ideas then in circulation — but there is no question that he was right to be cautious. That is to say that conservatism might have been *dormant* when he wrote at the century's midpoint, but in no way was it *dead*. For soon after Trilling wrote, political demagoguery and "Red-baiting" by Joe McCarthy and Richard Nixon in the 1950s helped to reignite a vigorous, if unfocused and unreflective, resurgence of political conservatism that in spite of (or perhaps because of) numerous subsequent periodic swings from thoughtful sobriety to frightening political extremism, has nonetheless culminated in its powerful ideological and political positions in America today.

Yet for all the publicity and public affirmation generated by the witch-hunts of McCarthy and Nixon, most conservative commentators trace the roots of America's awakened political conservatism after its trouncing by Roosevelt not to those histrionics, but to a more thoughtful source: the 1953 publication of Russell Kirk's acclaimed study *The Conservative Mind*.[26] Lee Edwards, a fellow at the Heritage Foundation, a major conservative think tank, declared as much in a 2003 lecture: "With one book, Russell Kirk made conservatism intellectually acceptable in America."[27] In the *Chronicle of Higher Education* Edwards went further. "Kirk," he said, actually "gave the conservative movement its name."[28] Edwards' assessment of Kirk's importance to political conservatism was no exaggeration. Its accuracy is reflected in the fact that public usage of the term "conservative" was virtually non-existent before the appearance of Kirk's book. For example, when William F. Buckley published *God and Man at Yale* in 1951, he called himself not a conservative, but an "individualist." And when Barry Goldwater, a hero of the better-informed elements of political conservatism was elected to the Senate a year later, his preferred terms of self-reference were "progressive Republican" and "Jeffersonian Republican."

The most significant contribution of Kirk's work, however, is that it energized conservatism by giving it the historical and philosophical heft and reflective self-understanding it had lacked. More important was that it offered a coherent rationale for the values underpinning political conservatism's worldview. A sense of the influence of *The Conservative Mind* can be gleaned from its use as an ideological touchstone by political conservatives from the old-guard William F. Buckley to that scion of currently reigning neo-conservative royalty, William Kristol. Buckley expressly credits *The Conservative Mind* for the resurgence of political conservatism in America: "[It] is almost inconceivable to imagine, let alone hope for, a dominant conservative movement in America without [Kirk's] labor."[29] Indeed, a full quarter century after the appearance of *The Conservative Mind,* James J. Kilpatrick, the conservative self-avowed white supremacist[30] journalist, best known for his combative 1970s appearances on the weekly news show *60 Minutes,* virtually echoed Kirk's belief in the necessity for orders and classes in *Nation's Business* magazine: "Conservatives believe that a civilized society demands orders and classes [and] that men are not inherently equal."[31] Even at the dawn of the twenty-first century David Frum, a former economic speechwriter for President George W. Bush, would still pronounce Kirk to be "an artist, a visionary, almost a prophet."[32]

According to Kirk, political conservatism is based on six "basic canons" that are summarized below:

* Divine intent, as well as personal conscience, rules society.

* Tradition fills life with variety and mystery, while most "radical systems" are characterized by "a narrowing uniformity" and "egalitarianism."

* To be civilized, society needs "orders and classes, as against the notion of a 'classless society,'" although "ultimately, equality in the judgment of God, and equality before courts of law, are recognized by conservatives."

* Property and freedom are closely linked, but economic "leveling" is undesirable.

* Humanity's "anarchic impulse" and "the innovator's lust for power" must be controlled by "custom, convention, and old prescription."

* Social change must happen slowly and gradually.[33]

In subsequent years, Kirk would articulate these tenets in various forms and forums, but his "basic canons" would remain the same, and *The Conservative Mind* would retain them through multiple editions until his death in 1994. In an interesting examination of the landscape of political conservatism today, former Nixon White House counsel John W. Dean claims that by the mid-1980s many conservatives were coming to consider Kirk's work as "Old Testament conservatism" and that Kirk's canons of conservatism "now reside in the dustbin of history."[34] This is primarily because of the rise in the 1980s and 1990s of the religious right in America, represented by such figures and organizations as Falwell's Moral Majority, Pat Robertson's Christian Coalition, James Dobson's Focus on the Family, and the Family Research Council.[35] The discourse of the religious right as it is promulgated by organizations like these has taken political conservatism to a decidedly less considered, even less intellectual turn, shifting its focus from political and economic theory and analysis, to a near obsession with social and religious issues that are generally stated not in terms of legislative policies, but in moral and religious absolutes. As a result, the discourse of the religious right today has no place for — nor places any value upon — thoughtful analysis or even deep thought, except to buttress its own unquestioned conclusions. In other words, the religious right seems to value only assent to its theocratic moral absolutes. Any analysis, no matter how careful and thoughtful, that does not affirm the beliefs of the religious right has no home there.

But whether at the present moment conservatives refer to or even read Kirk's writings is immaterial; what is clear is that the tenets of political conservatism that he identified virtually define conservative political discourse today. Indeed, one would expect that most Americans share Kirk's stated beliefs if taken in their most benign formulations, regardless of personal political identification. For instance, in a nation in which nine out of ten people believe in God,[36] one would expect that most would agree to one degree or another that there is a divine intent that governs society. One would expect that most Americans would also agree that respect for tradition is important to the conduct of healthy lives in a healthy society, that abrupt and sudden drastic change can be disruptive and even destructive both to society and to individual lives, and so on. Yet when we consider the actions and policies that have resulted from these principles, we find that in spite of the pious "faith" pronouncements of many political conservatives, some of the most basic principles of political conservatives appear to actually fly in the face of the teachings of Jesus and the most fundamental biblical precepts.

For one, conservatism's insistence on gradual change, even in cases of egregious social injustice, has too often served to delay justice, thus often maintaining injustice (this is reflected in the legal maxim, "justice delayed is justice denied"), as in the shamefully slow abolition of de jure white supremacy in the United States, which remained legally enshrined in some jurisdictions in America in one shape or form until the passage of the Civil Rights Law of 1968. By most accounts political conservatives have counseled gradualism only when its purpose is to slow — or stop altogether — social and political changes that challenge their interests.[37] This is undoubtedly what Martin Luther King had in mind when he decried "the tranquilizing drug of gradualism" in his epochal "I Have a Dream" address. And there is also little question that King was specifically rejecting the gradualism of conservative political philosophy when he wrote "the time is always ripe to do right" in "A Letter from a Birmingham Jail," his eloquent reply to those, including Rev. Billy Graham, who counseled him to slow his efforts to dismantle apartheid in America. Indeed, despite Kirk's claims that "equality [of all persons] in the judgment of God, and equality before courts of law, are recognized by conservatives," it is political conservatives who not only have been slowest to accept full rights for all, but who have also been the most vociferous and violent opponents of equal rights for every American, especially those of African descent. In fact, without political conservatives' systematic efforts to deny African Americans the fullness of their rights as U.S. citizens there would have been no need for the civil rights movement in the first place. And distorting the belief that divine intent governs society into the specious notion that a particular ruler or leader, political party, or set of policies is divinely sanctioned can devolve into disastrous, even deadly, demagoguery, as in President George W. Bush's assertions that God told him to embroil our nation into a terrible war of choice that has cost the lives of tens of thousands of innocents on two continents.

As troubling as these principles can be, however, there is one that is even more disquieting: the notion that maintenance of economic classes is a necessary, even desirable, component of a "civilized" American society.[38] Kirk's emphatic declaration of the importance of the maintenance of classism in America is made even more disturbing by his dismissal of egalitarianism.

Egalitarianism is not "narrowing conformity,"[39] as Kirk portrays it, nor does it hold that every person's material conditions should be made the same in any respect. Rather egalitarianism maintains that everyone ought to be treated as equals — as possessing equal fundamental worth and moral status. In practical terms, capitalist economies such as the United States would seek to reduce gross systemic disparities in income, wealth, and economic opportunity and mobility.[40] Not only does egalitarianism constitute basic moral fairness, it is also a fundamental tenet of biblical ethics, as we shall see. Thus Kirk's dismissal of egalitarianism as "narrowing uniformity" flies in the face of some of the most foundational principles and pronouncements of the ethics of the Judeo-Christian biblical tradition that have as their unabashed aim the narrowing of class disparities, and most certainly not the perpetuation of them, as we will see below. Like many adherents of political conservatism today, it seems that Kirk mistakenly equates efforts by duly elected government officials to reduce the vast disparities of poverty and wealth in America with Soviet-style compulsory economic collectivism. Yet it is an understandable mistake, given the Cold War era in which Kirk wrote and the great impact the 1944 publication of Friedrich von Hayek's *The Road to Serfdom*[41] was then having on conservative political thought.

Friedrich von Hayek was a prominent Austrian economist (and second cousin to the renowned philosopher Ludwig Wittgenstein) who lived through the European theater of World War II and there faced first-hand the threat of Nazism (whose formal name was National *Socialism,* as Hayek never let his audiences forget). These experiences predisposed Hayek to see any mode of governmental intervention in economic matters as Soviet-style "collectivism" and thus a danger-filled step on the slippery slope toward totalitarian governmental domination of social and political life. Those experiences inculcated in Hayek the deeply held — and ultimately unsupportable — belief that only small government with little social reach and the totally unregulated markets that characterize completely laissez-faire economies can be consistent with democracy. For Hayek, the market, and never government, was to be the final arbiter of all things economic. His thinking was based upon Say's Law, the principle articulated by the eighteenth-century French economist, Jean-Baptiste Say

(1767–1832).[42] Say's Law simply states that "a product is no sooner created, than it, from that instant, affords a market for other products to the full extent of its own value."[43] Since market imbalances always correct themselves, argued Say, there is never a need for a government to intervene in the workings of markets. As consistent as Hayek's thought was with Say's, however, it was Hayek's painful personal experience of European totalitarianism rather than his academic reading of Say that most deeply influenced his thoughts on political economy.

An example of the way the personal experience of the brutality of communism comes to be expressed as an ideological obsession with totally laissez-faire, unregulated markets is seen in the influential right-wing political philosopher Ayn Rand. Rand, born Alice Rosenbaum in St. Petersburg, Russia, in 1905, saw her small-businessman father lose all that he had to the Bolshevik expropriations, including even the indignity of the seizing of a few bars of soap that he had hoarded. She experienced firsthand the shortages, rationings, and recurrent indignities of a centralized planned economy. As a result, Rand came to hate anything that could be even vaguely construed as resembling centralized market planning. For Rand that included every type of market regulation, no matter the excesses it might be designed to correct or protect against. For Rand, like Hayek, the only protection against market ills was total market libertarian freedom,[44] a position espoused by Milton Friedman (whom we will discuss in Part II), the influential economist and hero to political conservatives, strongly promoted today by Congressmen Ron Paul (R-TX) and his son Rand Paul (R-KY).

In *The Road to Serfdom.* Hayek argued that the causes of the vast disparities in wealth and income in democratic societies was not the result of economic injustice or exploitation, but was instead the result of "natural forces," the effectuation of social Darwinist "survival of the fittest" in the marketplace, to use Herbert Spencer's famous phrase. *The Road to Serfdom* was surprisingly commercially successful in the United States. Its ideas became so influential in conservative political circles that today it stands as a seminal text of political conservatism.

Returning to Kirk, for him, as for Hayek, it is not the existence of extremes of wealth and poverty that is unjust; what is unjust for Kirk is governmental intervention of *any kind* in the supposedly natural selection process of the unfettered market that ordains some as rich and some as poor. It was this laissez-faire absolutism that rendered Hayek, and Kirk in his wake, unable to differentiate between lawful actions undertaken by democratically elected governments to protect their societies from becoming full-blown plutocracies and the violent despotism of politburos.

Despite Kirk's and Hayek's claims to the contrary, however, any clear-eyed consideration of economic egalitarianism reveals that its goal is not the narrowing of disparities of poverty and wealth for the simple sake of it; nor is it by any measure a precursor to communism or some kind of socialist state. Nor is its purpose to achieve social "uniformity," whatever Kirk means by that. The intention of economic egalitarianism is quite simple, quite admirable, and quite biblical: to stabilize human society by improving the quality of life and life chances of all people. Egalitarianism is as consistent with the basic biblical ethics of removing systemic barriers to upward economic mobility and narrowing the yawning chasms between economic classes as the economic philosophy of political conservatism is not. This is confirmed by Deuteronomy 15, Leviticus 25, the Holiness Codes, certain Gospel sayings of Jesus, and numerous other egalitarian biblical prescriptions that we will explore shortly.

To understand why the economic dimension of political conservatism came to be so stridently anti-egalitarian — and in that sense, stridently anti-biblical as well, at least with regard to class and market issues — it is necessary to look to the organizations, intellectuals, activists, and strategies that were marshaled in support of political conservative goals long before Russell Kirk put pen to paper.[45]

CLASSES AND CONSERVATISM

If Trilling and other important social commentators, such as the Harvard political scientist Louis Hartz,[46] saw a liberal consensus in America at the century's mid-point, in the aftermath of the stock market crash of 1929 a consensus was nowhere to be seen, for political liberalism confronted a major challenge from business leaders who were outraged by the opposition presented by Franklin Roosevelt's New Deal policies to the laissez-faire, hands-off-the-market economic policies that had effectively precipitated the crash. Why the conservative outrage? Because many of the prevailing policies that the New Deal imposed limitations upon were the very laissez-faire policies, with their lack of regulatory market protections, that had allowed so many members of the business elite to accumulate their wealth — and maintain it for generations. And there was another reason for their outrage. In addition to endangering their wealth, these rich businessmen saw governmental oversight of markets as an insulting challenge to the positions of power and leadership in America that they believed rightfully belonged to their class.

Big Business had historically had a rocky, adversarial relationship with America's rank and file. Memories were still fresh of the unconscionable extremes to which corporations had gone to block the growth of unions, like the union-busting tactics at a Rockefeller-owned mine in Ludlow, Colorado, that resulted in the 1913 massacre of fifty-two women and children by corporate goons,[47] or Chicago's infamous 1886 Haymarket Massacre and numerous other incidents of corporate-sponsored murder, abuse, and forced starvation of union-seeking workers and their wives and children.[48] But in the decade or so immediately prior to the crash of 1929 businessmen had finally become respected leaders in America. Union unrest was relatively quiet, and leftist activists had been set to flight by the repression raised by the wave of anti-Bolshevik sentiments that followed World War I. This period of relative economic stability, coupled with a soaring, seemingly can't-miss stock market, made business leaders look like heroes. "The common folk believe in their leaders," wrote one commentator. "We no longer look upon the captains of industry as magnified crooks."[49]

But all this changed in the wake of the stock market crash of 1929. Businessmen were blamed for causing the widespread hunger, unemployment, and general hopelessness of the Great Depression by enriching themselves through greed and financial excess at the expense of ordinary citizens. They were parodied as fat cats and "economic royalists" who cared for nothing but profits, their own comforts, luxurious living, and maintenance of their preeminent class status. The New Deal's wresting of leadership of the economy from the business community was lauded by many who saw the New Deal as a much fairer deal for working-class Americans. Former U.S. senator and Democratic presidential candidate George McGovern reminds us that

> Roosevelt found "one-third of a nation ill-housed, ill-clad and ill-fed." He found not only much of the nation's workforce idled, but millions of workers without organization, representation, collective

bargaining rights, or unemployment insurance to protect them. He found older people haunted by the specter of insecurity and poverty in the closing years of their lives. He saw hardworking farm families losing their crops, their markets, their land, and their homes. As farmers lost their purchasing power, main-street businesses also went under. Banks were failing and closing their doors, wiping out the lifetime savings of families. . . . Roosevelt was determined to reduce the impact of the Depression on people's lives.[50]

However, America's business elites seethed; apparently Roosevelt's efforts to reduce the suffering of the masses meant little to the wealthy. The New Deal's regulation of the financial markets for the purpose of guarding against the fraud and excesses that had contributed to the Depression signaled a popular rejection of the old laissez-faire economic order that had largely left businessmen to their own financial devices. Kevin Phillips notes that "Franklin Roosevelt and the New Deal raised the top individual tax brackets, eliminated [Treasury Secretary Andrew W.] Mellon's fiscal favors, tightened inheritance taxes, and eliminated the personal holding companies through which some of the rich had deducted the expenses of their estates, stables, horses, and planes."[51] For this Roosevelt was widely reviled by America's wealthy elites as a "traitor to his class"[52] at whom wealthy denizens of "dinner parties in evening dress" went to movie theaters specifically to hiss when he appeared in newsreels.[53] *Time* magazine observed in 1936, "With few exceptions, members of the Upper Class frankly hate Roosevelt."[54] What this level of vitriol against Roosevelt betrayed was not a patriotic concern for constitutional freedoms. It showed that the true cause of their ire was the New Deal's circumscription of upper-class perquisites. But whatever their motivations, America's economic elites would not take the New Deal reforms lying down.

So in July of 1934 the du Pont brothers Pierre, Irenee, and Lammot, scions and corporate heads of the huge plastics manufacturer that bore their family name, organized a group of wealthy businessmen to oppose the challenge that New Deal policies posed to their financial interests. The group, which called itself the American Liberty League, was a "property holders' association," as Irenee put it — reflecting that its major concern was the maintenance of its members' material wealth. But du Pont was also careful to caution that the League's members should never characterize their raison d'être to be the protection of their wealth and property — at least not in public. So the League presented its activities not as the organized defense of its members' vast property holdings and financial interests that it actually was, but something much more benign and salutary in most quarters: as a patriotic defense of the Constitution, specifically a patriotic defense of the rights of private property and the right to the unfettered generation of profits without accountability. Whether those profits were generated justly or ethically seemed to matter little. Yet the fact that the League's real focus was defending its members' material interests rather than the Constitution showed in its complaints that "business," that is, the membership of the American Liberty League, "which bears the responsibility for the paychecks of private employment, has little voice in government." There was little doubt that it wasn't simply a voice that the League sought; there is little question that what it really sought was the right to take control of the nation's economic matters because, in the businessmen's estimation, only the business community was competent to run the country. As one corporate executive complained, "You can't recover prosperity by seizing the accumulation of the thrifty and distributing it to the thriftless and unlucky." Railed another, "The government and administration of these United States has been placed by a dumb, unthinking populace in the hands of notorious incompetents."[55]

In its quest to seize the nation's political leadership, the League challenged the New Deal as unconstitutional, as "a vast organism spreading its tentacles over the business and private life of the citizens of the country."[56] It denounced financial regulatory protections of citizens' interests as totalitarian and decried Social Security as "socialism," as the "taking of property without due process of law."[57] The League mobilized its members' vast wealth and waged an extremely well-financed campaign against the reforms of the New Deal and even sought to unseat Roosevelt at the polls. In a move with contemporary resonance, a radio ad entitled "Liberty at the Crossroads" featured a marriage license clerk telling a prospective bridegroom that in the future he would have to deal with federal debts created by Roosevelt's New Deal initiatives. "It's a low-down mean trick," the bridegroom whines. Then a voiceover, marked in the script as "The Voice of Doom," darkly intones, with an attempt to lend biblical gravity to its doomsaying with an evocation of Exodus 34:7:[58] "And the debts, like the sins of the fathers, shall be visited upon the children, aye, even unto the third and fourth generations."[59] Despite the businessmen's efforts, however, their candidate, Kansas governor Alf Landon, lost in Roosevelt's first reelection bid in the second most lop-sided race in the history of American presidential politics (only Barry Goldwater's rout by Lyndon Johnson was worse).

Although it counted many of America's wealthiest corporate elites among its members, and despite its strident appeals to patriotism, the League was never able to sell the American public on its self-serving message. With no real successes under its belt, the extraordinary collective wealth of its members notwithstanding, the American Liberty League folded in 1940.

The American Liberty League's characterizations of New Deal liberalism as manifestations of communism, socialism, totalitarianism, and just plain anti-Americanism were fallacious and intentionally misleading; equally so were its mischaracterization of efforts designed to reduce extremes of poverty and wealth as instances of "communistic" collectivism. Still, the seeds planted by the League's divisive and self-consciously disingenuous strategy have borne fruit that is still in use today by proponents of political conservatism. An instructive contemporary example of the currency of this seven-decade old strategy is the January 2011 conference entitled "Understanding and Addressing Threats to American Free Enterprise and Prosperity," hosted by Charles and David Koch, the billionaire owners of Koch Industries, the second largest privately owned corporation in America and a longtime major underwriter of conservative causes. A *New York Times* article noted that "the invitation sent to potential new [conference] participants, offers a rare peek at the Koch network of the ultra-wealthy and the politically well-connected, its far-reaching agenda to enlist ordinary Americans to its cause."[60] In terms eerily reminiscent of the rhetoric of the American Liberty League, the event invitation explains that the purpose of the conference is to "develop strategies to counter the most severe threats facing our free society and outline a vision of how we can foster a renewal of American free enterprise and prosperity." According to the *New York Times*. "Charles Koch, whose wealth *Forbes* magazine calculates at about $21.5 billion, argues in his [cover] letter that 'prosperity is under attack by the current administration and many of our elected officials,'" and repeatedly warns about the "internal assault" and "unrelenting attacks" on freedom and prosperity.

In an accompanying brochure Charles Koch warns that financial regulatory protections "threaten to erode our economic freedom and transfer vast sums of money to the state." The same *New York Times* article noted that at a similar Koch-sponsored conference in June 2010, "some of the wealthiest people in America listened to a presentation on 'a vision of how we can retain the moral high ground and make the new case for liberty and smaller government that appeals to all Americans, rich and poor.'"[61] Despite the fact that not one American who is not wealthy was invited to his exclusive gathering, Koch apparently tries to give the impression, by adding the closing phrase "rich and poor" to his letter, that somehow the interests of his ultra-wealthy crowd are the same as those who are vastly economically subordinate to his fellow wealthy elites, some of whom enjoy a greater income in one week than the average American makes in a decade. Thus almost three-quarters of a century after the American Liberty League folded, wealthy political conservatives are still clothing their campaigns to overturn obstacles to unbridled attainment of wealth in the League's intentionally misleading, self-serving rhetoric of patriotism and preservation of constitutional rights.

Whether explicitly stated or subtly implied, from the American Liberty League in the 1930s to the Koch brothers today, behind every claim by political conservatives of threats to "freedom" inevitably lurks the bugaboo charge of "communist" or "socialist" to be flung at every political thought, word, or deed that tries to achieve a more fair, just, and equitable economic environment in America. Newt Gingrich, former speaker of the U.S. House of Representatives, defines socialist policies as all policies that "favor increased central planning of the economy by politicians and bureaucrats instead of allowing entrepreneurs, businesses, and customers to make decisions in the free market."[62] By casting socialism with such a broad and intentionally misleading definitional net (with a Ph.D. in European history he undoubtedly knows better), Gingrich lays the groundwork for *every* governmental edict and regulatory protection that challenges conservative laissez-faire economic policies — or simply any policy political conservatives disagree with — to be demonized as an exercise in socialist centralized planning. What Gingrich fails to acknowledge, however, is that under his broad definition both Social Security and Medicare, the economic lifeblood of millions of Americans, would also be condemned as socialist policies.[63]

In fact, there is a long legacy of just such conservative attacks on both Social Security and Medicare. Henry Ford warned that Social Security could cost Americans their basic freedoms; Alf Landon called it a "cruel hoax" on the American people; both Ronald Reagan and George H. W. Bush attacked Medicare as destructive to democracy; David Stockman, Reagan's budget director, called Social Security "closet socialism"; George W. Bush actually attempted to *privatize* Social Security; and today conservative politician Representative Ron Paul, who chairs the congressional subcommittee that oversees the Federal Reserve, advocates completely abolishing Social Security.[64] Yet acknowledgment of the responsibility to care for those in society who are in need of care and assistance, which is the biblically consistent animating principle underlying both Social Security and Medicare, is hardly the same as socialism or enforced collectivism. In actuality, the governmental policies and initiatives that political conservatives deride as socialism almost always reflect the communitarian ethos of care for others in society, particularly for the poorest and most vulnerable, that is among the most foundational of biblical ethics.

In that the leveling charges of "communist" and "communism" at every policy with which they disagree is a regular stock-in-trade of political conservatives, it is appropriate to pause to consider what communism really is. In his magisterial study, *The Rise and Fall of Communism,*[65] the Oxford University historian Archie Brown explains that communism is "an all-encompassing system of beliefs." He offers six defining features of communist systems as seen in practice. I have summarized them below:

1. Non-democratic monopolizing of all political power under an official Communist Party.

2. Centralization of all policy decisions in a non-democratically selected central governing committee, whose decisions must be obeyed.

3. Complete state ownership of non-agricultural industries.

4. A "command" economy in which the decisions about the pricing and distribution of goods are dictated by Communist Party functionaries rather than by the functioning of markets (even regulated markets are excluded)'

5. The building of a communist state as a central aim with the features described above.

6. A sense of belonging to an international communist movement.[66]

Notwithstanding what has always been at best a tiny fringe element in American society, any clear-headed historical observation will attest that there has never been any action, any statement or even an implied political posture on the part of any elected or appointed official in either major political party that could be objectively viewed as sympathetic to even one of those basic communist principles, much less as seeking to subsume all American political activity under an international communist party or state.

The truth is that when the terms "socialist" and "communist" are used today, it is virtually never in an informed fashion and it is virtually never in response to any political action or pronouncement that can honestly and realistically be seen as pointing to a "communist conspiracy." In fact, there has never been any policy advanced by any credible elected official that can be realistically seen as an attempt to centralize all pricing mechanisms for products and commodities, or as an effort to abolish all American political parties, or as an attempt to throw away the U.S. Constitution and replace it with the summary edicts of a single authoritarian "communistic" party. Thus when those terms are used today they are virtually always strategic reinscriptions and cynical echoes of the same obfuscating rhetoric that has been used for the better part of a century by the American Liberty League and other politically conservative organizations to advance their own material interests. That is to say that charges of communism and socialism by conservative politicians against their political foes are almost without exception self-servingly strategic, which is to say *meaningless*.

In their zeal to demonize those who oppose their policies, political conservatives sometimes take this strategy to absurd extremes. A case in point: To commemorate the 2010 Thanksgiving holiday, Missouri Republican Representative Todd Akin contended on the floor of the U.S. House of Representatives that the Puritan pilgrims who journeyed to America, "came here with the idea that after trying socialism that it wasn't going to work. They realized that it was unbiblical, that it was a form of theft, so they pitched socialism out. They learned that in the 1620s."[67] The manifest ignorance of such a statement is astounding. For as even the most cursory reading of political history shows, the political concept of socialism did not originate until the late eighteenth century. In fact, the term "socialist" did not appear until 1827, when it was first used in a London magazine. Moreover, socialist political parties did not begin to gain influence in Europe until the nineteenth century.[68]

Actually, this tactic of conjuring the communist/socialist bogeyman to frighten American citizens into enlisting in their cause even predates the American Liberty League and its contemporaries. In 1870 farmers across the Midwest formed an organization they called the Grange as a workingmen's association to wage a collective battle against monopolistic price-gouging by railroad executives and wealthy grain elevator operators. A lawyer for the corporate interests wrote in the prestigious *American Law Review* that the Grange's suits for protective redress in the courts were an "assault on private property." He added that the Grange's efforts were "really directed, not against abuses, but against the rights of property" and that it was "perfectly clear that the Granger movement" — an association of heartland *farmers* — "was rank communism."[69]

Through the 1930s and 1940s organizations with conservative political commitments similar to those of the American Liberty League worked assiduously to develop and disseminate a conservative political vision and strategic rhetoric — including fear-mongering — that sought to limit the power of government while removing all obstacles to the expansion of the power and wealth of the corporate sector. These included the National Association of Manufacturers, which emerged as the leading opponent of the New Deal reforms; the Farmers' Independence Council, a conservative front group that, interestingly, could not identify a single farmer in its membership; the Foundation for Economic Education; and the American Enterprise Association, out of which grew the American Enterprise Institute, which today is one of the most influential think tanks in politically conservative circles.

Despite these efforts by political conservatives to discredit the government's oversight of economic activity in America with their charges of socialism and communism, by the 1940s the British economist John Maynard Keynes's advocacy of governmental fiscal activism had come to hold sway over U.S. economic policy making. The ideas about fiscal and monetary policy put forth in Keynes's magnum opus, *The General Theory*

of Employment, Interest and Money,[70] offered compelling intellectual justification for governmental intervention in financial markets for the purpose
of stabilizing them in times of economic upheaval and instability. The
acceptance of Keynes's ideas signaled bad news for political conservatives,
because governmental fiscal intervention was the very antithesis of political conservatives' laissez-faire policies and could only erode their economic
hegemony. We will consider Keynes's ideas in greater depth shortly.

Suffice it to say at this point that Keynes's influence was great enough
that the politically conservative corporate leaders and activists of his day
were so concerned to counter it that they sponsored a widespread dissemination of pamphlets and research reports touting their laissez-faire
ideas to their employees, to civic organizations, to elected officials, even
to ministers. However, this did little to tamp down Keynes's influence.
Deeply worried by the mounting authority of Keynes's *General Theory,*
corporate elites became convinced that they needed a "New Testament of
capitalism," a "Bible of free enterprise" to support the economic vision
of political conservatism. They eventually found their intellectual counter-
weight to Keynesian ideas in the work of the aforementioned Friedrich
von Hayek.

Although Hayek's views were not initially directed at the United States,
nonetheless his opposition to regulatory market protections fit well with
the rhetoric of political conservatives. Indeed, Hayek's political sentiments
and his scholarly research fit so squarely with the interests of America's
business elites that, realizing his potential usefulness to their cause, a
group of them prevailed upon him to move to the United States. The
Foundation for Economic Education sponsored both a professorship at
the University of Chicago for Hayek and bankrolled the formation of
the Mont Pelerin Society, an organization of intellectuals Hayek founded
to engage in dialogue and continuing research in political conservatism's
economic principles. As we saw above, Hayek's firm beliefs in political
conservatism's gospel of the free market are epitomized in *The Road to
Serfdom,*[71] Hayek's free market manifesto. That book and his subsequent
writings[72] offered exactly what the American businessmen had sought:
an intellectual justification for opposing all governmental controls on
the excesses of the corporate sector. A number of politically conservative organizations, especially the Foundation for Economic Education,
widely disseminated *The Road to Serfdom* and trumpeted its merits at every

turn, including organization of a U.S. book tour and sponsorship of a condensed version of it in *Reader's Digest*.

Although Hayek's dire warnings about governmental domination were specifically directed toward Nazism and Soviet-style "collectivism," in his wake some of today's political conservatives have mistakenly construed his writings as expressing opposition to all regulations and regulatory protections instituted by the U.S. government, especially those that affect financial markets. A recent example of this comes from the right-wing television talk show host Glenn Beck. In June 2010, Beck spent an entire program claiming that Hayek's denunciation of the Nazism that Hayek faced in embattled Austria in the 1930s and 1940s is applicable to twenty-first-century America: "And look at what we're doing! We have a government car company, government banks, we're talking about government oil companies, government is hiring all the workers. We are there, gang! And as Hayek so clearly demonstrated, this road only leads to one destination."[73]

But a recent essay reviewing Hayek's influence claims that, "unlike some of his champions in 2010, Hayek didn't oppose all forms of government intervention."[74] This truth has at times been ignored by Hayek's acolytes. Hayek himself declared that "the preservation of competition" is not "incompatible with an extensive system of social services — so long as the organization of these services is not designed in such a way as to make competition ineffective over wide fields."[75]

The reality is that Hayek's totalitarian predictions have not been fulfilled anywhere except in the fecund and fantastical imaginations of strident news entertainers like Glenn Beck. How far-fetched these assertions are is highlighted in a 2009 reminiscence of Hayek and his work by the economist and Nobel laureate Paul Samuelson. "Two-thirds of a century after the book got written," observes Samuelson, "hindsight confirms how inaccurate its innuendo about the future turned out to be." Referring to countries with socialized services and the totalitarianism Hayek insisted such policies would undoubtedly sink them into, Samuelson dismissively asks, "Where are their horror camps? Have the vilest elements risen there to absolute power? When reports are compiled on 'measurable unhappiness,' do places like Sweden, Denmark, Finland, and Norway best epitomize serfdoms? No. Of course not."[76]

Despite the misapplications of Hayek's work, both in his day and in ours, and despite his flawed predictions, he was a thinker to be reckoned with. He was awarded the Nobel Prize for Economics in 1974, and in 1991 President George H. W. Bush awarded him the Presidential Medal of Freedom, one of the top civilian honors in the United States. He remained a greatly influential, if greatly misapplied, presence in political conservatism until his death in 1997, never wavering in his belief in the inviolability of laissez-faire economic policies and totally regulation-free markets.

As for the contributions to conservative political thought by Hayek and others, notably Hayek's Austrian colleague Ludwig von Mises, an important economist in his own right, by the time Kirk wrote in the 1950s the foundational economic principles of political conservatism were clear: any and all governmental regulations, policies, and measures that had as their intent the lessening of the gap between America's haves and have-nots were deemed illegitimate, ineffective, and immoral. Conservatives recognized nothing good in the protective functions of regulations and ignored the harm that could be done to uninformed and unprotected consumers and citizens.

Thus what was to become modern political conservatism began as the collective and well-financed efforts of America's richest citizens to protect what they saw as their right to garner as much wealth as possible without social or legal accountability, no matter its impact on the rest of America. Their strategy was then, as it is now, to oppose any and all obstacles to that goal. Apparently political conservatives' grand design has never given serious consideration to alleviating the suffering of America's poor or to measures to remove structural impediments to upward economic mobility. It does not stop there, however. Not only does political conservatism include no questioning of the grave disparities of poverty and wealth in this nation, it justifies and explains away those disparities as the function of purely objective market forces or as a function of naturally meritocratic social Darwinian selection. Thus not only is laissez-faire acceptance of class inequities inherent to political conservatism, as Russell Kirk postulated more than half a century ago, keeping intact the disparities of poverty and wealth that cause class inequities is among its most cherished goals.

CLASS AND THE GOSPEL OF JESUS

Whether political conservatism's commitment to the maintenance of economic classes is a good thing or is necessary for the maintenance of healthy societies, as political conservatism claims, is a fair subject for secular debate and discussion. To be sure, there are worthy secular arguments to be made both pro and con. Of course, in a free society people are free to believe — or not believe — as they wish. But for those who profess to believe in the teachings of Jesus, it is a point that emphatically is *not* open to debate.

This is an uncompromising assertion to be sure, but it has nothing to do with theology or religious doctrine. As I said at the beginning of this chapter, my approach to this issue is based upon what I believe to be an intellectually honest reading of the Gospel of Jesus that takes seriously the implications of his historical context while strenuously resisting the popular temptation to spiritualize his every saying, even those that clearly are *economic* in nature. Thus my reading of Jesus does not emanate from my subjective opinion alone. It is a reading that takes pains to acknowledge what plainly appears on the pages of the Gospels: that a principal feature of the kingdom of God, which was so central to Jesus' teaching, is that it will sweep aside all forms of gross class disparity, political hierarchy, and social elitism in this world; that the class differences that made some rich and some poor, some free and some slaves, some secure and some held fast by fear and insecurity are, in the teachings of Jesus, to be replaced by abundant life for all in *this* world, with no one person or class lording over another.[77] The Gospel narratives also convey that the way the just and equitable socio-economic life of the kingdom of God was to be accomplished was by engaging in behavior that seems to have no home in the economic philosophy of political conservatism and its laissez-faire absolutism. These include unselfishly collectivistic, non-exploitative, egalitarian, non-authoritarian social relations, and personal acceptance of responsibility for others. These ethics are summarized below.

- *The kingdom of God as unselfish and collectivistic:* This is the overriding ethos of Jesus' teachings. It is expressed in such of his sayings as "love your neighbor as yourself" and "as you have done it to the least of these my brothers [and sisters] you have done it to me." That selflessness should be normative in his followers' practice is further indicated in this instruction to his disciples: "And preach as you go, saying,

'The kingdom of heaven is at hand.'. . . You received without pay, give without pay" (Matt. 10:7–8).

• *The kingdom of God as non-exploitative:* Jesus severely condemns self-ish and unjust economic actions and relationships in the story of the servant who had a man arrested because the man was unable to imme-diately repay a loan when it was demanded of him (Matt. 18:23–35). Because, as we will discuss shortly, accumulated riches were perceived prima facie to be proof of theft or exploitation in Jesus' setting in life, his saying, "How hard it will be for those who have riches to enter the kingdom of God" (Mark 10:23) is also a searing reproach to exploitative economic practices.

• *The kingdom of God as non-authoritarian:* In his scathing indictment of the religious establishment in Matthew 23, among the things Jesus denounces is their authoritarianism: "Woe to you, scribes and Pharisees, hypocrites! because you shut the kingdom of heaven against men; for you neither enter yourselves, nor allow those who would enter to go in" (Matt. 23:13). In this same diatribe he also denounces their concern for institutional economic matters at the expense of justice and mercy (Matt. 23:23). Moreover, in Mark 10:41–45 he issues this admonition to his disciples when they express hierarchical aspirations: "whoever wishes to be first among you must be servant of all" (v. 44).

• *The kingdom of God as responsibility:* In response to the question "Who is my neighbor?" Jesus tells a parable in which a Samaritan man on the Jericho road encounters a Jewish man who has been assaulted, robbed, and left for dead. The Samaritan stops to aid the Jewish man and then carries him to an inn to be nursed to health, leaving sufficient money with the innkeeper to pay for the man's care. However, stopping on the Jericho road for anyone was more than an altruistic, self-sacrificial act; it was also a dangerous act. Not only was the Jericho road noto-rious for bands of predatory bandits, the topography was so devoid of vegetation that the run-off from the area's meager rainfall created multitudinous chasms in which bandits would lie in wait, unseen, often just yards from the road and their potential prey. Thus simply travers-ing the Jericho road was dangerous, but by stopping at the site of a recent assault, then making himself an even more vulnerable target by laboriously carrying a grown man along the dangerous route, the

Samaritan was committing more than a mere act of courage; he was literally putting his own life at risk to help a stranger in need without regard for the stranger's ethnicity or class. The Samaritan's act was even more commendable in that Samaritans and Jews were traditional enemies. For the Samaritan, however, there was a factor that more deeply tied him to the Jewish man than the social chasm that separated them — recognition of his responsibility for the injured Jew based on nothing more than their shared humanity. At the end of the parable Jesus answers the question "Who is my neighbor?" with this response: "Go and do likewise" (Luke 10:29–37). That is to say, go out and do what this Samaritan did: treat everyone as neighbors, acting out of a sense of responsibility that recognizes only needs, not differences.

◆ *The kingdom of God as egalitarian:* In Mark 12:29–30 Jesus is narrated as quoting Deuteronomy 6:4: "You shall love the Lord your God with all your heart, and with all your soul, and with all your mind and with all your strength." He then does something that is seen nowhere in antiquity before him: he couples Deuteronomy 6:4 with Leviticus 19:18: "You shall love your neighbor as yourself," the latter of which culminates with a series of prohibitions against exploiting and oppressing the poor (cf. Lev. 19:33–37), which must be factored into the verse's meaning. Jesus' equation of love of one's own interests, needs, and concerns with love for the interests, needs, and concerns of others is a beautiful sentiment. But the context of the statement makes it clear that he was not simply teaching how one should *feel;* he actually was teaching how his followers should *act.* However one approaches Jesus' statement, when seen in practical terms, loving one's neighbor, that is, wanting the same for one's neighbors as one wants for oneself, when applied in the realms of economic and political interests is *egalitarian* by any definition. And egalitarianism implies striving to lessen economic class differences, not to maintain or enhance them.

◆ *The kingdom of God as egalitarian (continued):* Particularly germane to the egalitarian nature of Jesus' kingdom of God teachings is the famous parable of the mustard seed (Mark 4:30–32 and parallels). As the only parable that occurs in all three of the Synoptic Gospels, it assumes a representational importance for understanding the message of Jesus. Although better known as a parable about the impending growth of God's kingdom, deeper examination reveals compelling egalitarian implications as well. First, no self-respecting cultivator of land in first-century Israel would purposely sow a mustard plant in his field, not only because it is a noxious weed, but also because it would overrun his cultivated commercial crop. As the Roman chronicler, Pliny the Elder (23–79 C.E.), observed, "when it has once been sown it is scarcely possible to get the place free of it, as the seed when it falls germinates at once."[78] Second, to sow the typically unwanted mustard seed onto a cultivated field is to treat it as the equal of more highly valued, traditionally planted crops. Third, purposely sowing the mustard seed in the midst of other plants (no one devoted an entire field to a noxious weed) intentionally violates the prohibition of Leviticus 19:19: "You shall not sow your field with two types of seed" (cf. Deut. 22:9–11). Fourth, despite its insignificant size (mustard seeds typically are the size of specks of dust), the mustard seed grows taller than other cultivated crops, certainly taller than the staple crop, wheat (the mustard bush typically stood as high as four feet with branches that spread a similar width).[79] Therefore the significance of the mustard seed for Jesus' parabolic purposes and the reason he chose it to communicate his message is that despite its devalued stature and its lack of commercial value in such settings, the mustard plant offers what traditionally valued plants do not: a home to those whom Jesus calls "the birds of the air," those without fields of their own or who, for whatever reasons, are unable to care for themselves.[80] Thus the mustard plant offers a home (i.e., a "nest") to "the birds of the air," that is, the poor and landless[81] in a cultivated field where birds — the poor — typically are never welcome, because every kernel the "birds" consume for sustenance means there is less for the cultivator of the land to harvest, and thus impinges on his profits and wealth. In this way the portrayal of God's kingdom as a tiny mustard seed is a metaphor for egalitarian inclusion of even the neediest in the largesse of God's kingdom on earth.

Nothing in the egalitarianism that is reflected in these or any other Gospel sayings of Jesus reflects any desire to achieve or impose the "narrowing uniformity" or "economic leveling" that political conservatives associate with fair and equitable egalitarian goals. Instead, the egalitarianism that is espoused in the sayings of Jesus declares everyone's right to equal access to the necessities of life and equalizes their opportunity to experience life's good things. Moreover, it must not be overlooked that if the farmer figure in the parable of the mustard seed had not been willing to transgress the constraints of Leviticus 19, there would have been no home or sustenance for those who were bereft of one (as represented by "the birds of the air"). Thus a further indication of Jesus' egalitarian vision, one of great significance, is that it also entails removing structural and institutional class barriers that stand in the way of equality of opportunity for everyone who seeks to eat the good fruit of the tree of life.

In the modern era we call this *distributive justice,* the just and fair distribution of goods in society.[82] This includes not only distribution of material goods, but also psycho-emotional goods such as peace of mind and a sense of material and physical security. In modernity, the ways and means of developing social and political processes that promote egalitarianism and distributive justice get their most extensive treatment since the towering Immanuel Kant (1724–1804) in the work of the American political philosopher John Rawls (1921–2002).

In his adult life Rawls pointedly professed no particular faith commitments,[83] yet the profound egalitarianism of his vision seems closely aligned with the egalitarian vision of Jesus. His entire career was spent laboring to develop practical, workable principles of fully equitable social and economic justice in American society that would impartially situate every member of society as full equals: on the one hand, by removing unfair advantages to economic advancement and, on the other, by dismantling structural barriers that deny equitable access for all to crucial social and material goods. The fruits of his profound and unstinting vision of social and economic egalitarianism are contained in his masterwork, *A Theory of Justice,*[84] which is almost universally praised as the greatest work of political philosophy of the twentieth century, if not since Kant's *Critique of Pure Reason.* Underlying Rawls's philosophy is the notion that the fairness of a society — in biblical terms, the "justice" or "righteousness" of a society — can be measured, and should be judged, by its treatment of its most vulnerable and least advantaged members.

This focus on distributive justice is consistent with Jesus' Gospel teachings. His pronouncements about the kingdom of God include many references to God, of course, but an important aspect of the focus of those sayings is always the just distribution of social and economic goods: the needs of the people, how they should live, how they should be treated, how all the good things of life should be made available to them. For example, we see this in his instruction as to how his disciples should conduct themselves: "And preach as you go, saying, 'The kingdom of heaven is at hand.' *Heal the sick, raise the dead, cleanse lepers, cast out demons. You received without pay, give without pay*" (Matt. 10:7–8). In other words, the kingdom of God that Jesus preached is not an abstract notion; it is concretely relational. And it seems beyond question that if its relational principles of non-exploitation, non-authoritarianism, and egalitarianism were lived principles, great disparities of poverty and wealth would never form, much less become stratified into classes. The egalitarian nature of Jesus' vision is reflected in the sampling of his Gospel sayings below:

- *He strongly taught against the undue amassing of wealth:* "Do not store up for yourselves treasures on earth," (Matt. 16:19) and "Be on your guard against all kinds of greed" (Luke 12:15).

- *He indicted wealthy elites outright:* "It is easier for a camel to go through the eye of a needle than for someone who is rich to enter the kingdom of God" (Matt. 19:24).

- *He pronounced against wealthy elites* in the midst of his paradigmatic ethical teachings in the Beatitudes, which shows how significant class issues were for Jesus: "Woe to you who are rich. . . . Woe to you who are full now" (Luke 6:24–25).

- *He taught of the egalitarian nature of the kingdom of God,* which equally welcomed everyone to the kingdom banquet table and offered its fare to all in equal measure. This is clearly reflected in the banquet parable in the Gospel of Luke (14:16–24).

There is an unmistakable implication underlying all these representative pronouncements: that there is no room for classism, elitism, or privileged entitlement in Jesus' conception of the kingdom of God.

Perhaps the greatest significance for our purposes is the promise of lowering, if not removing, class barriers that underpins Jesus' proclamation that the primary reason he has been designated a messiah (i.e., "anointed") is to "preach good news to the poor" (Luke 4:18). This welcome news "to the poor" (*ptochois*, the Greek plural noun for "poor" here, indicates a collective or class identity) could not simply be that those who were currently poor would no longer be poor, for that would leave in place relations and structures that would simply create more poor people, for whom it certainly would not be good news. Jesus' pronouncement must also mean that what he heralds and affirms is the transformation, if not the total dismantling, of the systemic and institutional barriers that make people poor and keep them poor. And if the "poor" as a class is to cease to exist (that is, if access to goods and resources comes to be distributed in the just and equitable fashion that the Bible intends, an ethos we will explore shortly), the "rich" as an elite upper class would cease to exist as well. In fact, with the admonition "Woe to you who are rich," Jesus summarily rejects altogether the ethical legitimacy of a wealthy upper class. In other words, Jesus' declaration of "good news to the poor" proclaimed his rejection of the extreme disparities of wealth and power upon which the class distinctions of "poor" and "rich" are based.

However, it should be stressed here that there is no reason to construe Jesus' alleviation of the class categories of rich and poor to mean that there would be no differentials of wealth in society; nothing in Jesus' pronouncements implies that. Rather it means that there should be no permanent economic stratification and no structural impediments to economic mobility and opportunity. This is most clearly reflected in what scholars widely recognize as Jesus' invocation in Luke 4:18 ("the acceptable year") of the Jubilee legislation of Leviticus 25, which declares that in every fiftieth year all land was to be returned to its original family owners, i.e., those families whose ancestors had originally settled it.[85] The "socioeconomic implication of the Jubilee legislation," writes David A. Fiensy, "was that the land should be approximately evenly distributed with no one becoming wealthy to the impoverishment of others." He concludes, "Thus the Jubilee legislation protected against the permanent alienation of one's patrimony and against amassing large tracts of land by a few people. *The ideal was rough equality.*"[86]

Because land was the primary source of wealth in the agrarian mode of production, Jesus' invocation of a text designed to guard against the formation of classes comprised of landed and landless is further proof of the egalitarian nature of his ministry and of his uncompromising opposition to the continued existence of socially inscribed and enforced economic classes. Although he does not specifically mention overtly economic factors, the apostle Paul, writing less than three decades after Jesus' death, seems to reflect a similar understanding of Jesus' ministry as militating against all forms of class distinction and differentiation:

> There is neither Jew nor Greek, there is neither slave nor free, there is neither male nor female; for you all are one in Christ Jesus (Gal. 3:28).

In sum, Jesus' vision of the kingdom of God includes an egalitarian socio-economic order that takes responsibility for the well-being of all. It refuses to be hindered from the task of serving the needs of the dispossessed and the vulnerable by official sanctions, traditional narratives of social control, or even by edicts from on high, if they stand in the way of the kingdom's goal of ensuring that the basic elements of a healthy and secure life are available to all. Many political conservatives, and every Christian in conservative ranks, hold some form of belief in the kingdom of God. Unfortunately, their acceptance of conservative political philosophy blinds them to the fact that as long as there are broad-based, often structured disparities of poverty and wealth and unequal access to the good things of life in society, Jesus' egalitarian vision will not be realized, for class barriers deny complete and unfettered access to the fullness of every social and economic good.

CONTEXTUALIZING JESUS AND CLASS

The sayings of Jesus that impinge upon economic class relations and economic conditions included blanket denunciations of riches and rich people that are so pointed that one might reasonably construe him as having declared unqualified class warfare against every rich person in every society at every historical juncture. Because of the extreme nature of Jesus' declarations, his teachings about class and economic relations usually either have been ignored or, at best, dismissed as quaint by all but a few marginal Christian groups, sects, and religious orders.[87] But when viewed in their own cultural context, Jesus' teachings on class and economic relations offer ethical and practical guidance that is both timeless and fully appropriate for the conduct of social and economic policy in our society today.

Jesus' notions of poverty and riches, his concept of what was acceptable and what was unacceptable in economic relations, was shaped by what cultural anthropologists call "limited good,"[88] a cultural worldview that was inherent in most peasant societies in antiquity, including that of first-century Israel. Aristotle had long since given voice to the limited good worldview: "For the amount of such property sufficient to itself for a good life is not unlimited."[89] As George M. Foster explains,

> Broad areas of peasant behavior are patterned in such fashion as to suggest that peasants view their social, economic, and natural universes — their total environment — as one in which all of the desired things in life . . . exist in finite quality and are always in short supply, as far as the peasant is concerned.[90]

It must be kept in mind that late antiquity was a world of rudimentary technology with no real economies of scale. Socio-economic mobility was extremely circumscribed and most persons were virtually powerless against the will and the whim of the powers-that-be.[91] In such a setting it was reasonable to conclude that the world contains only a finite amount of good things that can never be increased and that were forever gone once claimed, expropriated, or otherwise depleted. Given this belief in a limited amount of available goods and resources in the world, it was a small step to believe that if one person accumulated significantly more wealth than others, he did so by depriving those others of their rightful share of the world's goods. This would render the rich person unjust and dishonest, if not evil, in the eyes of those with less. As cultural anthropologist Bruce J. Malina explains, "That every rich person is a thief or the heir of a thief was a truism based upon the perception of limited good. If all goods are limited and people were created more or less on equal footing, then those who have more must have taken it from those who now have less."[92] That is why Plato (428–348 B.C.E.) could declare, "The very rich are not good,"[93] and eight centuries later the indictment of St. Jerome (Eusebius Sophronius Hieronymus, c. 347–420 C.E.) could be even more biting: "Every rich person is a thief or the heir of a thief."[94]

Since in the limited goods worldview all riches were unjust riches gained by greed, avarice, exploitation, or theft, then by extension rich people were also greedy, avaricious, exploitative, and guilty of theft. However, it was not only the fact of having accumulated riches that was seen as morally wrong; *even attempting to become rich* was equally as morally culpable, because in the limited good setting this was seen as consciously seeking to deprive others of their just due. That is why Jesus pronounced that even giving oneself over to the desire to accumulate wealth is antithetical to a right relationship with God: "No one can serve two masters. . . . You cannot serve God and mammon" (Luke 16:13). To guard against even the perception of the accumulation of riches from larger than normal harvests or other windfalls, many cultures utilized leveling mechanisms, such as throwing banquets for the entire community, that served to spread the wealth, so to speak.[95]

If we translate Jesus' sayings from his limited goods context into today's North American context, in which the potential production of goods is virtually unlimited, the cultural, technological, material, and political economy contexts change, of course, but moral and ethical content of Jesus' sayings remains the same: it is still ill-gotten, unjustly obtained, and unjustly maintained wealth to which Jesus' ire is directed. In this sense, the references Jesus made to "riches" and "the rich" in his day are today interchangeable with "the economically dishonest," and "the economically unjust."

Therefore, according to this contextualized understanding of Jesus' ethical paradigm, the existence of wealth by itself does not necessarily indicate injustice or dishonesty. Wealth becomes unjust for Jesus when it is used in an unjust fashion, or for unjust ends, or when it is greedily accumulated and not shared with those in need of material assistance. That is to say, wealth is unjust according to the ethics of Jesus when it is used in a way that disregards what he likened to the greatest of all commandments, to "love your neighbor as yourself." This is expressed in practical terms in Matthew 25 to include feeding the hungry, clothing the naked, and welcoming immigrant strangers, the last of which seems to be a particular sticking point for conservative politicians today. Performing these actions seems to be a categorical imperative for Jesus in that he declares that failure to perform them is tantamount to rejecting him and his teachings: "as you have not done it to the least of these, you did not do it to me." As a result, "they will go away into eternal punishment," while, he adds in a sort of clarifying addendum, "the just [*dikaosune,*] go into eternal life" (cf. Matt. 25:31–46). Therefore, according to Jesus' ethics shorn of their cultural delimiters, one could legitimately and justly become rich if the enriching enterprise involves no abuse of trust or dishonesty or exploitation or unjust advantage in practice. Put more simply, one can legitimately become rich under Jesus' ethics, but only if one has not garnered wealth at the expense of others, has not betrayed the trust of others or betrayed one's own soul with greed and avariciousness.

The New Testament Letter of James, which is full of ethical content (and which some attribute to James, the brother of Jesus),[96] offers an assessment of Israel's socio-economic class setting that echoes Jesus: "Let the lowly brother boast in his exaltation, and the rich in his humiliation, because like the flower of the grass he will pass away. For the sun rises with its scorching heat and withers the grass; its flower falls, and its beauty perishes. So will the rich man fade away in the midst of his pursuits" (James 1:9–11). Like Jesus, James's letter decries the status claims of the rich and the deference shown to them because of their wealth:

> If a rich man with gold rings and in fine clothing comes into your assembly, and a poor man in shabby clothing also comes in, and you pay attention to the one who wears the fine clothing and say, "Have a seat here, please," while you say to the poor man, "Stand here," or, "Sit at my feet" have you not made distinctions among yourselves, and become judges with evil thoughts? (James 2:2–4).

James's letter does not stop there. It specifically goes on to denounce rich elites for their economic exploitation of the lower classes:

> Come now, you rich, weep and howl for the miseries that are coming upon you. Your riches have rotted and your garments are moth-eaten. Your gold and silver have rusted, and their rust will be evidence against you. . . . Behold, the wages of the laborers who mowed your fields, which you kept back by fraud, cry out; and the cries of the harvesters have reached the ears of the Lord of hosts (James 5:1–4).

Not only is James's letter consistent with the New Testament pronouncements of Jesus, it elaborates them, thus elucidating the kinds of abusive practices that Jesus, echoing the tradition of Hebrew prophets like Isaiah and Amos, would surely have had in mind, as we will see in the next section.

The Meaning of Rich and Poor for Jesus

So what did Jesus mean by "poor" and "rich"? Nowhere in the Gospels does he define either term. Yet the Gospels do contain markers of his meanings. When we look to Jesus' use of the terms themselves and to the descriptions of the types of persons who fall under each term's descriptive umbrella, whether explicit or clearly implicit, or are otherwise associated with each, we can make important observations.[97] "The rich"

- are associated with undue pride and political might (Luke 1:51–53);

- have enough wealth to contribute big sums to the Jerusalem Temple, as opposed to a widow who after contributing a pittance had nothing left with which to buy food (Mark 12:41–44);

- are covetous, selfish, and greedy; a rich man is "he who lays up treasure for himself" (Luke 12:16–21);

- have much more of the "limited good" of society than they need and should rightfully possess, as indicated by the rich man who has so much ill-gotten gain that he can return it four-fold (Luke 19:1–10).

To summarize, the terms associated with "the rich" in the Gospels convey the presumption of the limited goods worldview that people became rich as result of greed, fraud, depriving the poor of the basic necessities of life, and prospering at the expense of those who cannot defend themselves.

On the other hand, "The poor"

- are classed with captives, the blind, the oppressed [*tethrausmenous*], and the indebted (Luke 4:18);

- are ranked with those who hunger, thirst, and mourn (Luke 6:20–21; Matt. 5:3);

- are listed with the blind, the lame, lepers, the deaf, and even the dead (Matt. 11:4–5);

- are grouped with the maimed (Luke 14:13, 21);

- are hungry and homeless (Luke 16:19–31).

Generally, then, the New Testament characterizes the poor as deprived of material necessities, often as the result of infirmities that render them unable to be economically productive. Some commentators, however, have downplayed the economic class dimension of the Gospel meaning of "poor." For instance, the cultural anthropologist Bruce Malina asserts, "These adjacent descriptions of the poor point to the poor person as one who has undergone some unfortunate personal history or circumstance. . . . Consequently, the poor would not be a permanent social class, but a sort of revolving class of people who unfortunately cannot maintain their inherited status."[98] What Malina seems to be saying is that poverty in first-century Israel was — and was in that setting understood to be — primarily the result of individual misfortunes, not the consequence of structural causes. He also seems to imply a not insignificant amount of upward mobility in that setting.

Yet the types of persons and the characteristics that are associated with the term "the poor" in the Gospels in every circumstance hold in common one undeniable overarching factor: their personal economic circumstance. Either they do not have enough of the basic necessities of life or they are totally bereft and, therefore, totally dependent on the charity of their peers for survival. In the final analysis, in every instance in the Gospels those who are poor share the circumstance of being powerless in the face of exploitation by rich elites, who controlled the political economy and profited disproportionately from it. It is in this sense in which "the poor" in Jesus' setting constitute a class that is comprised of the hungry, the vulnerable, the expendable, the homeless, and the helpless, all of whom barely subsist while the rich live lavishly.

Indeed, consideration of the historical evidence from first-century Israel affirms that "rich" and "poor" reflected not just cultural perceptions in that period, as Malina asserts, but rather primarily referred to hard economic realities. Almost half a century ago the scholar A. N. Sherwin-White famously observed that the economic dimension of the world reflected in the Gospels "presents two classes, the very rich and the very poor."[99] This has been essentially affirmed by the work of numerous biblical scholars in the last several generations.[100] Specifically, what were those hard economic realities that elicited from Jesus such consternation and concern? And what would Jesus specifically have had in view in terms of actual material living conditions by his use of "rich" and "poor"?

The Rich

The "rich" in Jesus' life setting were primarily comprised of two groups: the wealthy lay nobility and the priestly aristocracy. They are estimated to have together comprised between 5 and 10 percent of Israel's population. The priestly aristocracy, which included high priests, chief priests, and their families, derived the foundation of their wealth from tithes and offerings. The richest priestly families compounded their priestly remuneration by purchasing real property with it. Josephus, who hailed from a wealthy priestly family, reflects this in his description of the extensive lands his family owned.[101] This despite the prohibition in Deuteronomy 10:9 against priestly ownership of land, a prohibition, by the way, that seems to have had the express but ultimately unrealized purpose of keeping the hereditary priesthood from developing into the rich upper class that it became.

Other members of Israel's upper class included the lay nobility of Jerusalem, who were the wealthiest and most prominent families of that city, as well as large landowners in the agrarian regions, particularly in Galilee. Biblical scholar Harold Hoehner estimates that as the result of the land expropriations by Herod and his cohorts during his forty-five year reign,[102] by Jesus' day this landed elite class privately owned between one-half and two-thirds of all land in Galilee, some 2,605,850 acres (1,055,000 hectares). Most of the rich elites of Israel lived in Jerusalem, however,[103] which meant that most were absentee landlords. To give some sense of the scope of the upper class's landed wealth, the average size of a peasant holding was 4 to 6 acres,[104] whereas the average size of a large estate was 315 acres, with many significantly larger.[105] To give further perspective, it is estimated that it required only 100 acres for landed gentry to live comfortably, replete with tenants, day laborers or slaves to work the estate, and a full-time overseer to manage it.[106] The existence of such large estates in first-century Israel, with numerous tenants, hired workers, and managers, is reflected in several of Jesus' parables.[107]

Thus the upper class in Jesus' setting in life was essentially a wealthy landowning class whose landholdings provided them a quite substantial income stream. They either employed large numbers of laborers on their estates or leased all or part of their lands to tenants or sharecroppers. Tenant farmers paid a set rental fee. Sharecroppers typically remitted a percentage of the land's production in return for the right to cultivate a portion of a landowner's holdings. As the letter of James indicates, the rich were known to engage in fraud and economic abuse in these arrangements: "Behold, the wages of the laborers who mowed your fields, which you kept back by fraud, cry out; and the cries of the harvesters have reached the ears of the Lord of hosts" (James 5:4). The abusive behavior of the rich elites ranged from paying workers less or in a different form than was agreed; to extending loans, especially during droughts and bad harvest, for the purpose of foreclosing on the land that secured the loans;[108] to the use of violence to force peasants to sell their landholdings.[109]

Typically the rich elites in Jesus' setting in life lived luxuriously. Archeologists have unearthed mansions in the priestly quarter of upper Jerusalem of great size and luxury. One uncovered mansion covers some 6,500 square feet.[110] By way of contrast, the average size of a home in the United States in 2009 was 2,422 square feet. Country folk like Jesus and his Galilean compatriots would have witnessed such luxury on pilgrimages to the Jerusalem Temple on holy days like Passover or Yom Kippur, the most sacred day of the Jewish liturgical calendar. Later Jewish sources recount extraordinary shows of wealth by the Jerusalem Temple priestly aristocracy and their families. One report concerns a chief priest's widow who was so used to the extraordinary trappings of priestly wealth that she cursed the scribe who negotiated her widow's allowance because she was granted only four hundred denarii a day for luxury items (the average day's pay for a laborer was one denarius).[111]

The Poor

In contrast, the other of Israel's two economic classes, the poor, struggled to provide even the basic necessities for themselves and their families. Israel's poor, who constituted some 90–95 percent of the population, were primarily comprised of peasant farmers and landless workers, but also included "expendables," those whom society little valued, whose ranks included street beggars, the permanently infirm, petty criminals, underemployed itinerant workers, and those who lived solely by their wits or through charity. The percentage of expendables in agrarian societies typically constituted something like 5 percent of the population.[112]

From all indications, the lives of peasant farmers were lives of unceasing struggle to wrest a subsistence from the land. In addition to drought, plant and livestock diseases, periodic exhaustion of soil, and bad harvests caused by any number of factors, there were also structural reasons for the widespread poverty in Israel. After paying taxes out of their subsistence production to their Roman overlords and religious dues to the Jerusalem Temple and its reigning hierarchy, many peasant farmers had barely enough left to survive. Many were forced to borrow funds from rich elites in order to pay taxes or simply to make ends meet, which then left them vulnerable to default on land-secured loans. Default meant loss of their land and all their possessions. In extreme cases, it could lead to debt enslavement, as is reflected in Matthew 18:23–35. In cases of extraordinary default, the lender could sell the debtor's wife and children into slavery and then seize members of their extended family if the proceeds from their enslavement did not satisfy the defaulted debt. If the debt still was not satisfied, the lender could even enslave the debtor's neighbors. In one instance a whole village in first-century Egypt, which had a political economy similar to that of Israel, was emptied in this way because all of its inhabitants were either sold into slavery or escaped into the surrounding hills.[113]

Survival for the large population of landless workers was even more difficult and tenuous. Workers were almost always hired only by the day.[114] In Israel, as throughout the Mediterranean basin, their typical day lasted from sunrise to sunset, which ranged from almost ten hours a day on January 1 of our Gregorian calendar to more than fourteen hours a day in June. During the harvest seasons the working days were about twelve and a half hours long.[115] Examination of skeletal remains from the first century indicates that work for landless day workers could be so physically arduous that sometimes the rigors of their labor permanently deformed their bone structures.[116]

The going wage for day laborers was one denarius a day. The cost of living for a single adult in Jesus' day is estimated to have been one-half a denarius. With an average family size then of six, a denarius a day was virtually a starvation wage.[117] Thus the typical worker was ill-clad and usually hungry. Children were often brought to the harvest fields by their worker parents simply to follow behind and watch for gleanings with which to assuage their hunger.[118] Indeed, it appears that hunger was widespread. Estimates of the daily caloric intake of landless workers range from 1,400 to 2,500 hundred calories, which indicates that many may have suffered from chronic malnourishment.[119] Among the indications of this is that hunger is prominently mentioned in Gospel proclamations as diverse as the Beatitudes ("Blessed are you that hunger now," Luke 6:21); the Magnificat ("My soul does magnify the Lord . . . for he has filled the hungry with good things," Luke 1:46); and the Lord's Prayer ("give us our daily bread," or "bread for subsistence," *arton epiousion*, Matt. 6:11).

Although it is crafted to speak to the privation of a much later time, John Kenneth Galbraith's exquisite prose quite aptly articulates the plight of the impoverished populace of first-century Israel: "This poverty was not the elegant torture of the spirit which comes from contemplating another man's more spacious possessions. It was the unedifying mortification of the flesh — from hunger, sickness and cold. Those who might be freed temporarily from such burden could not know when it would strike again, for at best hunger is yielded only perilously to privation."[120]

Thus when Jesus spoke in the Gospels about rich and poor with such uncompromising conviction, on both humane and ethical grounds he was decrying the vast chasm between the economic wealth and lifestyles of relative ease of Israel's rich upper class and the suffering and day-to-day struggle of its poor lower classes. Because the hereditary priestly class constituted most of Israel's rich upper class, he pointedly rejected the legitimacy of the priestly class in numerous instances.[121]

In summary, pronouncements of Jesus' opposition to the disparities of poverty and wealth that define classes literally permeate the Gospels.[122] Taken as a whole, the Gospels attribute to Jesus unquestionably egalitarian, anti-classist sensibilities. Jesus' numerous pronouncements of woes against the rich and his championing of the poor must be seen for what they are: unmistakable markers of an anti-classist egalitarianism that permeates, perhaps even dominates, his Gospel message.

CLASS AND THE HEBREW BIBLE

As basic as the concern for equity and justice was for Jesus, obviously biblical egalitarianism did not start with him. Jesus was rearticulating commands that stand at the heart of the Hebrew Bible tradition. These commands had three distinct purposes: (1) to lessen, if not fully elim-inate, the economic class differences that already existed; (2) to guard against the further development of economic class differences in society; and (3) to protect the poor and vulnerable against exploitation by the rich and powerful. In fact, the history of the Hebrew people is inter-spersed with vivid recountings of divinely inspired rejection of elitism, class distinctions, and class exploitation.

Recall that the Exodus, the root-event of biblical faith, is the recounting of the Hebrews' flight to freedom from the rigid and exploitive class hierarchy of Egypt. Having been redeemed from a system in which a tiny elite hereditary upper class claimed it as their birthright to lord over the masses, the Hebrews honored God for their deliverance by refusing to commit the sin of implementing a class system of their own. It was clear to them that to do as their oppressors had done would be to spit in the face of their salvation. Both Joshua 18:1–10 and Numbers 26:52–56 reflect the Hebrews' egalitarianism in their descriptions of equal distribution of land and land ownership. Likewise, the setting of the book of Judges is a relatively egalitarian society of small landowners.

Leviticus 25 and Deuteronomy 15 present divine prescriptions for combating the development of classes characterized by significant disparities of property and wealth by establishing a cut-off point beyond which disparities could not go. As we saw above, the Jubilee Year that is prescribed in Leviticus 25 stipulates that every fifty years all land, the principal means of wealth and sustenance in antiquity, was to be returned to its original family owners. Because land was then the major means of production, this would serve to give every family the same opportunity and the same practical means to provide themselves with the necessities for a reasonable standard of living.

Not only were the means of production and the opportunity of every family to earn a decent living equalized by Leviticus 25, it provided that the needy would not be forced to wait for the crumbs of the wealthy to dribble down to them, a prescription that one might reasonably construe as an early acknowledgment of the moral bankruptcy of any forms of "trickle-down" economics (which we will discuss in Part II). Leviticus 25 also made clear that providing equal access to wealth and every good thing for everyone was a divine command, a sacralized duty. As biblical scholar Warren Carter observes, "The redistribution of wealth [in Lev. 25] was to prevent the emergence of both an elite with massive wealth and power and a permanent poor class with inadequate means of support."[123] More than that, the Bible commanded that the Jubilee was always to begin on the Day of Atonement. The purpose of this, we can surmise, was to continually remind the people that the repentance they sought on that sacred day was not complete until their economic relationships were also set right (also see Leviticus 25:9).

Another biblical prescription whose purpose was to combat the development of permanent extremes of poverty and wealth is found in

Deuteronomy 15. This edict provided for the freeing of all slaves at the end of six years. But it did not stop there. It also directed that freed slaves were to be allowed to depart with a share of the goods and the wealth that their labor had helped to produce. Note well that this measure can also be understood as a rudimentary severance package, a directive that every corporate manager might keep in mind when laying off employees and especially when terminating their employment:

> And when you let him go free from you, you shall not let him go empty handed; you shall furnish him liberally out of your flock, out of your threshing floor, and out of your wine press; as the Lord your God has blessed you, you shall give to him. (Deut. 15:13–14)

Deuteronomy 15:1–6 also stipulates that at the start of the seventh or sabbatical year all debts are to be canceled. The purpose of this directive is to ensure that no one is relegated to lifelong membership in a debtor class. Its goal is plainly stated in verse 4 in the imperative voice: "There shall be no poor among you."

The Hebrew Bible stipulates other prescriptions that are calculated to soften and, where possible, to abolish the extremes of wealth, power, and unequal access to opportunities for economic betterment that characterize class distinctions. Exodus 23:10–11 directed prosperous landowners to suspend cultivation of their land every seventh year and to give to those in need unrestricted access to whatever the land produced during the fallow year, without requiring the needy to work the land on the owners' behalf or to give back any portion of their gleanings. That the poor received a free year of gleaned produce while the landowners were forced to forego it also served as a kind of economic leveling mechanism, although ultimately its leveling effects alone would not have been great.

The Sabbath we know as the weekly day of worship. Yet the implications of the Sabbath are much more profound and far-reaching than worship alone. The Sabbath is also a weekly reenactment of radical equality in this sense: that at least one day a week everyone, not just leisured elites, gets to rest and know leisure. More importantly, on the Sabbath God is acknowledged as the sole sovereign of all humanity — including the rich and the powerful. From this we can conclude that a major purpose of the Sabbath is to regularly, albeit temporarily, remove all class differences. That the Sabbath is held as holy, week after week, serves as a perpetual reminder that egalitarian values must govern all human relationships and interactions, both individual and collective. In other words, by its very nature, the Sabbath is the recognition of egalitarianism as God's holiest vision for humanity. In this sense it is a model of how life should be lived every day of the week.

Thus the early attempts by the Hebrews to develop an egalitarian social system did not just express their hatred of Egypt's brutal class hierarchy, nor can it be dismissed as merely a function of a primitive political economy. In a fundamental sense, the Hebrews' egalitarian social organization was the expression of their understanding of how God required them to live in the world as the reciprocal, covenantal duty their freedom from bondage placed upon them.[124]

The goal of reducing disparities of income and wealth between Israel's classes was also a primary goal of the biblical Law Codes,[125] which collectively promote and legislate distributive justice and economic parity. Following are a few of the Law Code's economic stipulations:

- Protecting the poor from exploitation by providing fair and just measures of weight and dry quantity (Deut. 25:13–15) as well as standardized measures of liquid quantity and physical length (Lev. 19:35–36).

- Protecting the earnings of hired servants by providing that wages be paid on the day they are earned (Deut. 24:14–15).

- Forbidding the charging of interest to poor borrowers (Exod. 22:25).

- Prohibiting partiality and bribes in the courts because such actions benefited the rich and disadvantaged the poor (Deut. 1:17; Lev. 19:15).

- Instructing that truly needy persons be lent whatever they required, with outstanding balances to be forgiven after seven years (Deut. 15:7–11).

- Instituting the year of Jubilee, the end of a fifty-year cycle, when all lands were to be returned to the families of their original owners and all bondservants released (Lev. 25:10).

- Sacralizing economic parity by allowing the poor to bring less expensive sacrifices to the Temple (Lev. 12:8: 14:21–22).

Removal of inequities that separated the people of Israel into socio-economic classes of rich and poor was a definitive focus of the biblical prophets like Isaiah, Jeremiah, Amos, and Micah. As Abraham Joshua Heschel observes in his seminal work *The Prophets,*[126] the peculiar genius of the biblical prophets is that prior to their proclamations, it was the virtually unchallenged popular belief that riches and might made right and that rulers and the very rich were granted their wealth and social locations by divine fiat. This notion of the divine right of rulers and ruling classes was endemic to the ancient view of the world, so much so that almost a millennium after the classical period of Israel's prophets, the Roman Tacitus (56–117 C.E.) could still boldly assert, "The Gods are on the side of the stronger."[127] But as Heschel points out, the declarations of the prophets turned that worldview on its head: "The prophets proclaimed that . . . God's special concern is not for the mighty and the successful, but for the lowly and the downtrodden, for the stranger and the poor, for the widow and the orphan."[128] As one scholar explains it, "For the prophets, poverty is an evil created by the wealthy who engage in immoral practices to enrich themselves in land and property."[129]

The primary concern of the prophets was *mishpat,* justice. That includes economic justice. The prophets' outrage at the exploitation of the poor and the weak by the rich and the mighty, and the widening of the chasm between the quality of life and the possession of material necessities of the different socio-economic classes that resulted from it, is reflected in numerous prophetic pronouncements. Below is a sampling:

> Woe to him who builds his house by unrighteousness, and his upper rooms by injustice; who makes his neighbors work for nothing and does not give them their wages . . . But your eyes and heart are only on dishonest gain. (Jer. 22:13, 17)

> Hear this, you that trample on the needy, and bring to ruin the poor of the land, saying . . . "We will . . . practice deceit with false balances." (Amos 8:4–5)

> Alas for those who devise wickedness and evil deeds on their beds . . . because it is in their power. They covet fields, and seize them;

houses, and take them away; they oppress householder and house, people and their inheritance. (Mic. 2:1–5)

The Lord enters into judgment with the elders and princes of his people: "It is you who have devoured the vineyard; the spoil of the poor is in your houses. What do you mean by crushing my people, by grinding the face of the poor?" says the Lord God of hosts. (Isa. 3:14–15)

Ah, you who join house to house, who add field to field, until there is room for no one but you, and you are left to live alone in the midst of the land! (Isa. 5:8)

Even many Psalms — plaintive, liturgical, and full of thanksgiving though they variously may be — nonetheless reflect the Hebrew Bible's ethos of opposition to economic classism and the pronounced disparities of poverty and wealth that attend it. For instance, Psalm 10 likens economic exploitation of the poor to being attacked by a beast: "Their eyes stealthily watch for the helpless; they lurk in secret like a lion in its covert; they lurk that they may seize the poor; they seize the poor and drag them off in their net" (Ps. 10:9). The "royal" psalm, perhaps a coronation ode, contains a description of the responsibilities of the ideal righteous ruler. In the psalm's twenty verses, the king's responsibility to justly address the plight of the poor and the needy is mentioned nine separate times, beginning with these petitions to God: "May he judge your people with righteousness, and your poor with justice. . . . May he defend the cause of the poor of the people, give deliverance to the needy" (Ps. 72:2, 4).

In contradistinction to the support of laissez-faire economic principles by political conservatives and members of the religious right, including their virtual sacralizing of anti-regulatory notions, we see in these biblical texts a pronounced practical acknowledgment of the necessity for imposing market regulations in society to protect all consumers, especially the poor and the unsuspecting. This is particularly evident in the Law Codes and the pronouncements of the prophets. Thus in a real sense the imposition of regulatory protections for markets of exchange — including financial markets — are a divine mandate.

In summary, with the exception of the biblical book of Proverbs, which, because of its bourgeois didactic character, is more concerned with the personal failings that cause poverty than with its social or structural causes, every section of the Bible shows a clear and critical concern for the alleviation of gross disparities of poverty and wealth and consumer protections. Even this brief survey of the Hebrew Bible clearly demonstrates that the biblical ethos fundamentally militates against unjust, exploitive practices that create and maintain stark class disparities of material riches and power. It not only decries pronounced class distinctions; it also gives numerous detailed prescriptions for curtailing, if not abolishing, them.

However, nowhere does the Bible claim that *every* wealth differential is the result of exploitation or theft or some other transgression. It recognizes that natural advantages and disadvantages, physical handicaps, mishaps, and personal and collective misfortunes are often the cause of disparities of wealth. In the biblical perspective the transgression, or sin, if you will, arises when the more fortunate members of society cause or even allow these disparities to lead to circumstances in which some lack the necessities for a decent quality of life, while others have much more than they need, yet refuse to share their abundance in any truly significant measure. The transgression is compounded when these disparities become permanent and are passed from generation to generation in the form of stratified classes. Even the biblical writers' relegation of women to secondary status was not understood as contradicting this bedrock principle, because in the unquestioned patriarchy of the biblical writers' ancient settings in life, it was taken for granted that since every woman was by law part of a man's household, women also benefited from these biblical stipulations.[130]

Moreover, in the whole of the Hebrew Bible there is not one "socialist" or "communist" biblical prescription that calls for the abolition of private property. Legitimate ownership of real property was acknowledged and encouraged. It is important that this be expressly stated, because many politically conservative defenders of the need to maintain divergent economic classes will surely reject biblical pronouncements about class and economic ethics as primitive, naively "communistic," or as somehow otherwise opposed to free enterprise. This would then allow them to declare the biblical witness an unsuitable basis for their economic principles or an unsuitable standard by which to judge their market activities. One would hope that political conservatives would not follow that route. Thoughtlessly overlooking these principles in the bustling course of unreflective practice can have consequences that are destructive enough, even without malicious intent. But cynically, intentionally casting aside the economic ethics and mores of the Hebrew Bible in their quest for the accumulation of wealth would mean that political conservatives have consciously chosen to reject the same Bible as a standard for their economic behavior that they so publicly claim to be their standard in other dimensions of social life. Such a rejection has frightening implications, for in practical terms it would signal that the economic philosophy of political conservatives has effectively eschewed the most fundamental ethics of the Euro-Western ethical tradition as well as the most fundamental biblical limits on greed, exploitation of their neighbors, and every manner of selfish acquisitiveness. But alas, when we more closely examine the economic philosophy of political conservatives in chapter 4, we will see that this is already the case.

– 4 –

A Camel through
the Eye of a Needle (Part II)

*Class, Political Conservatism,
and Anti-Christian Economics*

*The modern conservative is engaged in one of man's oldest exercises in
moral philosophy: that is, the search for a moral justification for selfishness.*
— John Kenneth Galbraith

THE MEANING OF RICH TODAY

As we saw in Part I, the meanings of poverty and wealth, rich and poor
were unambiguously clear to Jesus and the biblical prophets. In the various texts ascribed to them, all described the realities that defined economic
class disparities in their respective settings in life in concrete ways: hunger
versus plenty, thirst versus flowing wine, sumptuous lodgings versus dispossession, great wealth taken for granted versus trepidation about daily
needs. But the Bible's recounting does not stop there. It also makes quite
clear what constitutes economic justice and injustice, economic equality
and inequality, and describes in unmistakable terms, particularly in the
prophetic texts and Law Codes, what types of actions constitute market
abuses, inequities, and exploitation. Today, however, the meanings of poverty, wealth, and other terms of socio-economic measure are not always
as clear. This is especially the case when speaking of economic classes
in the United States. Terms like "middle class," "lower class," and "upper
class" are bandied about in today's political discourse with great frequency,
but their parameters are seldom defined. For our purposes, how might we
arrive at a usable definition of economic classes in the United States today?

141

The most often used, and in many quarters, the most useful economic measurement of class in the United States is income quintiles. In this mode of analysis Americans are divided by pre-tax salary and wage income into five gradational groupings, or quintiles, each representing 20 percent of household incomes, from the highest household incomes to the lowest. In rough class terms, these quintiles represent the upper class (top quintile), upper middle class (second quintile), middle class (third quintile), lower middle class (fourth quintile), and lower class (fifth quintile). However, in actual dollar terms the parameters of the quintiles vary from year to year according to fluctuations in Americans' earning patterns. According to the 2009 Congressional Budget Office data, in 2007 the average income of the bottom quintile, or lower class, was $18,400, the average income of the middle quintile was $64,500, and the average income of the highest quintile, or upper class, was $264,700.

Strictly speaking, in this pre-tax income quintile schema the middle class is easy to identify, as is the lower class. But the designation of upper class hides more than it reveals. To simply identify someone as a member of the upper economic class doesn't tell us if he or she earns $300,000 or $300 million. Moreover, because government income figures take into account only salaries and wages, they only tell half the income story. An important source of income left out of the story is that which comes from capital gains. Capital gains are profits realized from transactions in investments such as stocks, bonds, and real estate. What is significant about these kinds of investments is that all of them are disproportionately owned by America's most wealthy citizens. Thus when speaking of the upper class or the wealthy, we must speak not only in terms of wages and salaries; we must also include in the income equation capital gains and investment income such as dividends. This is important because the discussion of the role of political philosophies in the maintenance of class inequities is ultimately a discussion about concentrations of economic power and resources, about who disproportionately controls the wealth in America. In order to get a truer sense of the distribution of wealth in America we must refocus our gaze from the upper quintile in general to the upper reaches of that quintile, that is, to the richest of the rich, the ultra-wealthy.

In 2007 the top 1 percent of households in America, that is those with average incomes over $398,900, took home some 24 percent of all income in America.[1] This is quite astonishing. Yet in 2007 the richest tenth of a percent of American families (0.1 percent, i.e., one in a thousand) on average took home $7.1 million dollars, or 12.3 percent of national income. When we further sharpen our focus to the wealthiest hundredth of a percent of American households (0.01, i.e., one in ten thousand, just 15,000 families), the average 2007 income jumps to more than $35 million per household, or 6 percent of national income. That is correct: just 15,000 out of an estimated 111,162,259 total American households received some 6 percent of total income in America.[2]

This wealthiest hundredth of a percent of American households (0.01, i.e., one in ten thousand) represents the richest and most powerful figures in America today. By virtue of their wealth they constitute what political commentator David Callahan calls "super-citizens" in that as a class they wield vastly disproportionate power and influence in the American political landscape because of their wealth. Thus when we speak of the rich and the wealthy, it will actually be the ultra-wealthy, defined here as the richest 0.1 percent (one in a thousand families) to the 0.01 percent (one in ten thousand) of American income earners to which we will refer.[3]

Special notice in this regard should be given to a significant cohort of the ultra-wealthy class: corporate CEOs. For the last twenty years or so the average salary of a CEOs of major American corporations has ranged as high as 419 times the average worker's salary. In the last decade or more the differential has hovered at the 300–to-1 level, still an incredible multiple. For example, in 2004 the average CEO was paid $9.84 million in total compensation, while the average worker was paid $33,176. That means that the average worker would have to work three hundred years to make what the average CEO makes in one year. In a March 2009 speech to the AFL-CIO Executive Council, Vice President Joseph Biden decried the enormity of the salary differential between CEOs and workers: "It's just not right, it's just not right, and everybody knows it . . . when the average CEO makes $10,000 more every day . . . than what the average worker makes every year." Yet ironically, these wealthy CEOs, who apparently see nothing wrong with receiving huge multiples of workers' salaries, are disproportionately represented among the ranks of those who most heavily influence the economic and business policies that are responsible for perpetuating America's vast economic inequality.

It is important to acknowledge, however, that not every member of the ultra-wealthy class subscribes to the principles and concerns of political conservatism. Some of America's wealthiest citizens have staked out very liberal positions in social, religious, environmental, and political matters and have contributed significant financial resources to those causes. The huge role that ultra-wealthy contributors played in the 2008 election of Barack Obama as president of the United States is proof of that.[4] Yet it must also be acknowledged that typically even the ultra-wealthy who are liberal in other causes give little attention to issues of economic class inequality in America; as a group they have historically shown exceedingly little willingness to dismantle their class privileges. Even as we keep in mind that the ultra-wealthy are not an ideologically homogenous group, it must be acknowledged that in the final analysis their inattention to the nation's extreme disparities of poverty and wealth contributes to their maintenance. Whether America's wealthiest citizens engage in willful and systematic efforts to keep America's economic status quo in place or tacitly support it by refusing to take measures designed to change it, the final result is the same: the vast chasm between rich and poor in America, the likes of which are so passionately condemned by the biblical witness, continues unabated.

AMERICA'S CLASS SOCIETY

When we shift our gaze from biblical times to present-day America, we behold this jarring sight: despite the uncompromising anti-elitist, egal-itarian disposition of both the Hebrew Bible directives and the Gospel pronouncements of Jesus, the economic policies promoted by political conservatives do just the opposite: without question they are skewed to serve the interests of America's wealthiest citizens. More jarring yet is the fact that most political conservatives publicly profess some form of bibli-cal faith. Just as blasphemous — there is little doubt that the prophets Amos or Micah or Isaiah would call it that — is the reality that at best only secondary consideration has been given to the interests of America's least privileged and poorest citizens. This despite unambiguous biblical imperatives like Leviticus 15 ("there shall be no poor among you") and Matthew 25 ("as you have not done it to the least of these . . . you have not done it to me").

Our shifted gaze would also see with tragic clarity a sight that is even more jarring: that conservative politicians have opposed at their inception virtually every modern policy initiative ever proposed for the purpose of aiding and protecting this nation's most vulnerable and economically disadvantaged citizens. This has been particularly true if those policies entailed any economic sacrifice, real or imagined, on the part of America's wealthiest citizens. Even a partial listing of such policy initiatives that political conservatives have opposed is hair-raising: Social Security, Medicare and Medicaid, unemployment compensation, the right to form labor unions, government guaranteed student loans, child labor laws, the minimum wage, workplace safety regulations, guaranteed bank and savings deposits, oversight to insure the purity of our food and drugs, the environmental protection movement, the Equal Rights Amendment, civil rights legislation, even anti-lynching legislation. The sad truth is that no matter their party affiliation, political conservatives have opposed virtually every policy proposal that might somehow narrow the gap between rich and poor.

Another shift in our gaze will reveal a sad fact of more recent vintage, yet of similar consequence: that more than in any previous modern American presidential administration, political conservatism's economic hallmark of privileging the interests of the very wealthy over the interests of ordinary Americans were embodied in the policies of the presidential administration of George W. Bush. This includes tax policies that have disproportionately benefited America's richest citizens, deregulatory measures that have privileged corporate interests over the common good, and generally lax enforcement of the investor and consumer protections that Bush found already in place. Not only have these actions gone far in maintaining the existing class disparities in wealth in American society, they have actually intensified them. This outcome is so thoroughly consistent with political conservatism's goal of maintaining class wealth differentials that it is difficult to reach any other conclusion than that this result was the studied intention of the Bush administration in the first place. Of course this is a charge that political conservatives will hotly contest. Yet Jesus' saying — "You will know them by their fruits" (Matt. 7:16.) — in this case is quite appropriate, for despite the disastrous consequences of Bush's economic policies for the nation as a whole, under his watch the richest Americans literally got richer — much richer — while everyone else got poorer. This is true even if one ignores Bush's generous corporate largesse, in the form of the relaxed regulatory environment of his administration, and considers only his tax policies. As the result of Bush's tax policies, as of 2006 households with incomes over $1 million enjoyed an increase in after-tax income that in basic percentage terms was some twenty times greater than was received by those in the bottom fifth of the nation's income spectrum and almost two and a half times of what was received by the middle fifth — the middle class. A joint Urban Institute–Brookings Institution study estimated that by the end of 2010, when Bush's tax policies are fully operative (some were scheduled to begin in 2008 and thereafter), final data will show that those with incomes over $1 million will receive a percentage tax benefit over *a hundred times greater* than Americans whose income lands them in the lowest fifth of U.S. households.[5]

Bush publicly justified his tax cuts (which he coupled with severe reductions in funding for many programs that primarily benefited the poorest Americans) with the claim that they would stimulate economic activity and would actually increase government revenues, which was simply a reprise of the claims of Ronald Reagan's supply-side economics. Bush was breathtakingly wrong, of course, as were Reagan's supply-side policies before him; Bush's tax cuts (which, because they did not pay for themselves, ended up costing the government billions of dollars in lost revenue) and his philo-corporate policies plunged the nation into its worst economic crisis since the Great Depression. But why was Bush able to sell the nation on this mélange of economic policies that clearly further enriched the already rich to the detriment of all others? One only has to look to the presidency of Ronald W. Reagan for the answer.

THE THEORETICIAN OF UNACCOUNTABILITY

When Ronald Reagan became president of the United States in 1981, what laid the groundwork for the economic policies that came to be called "Reaganomics" were not political machinations. It was not even the soaring inflation and double-digit interest rates that had bedeviled the nation under his predecessor, Jimmy Carter (the prime rate peaked at 21.5 percent in December 1980, the highest level under any U.S. president). In large measure what laid the groundwork for Reagan's economic strategies that conservatives use as a touchstone to this day was an eighteenth-century theory and the work of a diminutive, argumentative, twentieth-century academician named Milton Friedman.

Five-foot-three, bald and bespectacled, Milton Friedman (1912–2006) fit the very stereotype of a lifelong academic. Yet he was anything but typical. Friedman began his professional career in the U.S. Treasury Department as a Keynesian who actually admired some of Franklin Roosevelt's New Deal jobs programs; while there he developed the idea of the withholding tax. Eventually, however, he became a disciple of Friedrich von Hayek and adopted Hayek's uncompromising anti-government libertarianism, whereupon he pronounced the withholding tax the worst mistake he ever made and completely turned against all forms of political intervention in markets and economic fortunes.

In 1946 at age thirty-four Friedman joined the economics department at the University of Chicago, which he would help to make the preeminent bastion of laissez-faire economics. There he began to investigate the role of the money supply in the economy and to launch what became a lifelong attack on the U.S. government's fiscal policies, an uncompromising opposition to governmental market regulations and opposition, well, to government *in general*.

In his writings Friedman argued that the primary determinant of both economic prosperity and economic recession is the supply, or amount, of money that is circulating in the economy at any given time. In a nutshell, this means that if there are too many dollars in circulation chasing too few goods, the result is price inflation. Conversely, if there are too few dollars chasing too many goods, the result is falling prices and a downward spiraling economy. Because of his belief that it is the money supply that is the lone key to economic health, Friedman argued that the government should solely focus its economic efforts on maintaining price stability by managing the money supply. In fact, Friedman opined, government interference in the economy to balance market supply and demand or to curb market excesses can accomplish nothing except upsetting the markets' natural balances. Put more simply, the only appropriate roles of government in the working of the economy, according to Friedman, are to adjust the amount of money in circulation through the Federal Reserve Bank or to just stay out of the way of the markets' natural movement. In greatly simplified form, of course, this was the basis of Friedman's theory of monetarism, which was first substantively introduced in his 1963 book, *Monetary History of the United States, 1867–1960*,[6] which he co-authored with research partner Anna Jacobson Schwartz. Because of the wide divergence of his theories from the conventional wisdom of Keynesianism's insistence on the necessity of governmental fiscal intervention to maintain healthy markets, for years Friedman was treated like a crank. But little by little, and especially after the publication of his *Monetary History*, fellow academics and governmental policy makers alike began to see value in his monetarist theories.

By the 1970s Friedman and his monetarist theory came to hold sway in major economic policy circles. Especially after the fulfillment in the 1970s of his 1967 prediction of "stagflation"—the simultaneous rise of inflation and unemployment (according to the prevailing economic wisdom this was not supposed to happen)—Friedman was arguably the most influential economist of his time. In 1976 he was awarded the Nobel Prize in Economics (an award he shared with Edmund Phelps of Columbia University, who separately had also predicted stagflation).

Yet despite his important contributions to economic theory, it was Friedman's public expressions of disdain for governmental programs in general—he felt that most governmental functions would be much better handled by the free market alone—that were most politically influential in political conservative circles, although those views were his most theoretically questionable. Paul Krugman explains how this came to be the case:

> Friedman's effectiveness as a popularizer and propagandist rested in part on his well-deserved reputation as a profound economic theorist. But there's an important difference between the rigor of his work as a professional economist and the looser, sometimes questionable logic of his pronouncements as a public intellectual. While Friedman's theoretical work is universally admired by professional economists, there's much more ambivalence about his policy pronouncements and especially his popularizing.[7]

Krugman's assessment is telling. Paul Samuelson, a fellow Nobel economics laureate, was a lifelong friend of Friedman. Nonetheless, he described Friedman as "a libertarian to the point of nuttiness." Friedman's extremist tendencies can be seen in his best-selling 1962 book,

Capitalism and Freedom. Therein, Friedman actually advocated abolishing medical licensing to let the free market weed out incompetent and unscrupulous medical practitioners and to lower medical costs. He also advocated abolishing the Food and Drug Administration with its crucial regulatory consumer protections. In its place he proposed giving up to the markets the crucial responsibilities of protecting the public from dangerous drugs, sickening substances, and subpar, even poisonous foodstuffs. These proposals were based upon Friedman's general conviction, shared by all political conservatives, that markets have an underlying, almost magical rationality that will, in time, correct all economic ills, and many social ills, too. Still Friedman's proposals were stunning for their apparent lack of concern for the terrible cost that such actions would exact in human suffering. Clearly the extensive biblical dictates for protecting the poor and the vulnerable had little place in Friedman's formulations. In his weekly *Newsweek* column he glorified the "robber barons" of the Gilded Age, turning their selfish predatory practices, which at times devolved into outright murder, into virtues: "there is probably no other period in history, in this or any other country, in which the ordinary man had as large an increase in his standard of living as in the period between the Civil War and the First World War, when unrestrained individualism was most rugged."[8]

Despite his over-the-top economic pronouncements and the great suffering, at least in the short term, that some of his major proposals could cause, Friedman's economic theories, particularly his monetarism, remained highly influential in conservative political circles. Speaking to the lessons learned from Friedman's theory of monetarism, Lawrence Summers, director of the White House Economic Council under Barack Obama and treasury secretary in the Clinton White House, declared, a bit hyperbolically, "Any honest Democrat will admit that we are now all Friedmanites."[9] What Summers's assessment of Friedman does not reflect is the wane of the overall influence of monetarism at the end of the 1970s when both the Federal Reserve Bank and the Bank of England abandoned monetarist management of their economies as ultimately unworkable. After Friedman's death in 2006 Paul Krugman offered this assessment of Friedman's legacy:

> Friedman had the intellectual courage to say that markets can too work, and his showman's flair combined with his ability to marshal

evidence made him the best spokesman for the virtues of free markets since Adam Smith. But he slipped all too easily into claiming both that markets always work and that only markets work. It's extremely hard to find cases in which Friedman acknowledged the possibility that markets could go wrong, or that government intervention could serve a useful purpose. Friedman's laissez-faire absolutism contributed to an intellectual climate in which faith in markets and disdain for government often trumps the evidence.[10]

Thus Friedman's important theoretical contributions to his field notwithstanding, his legacy with regard to the vast class disparities of poverty and wealth in America is highly problematic. Friedman argued against governmental responsibility to assist America's poorest and most vulnerable citizens and rejected virtually every aspect of America's safety net for them, including Social Security and Medicare and Medicaid. Unfortunately, for many the acclaim garnered by his more extremist notions and his stature as a theoretician of laissez-faire absolutism made him, in effect, a theoretical cheerleader for *governmental unaccountability* in matters pertaining to the marketplace. Nowhere in Friedman's influential work was it advocated or was there room for the government to protect the vulnerable from exploitation or for helping the cause of the poor. In this sense, in large measure it was Milton Friedman's public advocacy of laissez-faire absolutism that made the political and theoretical space for Ronald Reagan to declare, without being labeled a kook, "Government is not the solution. Government is the problem." In other words, it was Friedman's work that made space for Reagan's "supply-side" doctrine.

I have written about Friedman here at some length not only because of the credibility his monetarist research has given to laissez-faire absolutism in politically conservative circles, but also to demonstrate the common philosophical — and strategic — thread that runs from the public pronouncements of the earliest opponents of the New Deal's economic and social policies, to the rhetoric of its twenty-first-century opponents. Like the American Liberty League, like Hayek and the numerous political conservatives before and after him, Friedman embraced the premise of Say's Law that had already been brought into serious question, if not fully discredited, by the Great Depression. This is the same Say's Law that Ronald Reagan's much touted supply-side economics is based upon. Although today its name is never spoken, nonetheless it is Reagan's supply-side model that is the touchstone for the economic policies for virtually all political conservatives today.

THE RISE OF SUPPLY-SIDE ECONOMICS

It will be helpful to begin our examination of supply-side economics with a little background.

To recap our discussion in Part I, supply-side economics is based upon Say's Law, the principle articulated by the eighteenth-century French economist Jean-Baptiste Say (1767–1832). Say's Law states that "a product is no sooner created, than it, from that instant, affords a market for other products to the full extent of its own value."[11] Put more simply, Say's Law says that demand and supply are always in balance because supply creates its own demand. Put more simply still, the ongoing demand for goods that is created by the need for people to spend their money on *something* will keep the economy consistently moving. As a result of the wealth generated by this theoretical market equilibrium, there would always be new investment capital being injected into markets, thus keeping market supply and demand in balance. This being the case, argued Say, there is never a need for intervention in the workings of the markets, because market imbalances will always correct themselves. For that reason as well, full employment (or close to it) in laissez-faire economies would always be the norm, not the exception. Like eighteenth-century Scottish philosopher Adam Smith, whose acolyte he was, Say believed that markets are ruled by an omnipotent, unfailingly wise "invisible hand," to use Smith's widely misunderstood and overstated term.[12]

What concerns us here is not the history of Say's Law, but rather the claims it makes about governmental economic policy: that outside — read "governmental" — intervention in markets, even when the intervention is designed to combat fraud and illicit activity, can never be constructive, only destructive, accomplishing nothing except upsetting the markets' "natural" balance, with inevitably dire economic consequences. This is the claim that is echoed by conservative economic gurus Hayek and Friedman. This claim has provided an important legitimation for the laissez-faire arguments political conservatives have used ever since to justify their quest to be free of social and legal accountability in their pursuit of wealth and profits.

The claim of Say's Law that all governmental hands should be kept out of economic markets was accepted as received wisdom in Europe and in the United States from the eighteenth century onward. The effect of such widespread acceptance of Say's Law's opposition to governmental regulatory market protections was that it helped to maintain wide disparities of poverty and wealth by making space for the most powerful and most unscrupulous operators to exploit, manipulate, and assert unfair advantage toward weaker competitors and uninformed consumers, without restraint or accountability. It has resulted in severe price gouging and extraordinary human rights and labor abuses.

The justification offered by Say's Law for conservative laissez-faire opposition to market protections was finally brought into ill repute by the failure of the world financial markets to self-correct after their collapse in 1928 (as Say's Law said they would), which sank the United States and most Western economies into what became the Great Depression of the 1930s. With the Depression's discrediting of the claims of Say's Law, economists grasped for another way to explain — and to remedy — America's economic plight. They found both in Keynes's *General Theory of Employment, Interest and Money*.

As we saw earlier, Keynes's *General Theory* was despised by those who felt their interests were better served by the maintenance of unregulated markets, for the simple reason that with compelling logic and supporting data Keynes dismantled the central claim of Say's Law by theoretically demonstrating that the Depression was not a unique and aberrant contradiction to Say's Law. On the contrary, Say's Law failed because supply simply cannot be counted on to create its own demand. If supply does not create its own demand, then how can markets correct themselves when demand for goods lags behind supply? They cannot, not without assistance, answered Keynes. That is why according to Keynes and *contra* Say's Law, government intervention to maintain balanced and orderly markets *was* warranted and necessary, particularly when demand for goods needed stimulating in order to spur production and support employment.

For Keynes, market intervention included monetary measures such as tightening and loosening the supply of money and credit (which Friedman later developed to new levels of technical usefulness), but Keynes's principle means for balancing supply and demand were fiscal measures such as targeted government spending and strategic raising and lowering of tax rates to expand or contract demand for goods. Of course, these measures were blasphemy to the laissez-faire market sensibilities of political conservatives, not only because political conservatives opposed all tax increases in principle, but also because they decried them as a direct assault on the free market system that they claimed was akin to communistic centralized planning. The stridency of such charges notwithstanding, the influence of Keynes's economic theories, which came to be known simply as Keynesianism, eventually thoroughly superseded Say's Law and conservative theories that were based upon it, so much so that upon Keynes's death in 1946 the London *Financial Times* declared, "To find an economist of comparable influence one would have to go back to Adam Smith."

Keynes's influence continued to grow after his death. By the 1960s Keynesian interventionism had become more than influential; it had become a mainstay of U.S. governmental economic policies. So great was the impact of Keynes's ideas on President John F. Kennedy that Arthur Schlesinger pronounced Kennedy "the first Keynesian president." Walter Heller, chairman of Kennedy's Council of Economic Advisors, reflected Kennedy's sentiments: "We now take for granted that the government must step in to provide the essential stability at high levels of employment and growth that the market mechanism, left alone, cannot deliver."[13] The title of a 1965 cover story in *Time* magazine said it all: "We Are All Keynesians Now."[14] The article observed, "Now Keynes and his ideas, though they still make some people nervous, have been so widely accepted that they constitute both the new orthodoxy in the universities and the touchstone of economic management in Washington."

Keynesianism's use of tax policy, targeted governmental spending, and other governmental fiscal market interventions for the purpose of stimulating markets and enhancing economic growth increasingly were the bane of the corporate rich, who wanted no guidelines and no limits on their freedom to maintain and enhance their economic preeminence. Conservative politicians and lobbyists mounted an ongoing battle against Keynesian governmental policies from the 1940s through the 1960s, yet they had no coherent theoretical hat to hang their opposition upon.

Then, as we saw in the last chapter, in the 1970s during the Jimmy Carter administration Keynesianism fell into serious disrepute when it was unable to explain or stop the economic phenomenon known as "stagfla-tion" — the simultaneous occurrence of high unemployment and high price inflation. (Recall that it was Milton Friedman's prediction of stagfla-tion that brought him to acclaim.) According to Keynesian theory, nothing like stagflation was supposed to happen; prices were supposed to be con-strained from rising by the decreased demand that was supposed to result from high unemployment. Yet the Keynesian scenario did not hold. As a result the government's fiscal efforts were powerless to rein in the effects of stagflation.

Political conservatives seized this crisis as an opportunity to discredit Keynesian fiscal policies as the real cause of the economic crisis. They portrayed Keynesian market interventions as harmful to the nation's eco-nomic health and used the opportunity presented by stagflation to declare Keynesian policies as profligate and downright unjust. For these conser-vative critics, economic ups and downs had nothing to do with cyclical vagaries of demand or what economists call "real business cycles." Instead, as far as these critics was concerned, stagflation and, in fact, every eco-nomic problem, was the result of a *general failure* of Keynesian market interventionist policies. In short, political conservatives claimed that every effort by the government to rein in, assist, or otherwise affect the mystical "invisible hand" behind the markets had miserably failed, and the econ-omy was suffering for it. Now, they announced, it was up to conservatives to do something about it.

This claim that only the economic policies of political conservatives could save America's economy from ruin became an essential component of the political rhetoric of then presidential hopefuls Ronald Reagan and George H. W. Bush during the 1980 presidential election and beyond. The pithy pejorative they appended to their political opponents — "tax and spend Democrats" — expressed political conservatives' traditional dis-taste both for taxes in general and for the use of tax revenues to fund social safety net programs for the non-rich. But not only did their rhetoric ignore the responsibility for caring for society's poorest and most vulner-able members, it ultimately demonized them, as did Ronald Reagan and his acolytes, as we will see shortly. With Keynesianism on the wane conser-vatives, now emboldened by the legitimacy gained from the association of the acclaimed Friedman with their camp, rushed to fill the void by trumpeting their own brand of laissez-faire, hands-off economic policies, something they called supply-side economics.

ENTER "TRICKLE-DOWN," OR MASQUERADING GREED AS A SOCIAL GOOD

If Kennedy was our first Keynesian president there is little doubt that Reagan was our first supply-side president. It is important to understand supply-side economics because although political conservatives no longer use the term, the precepts, principles, and policies that constituted the supply-side approach are the same principles that motivated the economic policies of George W. Bush, and they are the same principles that dictate conservative economic policies today.

The principles of the ideology (the reason I do not call it a theory will be clear soon enough) of supply-side economics, more popularly known as Reaganomics, were laid in the 1970s by a handful of political conservatives, including two luminaries at the *Wall Street Journal* (Robert Bartley and Jude Wanniski), two academic economists (Robert Mundell and Arthur Laffer), all of whom were later joined by Jack Kemp, a former NFL quarterback turned junior congressman from upstate New York. Bartley, Wanniski, Mundell, and Laffer largely evolved their ideas over a series of dinner meetings at a prominent restaurant in New York City's Wall Street district. An early description of the "supply-side" economic precepts that evolved from those dinner meetings was offered by Wanniski. Supply-side economics, he claims, "go[es] back to an older style of economic thought in which the incentives and motivations of the individual producer and consumer and merchant are made the keystone of economic policy."[15] The "older style" to which Wanniski refers is, in essence, none other than Say's Law.

Basing their assertions on their resurrection of the effectively discredited claim of Say's Law that supply creates its own demand, the budding supply-siders argued that economic growth can be most effectively produced by increasing the nation's supply of wealth by cutting taxes. Lowered taxes, they argued, would actually raise federal tax revenues because if taxed less, people will work harder, earn higher incomes, and thus pay more in actual tax revenues despite the lowered tax rates. With higher after-tax incomes consumers will have greater purchasing power with which to fuel further economic growth. And with more economic growth would come more jobs. Arthur Laffer, the economist who conceived the so-called Laffer Curve, the economic model upon which all supply-side claims rest, summarized it this way: "Tax something, and you get less of it. Tax something less, and you get more of it."[16]

This approach to economic policy came to be known as "trickle-down" economics, because of its basic premise that lower tax rates will result in wealth trickling down from the rich to the benefit of the rest of society. The term is attributed to the Depression-era remark of the humorist Will Rogers: "money was all appropriated for the top in hopes that it would trickle down to the needy."[17] Another folksy adage better expresses the gist of trickle-down economics, albeit crudely: If the horse has better hay to eat, the birds will eat better, too. Princeton historian Sean Wilentz explains, "The idea is that further enriching the already rich would eventually produce great economic benefits for lowlier Americans."[18] Rather than question these characterizations, conservative economist George Gilder effectively echoed them in *Wealth and Poverty,* his 1981 best-selling paean to supply-side principles. "A successful economy," he wrote, "depends on the proliferation of the rich." The "function of the rich," he gushed, is "fostering opportunities for the classes below,"[19] which is simply a restatement of Will Rogers's maxim in more sophisticated terms.

Indeed, no less than David Stockman, Reagan's highly influential director of the Office of Management and Budget, admitted that the premise of the supply-side approach and its calls for drastic tax reductions for wealthy individuals and corporations was simply the elitist "trickle-down" mentality: "It's kind of hard to sell 'trickle-down,' so the supply-side formula was the only way to get a tax policy that really was 'trickle-down.' Supply-side is 'trickle-down' theory."[20]

What Gilder, Stockman, and others affirm is that supply-side economics depends upon the continued existence of an extremely wealthy class in American society. In a nutshell, that is the purpose of supply-side economics in its past and present incarnations: to maintain a very wealthy, privileged group of Americans. That is simply another way of saying that supply-side economics is predicated upon and depends upon the continued existence of extreme economic inequality in America. What is the "supply" that is expected to trickle down from the rich after their taxes are cut? It is wealth, to be sure, but not simply wealth. In the words of

John Kenneth Galbraith, it is "the residual after luxurious consumption."[21] Or, put another way, *it is what is left after the rich have satisfied all their wants.*

Founding supply-sider Arthur Laffer acknowledges that supply-side principles increase income inequality. But incredibly, he explains this as a *positive* development: "The increasingly unequal distribution of income during the era of supply-side economics [roughly 1980–2005] was the result of many millions of Americans becoming fantastically, unthinkably rich, not a result of the poor getting poorer."[22]

This highlights a central truth of supply-side economics: for all the economic models and journalistic literature touting its efficacy, for all its claims about doing what is right and good for the American people, there is exceedingly little evidence that either the formulators of the supply-side approach or its advocates ever gave significant consideration to whether wealth really would trickle down from the coffers of the very rich to the lowers reaches of society. Indeed, the principal feature of the trickle-down supply-side approach is that its primary tool of economic policy — reduction of taxes on income and capital gains — is solely aimed at an extremely small group of people: the wealthiest Americans. As the economist James K. Galbraith explains, "[Its] only relevant issue is whether that small group of people would control a large enough part of total income and whether they could be induced, by changing the structure of taxes, to save *and* invest it."[23]

Although he elevated conservative economic principles to a prominence they had not known since the days of Herbert Hoover, Reagan's supply-side doctrine was just a new name for the old conservative strategy of serving the interests of the rich. And since the implementation of Reaganomics, that strategy has well served those interests. Instead of wealth trickling down under Reagan's 60 percent reduction of the top tax rate for the richest Americans, the nation's wealth trickled up. Between 1981 and 1990 (Reagan's tax cut for the nation's top income earners was continued after he left office in 1988 by his successor, George H. W. Bush) the poorest 20 percent of Americans saw their after-tax family incomes drop by 12 percent. The wealthiest *1 percent,* however, saw their incomes increase by 136 percent.[24] Reagan's tax policies were so skewed toward the interests of individual and corporate wealth that a survey of 250 of the nation's largest corporations found that from 1981 to 1983 more than half of them *paid no taxes at all* in at least one of those years.[25] On the other hand, by 1986, under Reagan's supply-side policies, real hourly wages for the average worker had declined to levels lower than they had been through most of the 1970s. The nation's home ownership rate also declined. Moreover, despite supply-side prognosticators' grand claims, there were more farm foreclosures under Reagan than at any time since the Great Depression.

Reaganomics' legacy of heightened income inequality can be seen in myriad economic data. A 2006 Congressional Budget Office (CBO) study reports that in 2006 the top 1 percent of households had a larger share of the nation's after-tax income, and the middle and bottom fifths of households had smaller shares, *than in any year since 1979,* the first year the CBO data cover. This means that by 2006 the gaps in after-tax incomes between households in the top 1 percent and households in the middle and bottom fifths — that is, the households of most Americans — *were the widest on record.*

The CBO data show that the average after-tax income of the top 1 percent of American households in 1979 was 7.9 times higher than the middle fifth of American households (the middle class), but by 2006 that ratio had risen to *23.0.* The 1979 ratio between the after-tax incomes of the top 1 percent of American households to those of the poorest Americans — the bottom fifth of American households — was 22.6 times higher; by 2006 that ratio had risen to *72.7.* In other words, the income gap between America's upper economic class and most of the rest of the nation has tripled since the political ascendancy of Ronald Reagan's "trickle-down" reduction of taxes on the rich and relaxed regulations on industry, both the ongoing stocks-in-trade of political conservatism's economic policies today.

The lucky top 1 percent of all American households has seen their wealth grow inordinately since the rise to preeminence of conservative economic policies under Reagan. But it is when we look at the wealth of the wealthiest among that group that we see the real gap in income class-based growth. Even when adjusted for inflation the top 0.1 percent (the richest one in a thousand households) saw their average share of total household income grow since 1980 from 2.7 percent (just over $1 million) to 12.3 percent ($7.1 million), an average increase of *over 450 percent.*[26] The increase in the income share of the top 0.01 percent (the richest one in ten thousand households) has been even more spectacular. Since 1980 it has risen from less than 1 percent (less than $4 million) to over 6 percent of national income (more than $35 million per family).[27] This poignant observation puts the data into perspective: "If the total income growth of these years were a pie ... the slice enjoyed by the roughly 300,000 people in the top tenth of 1 percent would be half again as large as the slice enjoyed by the roughly *180 million* in the bottom 60 percent."[28]

Not only has the supply-side approach greatly increased income inequality; despite the grandiose promises of its supporters and adherents most reputable sources report that supply-side economics has added nothing to the public good. After an extensive study of the effects of supply-side policies from the Reagan era onward, the CBO concluded in a December 2005 report that any benefits to GNP that it might have accrued are dwarfed by the direct loss of tax revenue resulting from the tax reductions. In other words, supply-side tax cuts have not paid for themselves, or even come close. In the third edition of his textbook *Macroeconomics*, N. Gregory Mankiw, who would go on to be an economic advisor to George W. Bush, dismissed supply-side economics as, "An example of fad economics." He explained,

> People on fad diets put their health at risk but rarely achieve the permanent weight loss they desire. Similarly, when politicians rely on the advice of charlatans and cranks, they rarely get the desirable results they anticipate. After Reagan's election, Congress passed the cut in taxes that Reagan advocated, but the tax cut did not cause tax revenues to rise.[29]

Paul Krugman has demonstrated that despite supply-siders' claims of raising economic production, economic growth in the 1980s under the supply-side policies of Reagan and George H. W. Bush was essentially no greater than the periods that preceded and followed it, and in fact was slower than the rate of growth of the 1970s as a whole. This makes the outsize income gains by the truly rich during this period even more conspicuously unequal, because the increases in their wealth outpaced even the growth of the economy.[30] Thus there is no evidence that supply-side policies experienced any sustained success in any of their aims except one: they made the rich richer and the poor poorer.[31]

HOW DID SUPPLY-SIDE ECONOMICS WIN?

Supply-side economics was contrived to maintain a class of extremely wealthy Americans. It accomplished that in droves and along the way made the poor even poorer. The very existence of a wealthy class, it was supposed, meant that its wealth would somehow trickle all the way down to the lowest rungs of the economic ladder. Of course, focusing all efforts and attention on further prospering the already prosperous not only militates against basic biblical ethics, but also smacks of un-American aristocratic elitism. Furthermore, the lack of viability and theoretical efficacy of supply-side economics was not a surprise; indeed, it was suspected from the first. The MIT economist and future Nobel Prize winner Robert Solow called it "economic snake oil." Even Reagan's fellow 1980 Republican presidential aspirant, George H. W. Bush, mocked it as "voodoo economics." Why, then, despite the many indications that the supply-side economics would *not* benefit most Americans, did Reagan and his tax-cut worshiping acolytes, both then and now, pursue those policies with such relentless alacrity? The reason is that supply-side economics is not really a theory; it is an ideology evolved and crafted to serve the interests of America's wealthy elites. The economic concepts and equations it embraces are simply tools used to justify their ongoing quest to maintain America's unjust economic status quo. It is the same with its tax-cuts-for-the-wealthy political progeny today. This is why earlier I deemed it an ideological doctrine rather than an economic theory.

This is not simply my opinion. It is the estimation — sometimes strongly explicit, other times clearly implicit — of the founders and foremost proponents of supply-side themselves. For instance, it is clear that Leslie Lenkowsky, a Harvard-trained economist and early supporter of the supply-side approach, was unconvinced of its theoretical value. "Supply-side economics," he averred, "is less an economic theory than a philosophy, an ideology."[32] A perusal of claims by other early supply-side advocates seems to paint a similar picture. The attempt by a *Wall Street Journal* editorial writer to give supply-side economics historical heft by presenting it as basic to the very founding of the United States clearly describes it as an ideological, perspectival "approach" to governance rather than as a theory: "The supply-side approach was in fact so well known to the founders of the United States that it can claim to be the foundation of the American economic tradition." This same supporter attempts to forge a transparently *un*theoretical link between the nation's founding and the economic policies of Ronald Reagan: "Far from being radical and untried, the basic principles of 'Reaganomics' were common currency at the founding of the United States."[33]

Wall Street Journal columnist Jude Wanniski, the coiner of the term "supply-side" and one of its foremost architects, went further. He claimed that supply-side economics actually played a role in the birth of Jesus of Nazareth(!):

> Supply-side's birth coincided with the birth of Christ and Christianity. It was Emperor Caesar Augustus who decided to revive the idea of his adoptive father Julius and conduct a tax census of the empire. By identifying the whole of the citizenry, the burden of taxes could be spread, avoiding the necessity of burdening the few with the entire load. Joseph and Mary were en route to his home to be enumerated for this supply-side economic purpose when Jesus was born.[34]

Moreover, the political pundit Irving Kristol explicitly acknowledged the ideological nature of the supply-side approach to economic policy. Kristol, founder and editor-in-chief of the conservative periodical *Public Interest,* was a fervent supporter of supply-side economics. Yet he admitted in a 1995 essay that he attached no particular significance to supply-side economics as an economic theory, confessing that he actually held "a cavalier attitude toward the budget deficit and other monetary or fiscal issues." The reason he so relentlessly advocated supply-side in the pages of *Public Interest,* he confided, is simply because it was a useful ideological tool for accomplishing political ends: "The task, as I saw it, was to create a new majority, which evidently would mean a conservative majority . . . so political effectiveness was the priority, not the accounting deficiencies of government."[35]

Incredibly, Wanniski further reveals that beyond its ideological identity, for him and, one supposes, for other supply-side enthusiasts, there is even a theological, almost messianic mission and messianic self-identity underlying supply-side economics, at least as he understood it. Confessing that when he initially wrote *The Way the World Works,* his wide-ranging and closely argued exposition of supply-side principles, he was, "more than mildly megalomaniacal at the time," he admits: "I actually believed God had chosen me, of all people, to bring the *good news* of supply-side economics to mankind, thereby saving the world from economic decline."[36]

Thus by the admission of its founders and its earliest advocates, supply-side economics is at its root an ideology, an ideology based upon an effectively discredited economic theory that is in service to the central ideological goal of political conservatism: to maintain, and expand where possible, status quo extremes of poverty and wealth in America.

The ideological commitment of supply-side economics can most clearly be seen in the social vision reflected by the areas in which supply-siders invariably seek to reduce government spending to pay for tax relief for the rich. Their proposals for government spending reductions are almost always in the programs in which the rich have no interest: the social-welfare and safety net programs that millions of economically dis-advantaged, socially vulnerable, and health-challenged Americans depend upon, but for which the rich have no personal need.

I realize that I have leveled serious charges here. I am aware that one must tread lightly when purporting to ascribe intentions to public figures for the policies they advocate. That is to say, when it comes to policies regarding poor Americans I realize that not all political conservatives act out of disregard or willful disdain; some seem to act out of ignorance. Or, at the least, they plead ignorance. A case in point is Edwin Meese, Reagan's attorney general. When informed of a 1984 Harvard School of Public Health study that found that thirty thousand Americans had the stark choice of begging for food or starving, Meese publicly stated that he was not aware that there was hunger in America.[37]

Professions of ignorance notwithstanding, however, it is difficult not to detect a sense of disregard, disdain, or even malice for poor Americans underlying the policy choices of Reagan and his allied advocates of supply-side economics. In his first year in office, Reagan cut public hous-ing assistance funds in half. For several years thereafter he tried to kill *all* federal housing assistance for the poor. When told that his policies were causing a steep rise in the number of homeless Americans, Reagan actually claimed that those living on the streets were there because they preferred it. "People who are sleeping on the grates," he told the *Good Morning*

America television program in January, 1984, "the homeless ... are homeless, you might say, by choice." This was no aberration for Reagan. While
campaigning for Barry Goldwater twenty years earlier he displayed the
same apparent disdain for the plight of poor Americans. Referring to a
statement by John F. Kennedy in his 1960 presidential campaign, Reagan
intoned, "We were told four years ago that 17 million people went to
bed hungry each night. Well, that was probably true. They were all on
a diet."[38] And in 1974 when the kidnappers of the heiress Patty Hearst
demanded the distribution of food to poor people in Oakland, California,
Reagan said, "It's just too bad we can't have an outbreak of botulism,"[39]
a statement that was so exceedingly callous and so disdainfully elitist that
it could not even be justified as a joke.

The attitude of disdain for the poor was unapologetically present for
Jude Wanniski, who is arguably the central figure in the development of
supply-side principles. In a 1997 statement Wanniski effectively acknowledged the supply-side bias against poor Americans and defended it: "The
poor have become fat and happy, the rich impoverished. This is why we
are in the fix we are in. Everyone wants to be poor, because it has so many
more advantages."[40]

The callousness bred by the economic philosophy of conservative politics is even seen in supposedly more thoughtful and less doctrinaire
conservatives such as the prominent journalist George F. Will. In a December 1995 speech at the American Enterprise Institute, arguably the flagship
conservative think tank, Will mocked a portion of FDR's 1944 State of
the Union address that reflected the Bible's unwavering imperative that
those in power must care for the poor and the vulnerable: "We cannot be
content, no matter how high [America's] general standard of living may
be, if some fraction of our people — whether it be one-third or one-fifth
or one-tenth — is ill-fed, ill-clothed, ill-housed, or insecure."[41]

Incredibly, rather than affirm Roosevelt's call for all Americans to enjoy
the basic necessities of life, Will criticized Roosevelt for speaking to their
plight: "[Roosevelt's statement] was a summons to permanent discontent
on the part of citizens and government." Equally as incredible, Will went
on to complain about Roosevelt's so-called Second Bill of Rights because
it called for rights for all Americans to a useful and remunerative job,
adequate food and clothing, healthful recreation, good education, decent
homes, a decent living for farmers, adequate medical care, and a right to

freedom from unfair competition and from the economic fears that can attend old age, sickness, accident, and unemployment. Will showed no appreciation for Roosevelt's sense of care for the welfare of his neighbors or its resonance with the biblical admonition to love one's neighbor as oneself. According to Will, actively taking responsibility for making sure rank-and-file Americans have the opportunity to experience a decent quality of life is not the job of the presidency, or of any other branch of government, for that matter. He seemed totally unaware of the irony of attacking the efforts of an American president to help his constituents have a decent quality of life. Regardless of whether he was intentionally callous or not, Will's response, like Reagan's above, illustrates the elitist blind spot of political conservatism when it comes to the struggles and the plight of the non-wealthy. Apparently, the further down one is on the socio-economic ladder, the more invisible and less important one is considered to be under political conservative economic principles.

THE SPAWN OF SUPPLY-SIDE

Despite the claims of supply-side enthusiasts that their approach would benefit society in general, in reality at every step the principal beneficiaries of its policies have been the wealthy, especially the ultra-wealthy, for the following reasons. First, lowered taxes on income disproportionately benefits the rich, because they have more income. Second, lowered taxes on capital gains also disproportionately benefits the rich, because it is they who own most of the nation's capital. Third, reduced regulatory controls, especially in financial markets, almost exclusively benefit the rich, because they not only control most of the nation's financial capital, they also disproportionately possess the crucial information needed to make informed market decisions. Regulatory protections are indispensable for protecting ordinary citizens from deception, theft, exploitation, and misinformation in the normal course of buying and selling, because the average person seldom has access to the behind-the-scenes information that is necessary to protect them from bad investment deals, for instance, or misleading mortgage codicils, shoddy products, or habitual overpayment for services or goods.

Opposing regulatory protections and advocating a government too small to impose and enforce regulatory protections for the common good is a reckless and unconscionable violation of the responsibility to establish measures in the marketplace enjoined by the Bible upon those in governance and authority to protect the vulnerable.

In summary, the economic policy measures of Ronald Reagan stressed the "supply" or wealth possessing side of America's economic equation. That means that his administration was inherently philosophically disposed to aiming its policies toward the interests of America's wealthiest citizens. We have primarily discussed only the effects of Reagan's tax policies that favored the rich, but let us not forget that Reagan took other actions that also added to America's economic inequality. A case in point: he renewed corporate anti-unionism and reempowered it with his breaking of the Professional Air Traffic Controllers Organization in 1981. This reprise of corporate anti-unionism rivals the anti-unionism of the robber barons of the gilded age. On the one hand, it has vastly expanded the wealth of corporate management. Since 1980 the average CEO compensation has risen from about forty times that of the average worker to about four hundred times today. On the other hand, it has resulted in depressed workers' wages and lowered benefits and began a slide in union membership from 24.1 percent of the workforce in 1979 to 12.4 percent in 2008 (up from 12.1 in 2007), a decline of almost 50 percent.[42]

CONSERVATIVE ECONOMICS AND THE (UN)-AMERICAN ARISTOCRACY

The purpose of our discussion of Reaganomics and supply-side economics was to demonstrate that it set the paradigm for the economic policies that conservative politicians have followed since, with its singular focus on the interests of America's wealthiest citizens. This includes anti-government rhetoric, its insistence on tax cuts for the wealthy, and incorporation of the laissez-faire absolutism of Say's Law and the work of Hayek and Friedman.[43] When one surveys the effect of the economic philosophy of political conservatives one can see that, in effect, it has created an *American economic aristocracy*. Indeed, the trickle-down tax policies enacted by the George W. Bush administration, like those of Reagan, significantly strengthened the position of the American economic aristocracy by widening the income inequality between the upper class and the rest of

Americans, according to estimates in an Urban Institute–Brookings Institution Tax Center Policy Center study. That study looked at the results of the tax cuts enacted between 2001 and 2006. Witness the differences between the after-tax benefits enjoyed by the richest Americans and everyone else:

* The average after-tax income of households in the bottom fifth of the income spectrum increased by an average of *0.3 percent.*

* The average after-tax income of households in the middle fifth of the income spectrum increased by an average of *2.5 percent.*

* The average after-tax income of households in the top 1 percent of households increased by an average of *6.4 percent.*

Clearly, the greatest beneficiaries of the Bush tax cuts by far were America's richest citizens, those who least needed tax relief. The benefits received by other Americans, not even the nation's neediest citizens, even came close. In fact, the increase in income enjoyed by the richest Americans under the Bush tax plan by 2006 was more than *twenty times greater* than the benefits that the nation's poorest citizens received. Despite many political conservatives' regular public invocations of their Christian faith, this simply defies every biblical measure of justice and equality.

And Bush's policies continue to widen the economic chasm between America's richest class and every other American on the wealth ladder, for additional tax reductions were enacted after 2006, and some of those signed into law between 2001 and 2006 did not fully phase in until 2009. These were also heavily tilted toward people at the top of the income scale. These include the elimination of the tax on the nation's largest estates and the two income-tax reductions that began to take effect in 2006 and go almost exclusively to high-income households.

Although final figures were not available at the time of publication, the CBO has estimated that by the end of 2010, when all of the 2001–2008 tax cuts are operative, their combined result will have been to reduce taxes by 7.7 percent for those with incomes of more than $1 million, but only .07 percent for the poorest Americans. The middle class will have received an average cut of only 2.6 percent, less than a third of the benefit given to the rich. As a result, by the end of the decade the tax cuts enacted under the Bush administration will ultimately have become even more skewed toward high-income households than in 2006 — and will have increased income inequality to a still greater degree.

REMOVING THE RUNGS
ON THE UPWARD MOBILITY LADDER

Earlier the supply-side economist Arthur Laffer claimed that the dramatic rise in economic inequality in the last thirty years is "the result of many millions of Americans becoming fantastically, unthinkably rich." It would be nice if that were true. However, statistics show that the vast majority of Americans have never had even the semblance of a chance of entering the highest ranks of power and influence. In fact, most Americans never significantly rise above the station of their birth, much less enter the ranks of the rich. The truth is that the potential for upward economic class mobility in America is no higher than in France and Britain. This is an incredible fact, given that both France and Britain have had landed hereditary aristocrats and nobles for centuries longer than the United States has been in existence. In fact, a 2005 study released by the *New York Times* found that today Americans are more likely to end their lives in the same economic class standing into which they were born than was the case thirty years ago.[44] That same *New York Times* report cites a study by the Federal Reserve Bank of Boston as reaching similar conclusions. The Boston Fed found that fewer families experienced upward mobility in the 1980s than in the 1970s, and even fewer moved upward in the 1990s than in the 1980s. The severe economic recession in the United States that began in 2007, the effects of which continue to be felt at this writing in the first quarter of 2011, is poised to further reduce upward economic mobility in America.

Political conservatives like economist Thomas Sowell strongly argue that positing such limited economic mobility in America is incorrect because the use of income categories to analyze economic mobility is incorrect. He argues that it is "perhaps the most fertile source of misunderstandings about incomes." Sowell contends that a different picture emerges, one evincing much greater economic mobility, when the argument is structured in terms of "flesh-and-blood human beings," that is, by charting the movement of the incomes of actual persons, particularly by using Internal Revenue tax filing data.[45] Yet Sowell's method does not present a truly representative picture. Even children of the rich quite often begin their careers at a much lower income bracket than their family status and connections ultimately guarantee them in professional hierarchies once they have paid their entry-level dues. A more meaningful measurement is the mobility from the income and wealth status of one's parents, as in the *New York Times* study above. As economists Jacob Hacker and Paul Pierson point out, "In the United States, more than half of the earnings advantage (or disadvantage) of fathers is passed on to sons. In Canada, only about a fifth or less is. And almost all of the difference is accounted for by the fact that Americans are more likely to be stuck at the bottom or secure at the top."[46] Moreover, citing voluminous data, Hacker and Pierson argue that "the evidence is overwhelming that upward social mobility has *not* increased at the same time that inequality has skyrocketed." This observation applies to both individual and intergenerational mobility. "Over a typical decade, for example, just under four in five people stay in the same income quintile or move a single quintile up or down." On the other hand, "Only around one in ten had risen from the bottom 80 percent—down from around one in seven in the 1970s."[47]

Rather than bothering to question the conclusions of the economic mobility data *à la* Sowell, most conservatives simply dismiss these data outright, apparently based on a belief that either mobility patterns in America are inherently fluid or that class mobility is now based strictly on merit.[48] Both the *New York Times* and the Hacker and Pierson studies cited above debunk the former claim; the ascent of figures like the chronically underachieving George W. Bush is ample evidence of the falsehood of the latter. Yet even *true* merit is at least partly class based. The higher a family's economic status, the greater its access to the best educations and the social exposure and professional connections that accompany those educations. Moreover, recent studies show that the advantage of being born into a wealthy family, excluding the nation's wealthiest families, no longer lasts only two or three generations as was once believed. Now the advantage of a wealthy birth is closer to five generations. That means that it can take *four to five generations* for families without historical wealth to gain an equal footing with those that have long held it, according to the nonpartisan Economic Policy Institute.[49] Taken together, these factors mean that in reality most Americans have no realistic chance of entering the circles of power and wealth that make the policies that determine the very course of their lives.

Take education, for instance. At a time when education matters more than ever, access to the best educations and training remains tightly linked to class. Historically most of those in the greatest positions of power in America have come from the ivy-covered halls of America's top universities; it is a fact that the power brokers of this nation inordinately hail from Harvard, Yale University, Princeton, and other top-tier schools. The ranks of the nation's policy makers and business leaders are rife with graduates from these institutions, many with advanced degrees. It is no coincidence that both 2004 major party presidential candidates were graduates of Yale University or that both were members of the same Yale secret student society, or that America's current president, Barack Obama, is a product of Columbia University and Harvard Law School.

In principle, the doors of the nation's top universities are open to every American based upon achieved academic merit.[50] However, the reality is that out of the roughly 31,700 public and private high schools in America, only 930 — about 3 percent — had more than four students in their 1998–2001 graduating classes who attended Harvard, Princeton, or Yale. Yet *Worth* magazine, a monthly periodical dedicated to the interests of the very richest Americans, reports that the hundred top-rated American high schools sent 3,452 students to Harvard, Princeton, or Yale. In other words, three-tenths of *1* percent of America's high schools accounted for 22 percent of students at the top three universities. But here is where class comes into play: ninety-four of the top hundred American high schools are exclusive private schools with annual tuitions of $20,000 or more. And all of the six public schools on the list are located in communities that are among the nation's wealthiest.

Indeed, when the Educational Testing Service looked at students from the *poorest* 25 percent of the nation's population it found that only 3 percent of them made it to the nation's top 146 schools. On the other hand, it found that the children of the *richest* 25 percent of Americans comprised some 74 percent of the students at the top schools. More telling yet, the *entire bottom half* of America's total population accounted for only *10 percent* of students at the Big Three Ivy League schools.

At the end of the day, what this means is that students at the nation's top colleges are twenty-five times more likely to be rich than poor. And in recent years, the proportion of students from upper-income families at the most selective American colleges has consistently expanded. Moreover, David Callahan makes an observation that is worth quoting in its entirety:

> Attending an elite university seems to have much to do with getting rich, too. A 2008 analysis by *Forbes* magazine found that 141 U.S. billionaires had gone to just five top schools for either undergraduate or graduate degrees: Harvard, Stanford, the University of Pennsylvania, Yale and Columbia. And 1 out of 10 billionaires holds a degree from Harvard University alone. Ninety percent of billionaires in finance with MBAs got their degrees from only three Ivy League schools: Harvard, Columbia, and the University of Pennsylvania.[51]

These data are significant when considering the impact of wealth-based class disparities because although matriculation at elite schools opens doors to the highest levels of leadership and authority in America, entry to these institutions is circumscribed by access to wealth, and access to wealth is limited by class. It is a vicious circle. The poor continue to struggle while the rich continue running — and owning — things. At a time when manual labor can be farmed out to developing countries for as little as $2.00 a day, education and advanced skills training can mean the difference between a life of relative comfort and an existence of unrelenting struggle. Yet education, particularly the best education, is completely out of reach for virtually all but the most economically privileged Americans. In the constellation of causes for this distressing state of affairs, there is little question that socio-economic class inequities are among the most prominent. This is reflected in a 2010 study by the Delta Cost Project, a nonprofit group in Washington, D.C. Sadly, the study concludes, "While the United States has some of the wealthiest institutions in the world, it also has a 'system' of postsecondary education with far more economic stratification than is true of any other country."[52]

KNOWING THE TREE
BY THE FRUIT IT BEARS

How has our democracy come to such a sorry state of affairs? How has our society and our body politic come to be so dominated by the interests, wishes, and whims of the wealthiest Americans to the detriment of the rest of us? The answer, I think, is self-evident: the wealthy and powerful in America have remained rich and privileged and are becoming ever richer by using the perquisites, power, and influence afforded by their wealth to garner the bulk of the fruits of America's economic growth.

Let me illustrate this with several examples. The first I have chosen because it is such an egregious example: the proposal of George W. Bush to abolish the federal estate tax on inherited wealth.

Like the Jubilee provision of Leviticus 25, one of the purposes of the U.S. estate tax on multi-million dollar inheritances, particularly in the last half of the twentieth century, has been to try to guard against the perpetuation of a permanent American aristocracy of economic wealth. Because this flies in the face of political conservatives' studied goal of maintenance of significant class disparities of wealth, the estate tax has been an important target of destruction for them. In 2006 the Bush administration weighed in on the issue with its quite moral sounding contention that elimination of the estate tax was necessary to address the crisis of family farms being lost because heirs were unable to pay estate taxes on them. Yet under the existing laws farm couples could already pass family farms worth up to $4.1 million tax free to their heirs, as long as the heirs continued to farm the property for ten years. Thus 96 percent or more of all farms were already effectively exempt from estate taxes, making Bush's claim untrue on its face. So who would really benefit from this measure? The measure's intended beneficiaries: America's richest citizens. Fewer than three thousand, or about 1.9 percent of all estates in the entire country, would benefit from abolition of the tax on inherited wealth, and every one of those estates was valued in excess of $5 million.[53] However, the bias toward the rich in President Bush's politically conservative proposal was much greater than it appeared. Soon after the introduction of the measure, *Bloomberg Businessweek* magazine captured the extraordinary irony:

> The contrast in President Bush's new budget could not be more stark. On the one hand, he wants to eliminate what he likes to call the "death tax" — a levy imposed on a handful of the nation's biggest estates. On the other, he wants to end Social Security's lump sum death benefit — a $255 check that the families of many of the nation's poorest use to help pay for their funerals.[54]

Bush's assault on the estate tax was not just a lone politician's gambit. It was the public face of an effort underwritten by a handful of the wealthiest families in America to preserve billions of dollars of their personal fortunes. These families included the Koch and Mars families, who own the first and third largest privately held companies in the United States (Koch Industries and Mars, Inc., respectively), and the Walton clan, which owns approximately 40 percent of Wal-Mart, the world's largest retailer.[55] Between 1998 and 2006 these and some fifteen other super-wealthy American families spent nearly half a billion dollars on lobbying efforts against the tax for one simple reason: repeal of it stood to collectively preserve for them almost $72 billion in family wealth.[56]

When the American Farm Bureau revealed in 2001 that it could not identify one family farm that was actually threatened by the estate tax, thus revealing that Bush's stated motivation for repealing the estate was a lie, advocates of the estate tax repeal retrenched and re-presented it as an effort to save small businesses. However, in a June 2004 survey by the National Federation of Independent Businesses, small business owners ranked the estate tax as only their thirty-sixth most pressing concern out of a list of seventy-five, ranking it below "telephone cost and service" and "controlling my own time."[57] With the debunking of these false premises the push to abolish the estate tax can be seen for what it actually is: a measure driven by the interests of the wealthy that has cost the rest of the country billions of dollars in much-needed tax revenue yet has benefited no one but the nation's wealthiest citizens.

As the Bush estate tax cuts were set to expire at the end of 2010, the policy bias of political conservatives became even more clear. Even as the nation struggled to emerge from a serious financial recession amid a skyrocketing national debt, conservative politicians pushed for — and achieved — an even larger tax break for multi-million dollar estates. This despite President Barack Obama's publicly expressed opposition to it and despite the fact that most Americans opposed it as well, as reputable polls indicated. With the newest estate tax reduction, not only would the size of the personal estate tax exemption beginning in 2011 rise from the existing $1 million exemption to $5 million, the rate of taxation of estates over $5 million ($10 million now for married couples) would drop from 55 percent to 35 percent. This double whammy tax exemption windfall also includes exemption from all federal income taxes. This extraordinary two-year reduction in the estate tax rate will cost society some $207.5 billion, or just under $104 billion each for tax years 2011 and 2012, while offering virtually no stimulating effects for the struggling economy or for those Americans not fortunate or cunning enough to have amassed multi-million dollar estates. In fact, it is estimated that this measure will benefit *less than one-half of 1 percent (.005)* of all Americans in 2011.[58]

In short, the Bush administration's repeal of the estate tax and the victory of conservative politicians' even more wealth-friendly 2011–12 estate tax policy are classic examples of political conservatism's consistent bias toward the interests of America's wealthiest citizens and its unstinting efforts to maintain America's vast economic disparities.

A further and particularly illustrative example of the ideological bias of conservative economic principles is seen in the expansion of the purview of the Fourteenth Amendment to the U.S. Constitution. Toward the end of the nineteenth century, state governments were becoming increasingly concerned about corporations' price gouging, their often rapacious commercial policies, and their unchallenged degradation of natural environments. State governments were also greatly frustrated with the corporate elites' ongoing obstruction of federal efforts to institute basic regulatory protections. When the states began to fight back against unbridled corporate profiteering by instituting their own consumer regulatory protections against it, intense lobbying by corporate elites resulted in the Supreme Court issuing a surprising, even shocking ruling: that *corporations were persons,* thereby qualifying for protection under the Fourteenth Amendment. That amendment's central declaration, "nor shall any State deprive any person of life, liberty, or property, without the due process of law," was originally intended to protect the nation's beleaguered citizens of African descent, who were victimized, disenfranchised, and dispossessed daily with no viable mechanisms of legal recourse. Yet the Supreme Court allowed corporate elites to counter the states' efforts to rein in corporate profiteering by ruling that under the Fourteenth Amendment corporations were also "persons" whose "prosperity" — their immense wealth — should also be protected under the due process clause. In 1886 alone, the Court used this ruling to strike down some 230 separate state laws regulating corporations. In fact, the Court was so zealously engaged in protecting the interests of big business that it seems to have forgotten about America's vulnerable black citizens altogether. Between 1890 and 1910, of the 307

Fourteenth Amendment cases heard by the Supreme Court, only nineteen dealt with the rights of blacks.[59] The Supreme Court's decision to grant the protections of persons to corporations has morphed in the century after its enactment into layers of legal protection for corporations from culpability for their actions in the public domain, thereby collectively saving corporate coffers untold billions since the amendment's enactment and immeasurably enriching corporate managers and owners.

ECONOMIC CLASSES
AND HUMAN SUFFERING

The reason biblical witnesses consistently declare policies that intentionally spawn class inequality to be morally and biblically indefensible, notwithstanding the ingenious ways political conservatives contrive to defend them, is because they are destructive to innocent human lives in numerous and terrible ways. As the rich get richer, the life chances of the poor diminish, for class affects Americans' physical well-being in crucial and easily quantifiable ways. Every credible study has shown that the higher one's income, the longer the life expectancy. Upper-class Americans are less likely than middle-class Americans to develop and die from diabetes, stroke, heart disease, and many types of cancer. In turn, middle-class Americans experience far better health than the poorest Americans. And researchers report that this sad gap is widening. The primary factor in this health disparity in America is the high cost and lack of availability of healthcare to poor Americans relative to their more affluent countrymen. But there are other class-based health factors as well. For instance, the stress of the insecurity and the lack of affirmation that usually accompany jobs low on the occupational scale is more harmful than the stress of professional jobs that typically offer more security and greater appreciation of skills.[60]

In addition, the poor have less time and fewer resources to devote to health maintenance. And typically, the lower the income, the less healthful the diet. Professor Ichiro Kawachi of the Harvard School of Public Health explains that although "mortality rates even among the poor are coming down...the rate [of decline] is not anywhere near as fast as the well-to-do."[61] The result? The health gap between rich and poor in America, like the income gap, has gotten greater. In other words, generally speaking the vagaries of class have made poor and lower-class Americans less healthy, with lower life expectancies, while the health of more well-to-do Americans flourishes and improves.

A major cause of the acute health disparities in the United States is that adequate and affordable healthcare has never been available to all Americans even approaching the extent to which it has been available to wealthy Americans. Almost every president since Franklin D. Roosevelt and Harry Truman attempted without success to institute a national healthcare program that would make healthcare available for every American, regardless of wealth or class. Indeed, in that portion of Roosevelt's eleventh State of the Union Address, which he called an "economic Bill of Rights" but which came to be known as the Second Bill of Rights, he called for all Americans to have "the right to adequate medical care and the opportunity to achieve and enjoy good health."[62] This remained an unrealized, but closely held hope among progressive politicians. In 2009 President Barack Obama announced his intention to try to finally accomplish what Roosevelt had started: the achievement of a national healthcare plan. Obama's bill was passed after months of vociferous and virtually unanimous opposition by political conservatives. The Affordable Health Care Act was signed into law by Obama on March 23, 2010.

The provisions proposed by the Affordable Health Care Act are by no means a perfect or even a fully satisfactory solution to America's healthcare system ills. Yet if every provision of the Affordable Health Care Act is effectuated, 95 percent of Americans will be insured. The Affordable Health Care Act offers numerous other benefits to millions of middle- and lower-class Americans, including providing the largest middle-class tax cut for healthcare in history, thus reducing premium costs for tens of millions of families and small business owners who had previously been unable to afford coverage. It also prohibits insurance companies from dropping coverage when people get sick and prohibits the practice of invoking restrictive annual or lifetime limits on care. And crucially, it prevents the denial of healthcare for preexisting conditions, a strategy often used — and reportedly widely abused — by the insurance industry to protect their profits.

Despite the much needed assistance that the Affordable Health Care Act of 2010 offered the vast majority of the 32 million Americans who lacked healthcare, as well as the potential benefits to the quality and possibly the longevity of American lives that the Act provides, politically conservative members of the U.S. Congress reacted to the Affordable Health Care Act with extraordinary animus. They again employed the old strategy that the American Liberty League and other conservative organizations employed against Franklin Roosevelt and the New Deal in the 1930s, labeling Obama's healthcare initiative as "socialist," "communist," "un-American," even likening it to Hitler's Nazism. This despite strong evidence that Obama proposed his healthcare initiative as the result of his deeply held conviction that every American should have access to adequate healthcare, a conviction based at least in part on his experience with his own mother's struggles to secure adequate medical care in her dying months.[63]

There certainly are aspects of the Affordable Health Care Act of 2010 that are open to honest disagreement and debate. Indeed, honest debate is essential to our system of government. But what was little heard in political conservatives' at times venomous oppositional rancor to the healthcare bill was neither concern for alleviating the people's suffering nor concern for trying to give every American at least an approximation of the level of care and quality of life chances that are enjoyed by the most privileged Americans or even by members of the Congress themselves. However one looks at it, in the final analysis, adherents of political conservatism again vociferously opposed a governmental measure that is desperately needed by Americans who are not rich, never seeming to consider the potential toll of their actions on human suffering or their biblical responsibility to care for their neighbors.

THE SELFISH SIDE OF ECONOMIC POLICY

It is a sad truth that our grand democratic experiment is despoiled by the existence of a privileged aristocratic American class. It is a sadder fact still that it is the goal of political conservatism to maintain that aristocracy. The existence of a de facto aristocracy in America that continues to retain its privilege and preeminence is reflected in the fact that many of the vast concentrations of family wealth, social influence, and class alliances in America remain intact even though they have no de jure status. Indeed, as we saw above, the potential for upward economic class mobility in

America, much less the chance to enter into the ranks of the rich, is no higher than in France and Britain. What makes this fact more incredible is that America's economy has grown faster than Europe's for the last two hundred years, yet for most of the last century, in good aristocratic style the richest and most privileged families in America have lost little of their social and economic preeminence, even as others have joined their ranks.

When year after year, generation after generation, the lion's share of America's prosperity ends up in the hands of a tiny percentage of the American people, that is an aristocracy. When the richest 1 percent of the American people owns more wealth than the entire bottom 95 percent combined, that is an aristocracy. When tax laws are passed so the wealth of the wealthy can be gifted to their descendants while giving back little or nothing in estate taxes to the very public infrastructure that enabled them to amass their wealth in the first instance and that in a myriad of ways continues to enable and undergird the growth of their fortunes, those whose wealth is protected by these specially crafted measures comprise an aristocracy.

Although the form and perquisites of the de facto American aristocratic class are not directly upheld by law, they are upheld in practice by every conservative policy that puts the interests of the rich before all others and treats the interests of our poorest citizens as a nuisance. Ironically, in its stranglehold over the nation's wealth and power, America's de facto aristocracy is little different from the British aristocracy that American revolutionaries fought to free our nation from.

America's class hierarchy has no legal standing and there is a degree of mobility in its upper reaches, albeit extremely small, yet in actuality that hierarchy is virtually as deeply entrenched as if it were imposed by law, at least in part because throughout this nation's history laws have been routinely manipulated to provide tax and regulatory loopholes that serve the interests of the nation's wealthiest citizens. A case in point is the easing of restrictions on corporate contributions to political campaigns in *Citizens United v. the Federal Election Commission* by the predominately politically conservative U.S. Supreme Court's 2010 ruling. This ruling promises to intensify class divisions in America by opening an even wider legal space for cronyism and collusion between upper-class corporate elites and elected officials. It also promises to make the electoral process even more captive to the control of corporations. The ruling will render candidates for electoral office more beholden to corporate largesse and thus more vulnerable to defeat when they oppose corporate donors' interests. As the result of this controversial decision by the nation's highest court, electoral offices of any significance in the United States will become virtually off limits to everyone except rich elites — who overwhelmingly support politically conservative economic policies — and those who embrace the interests and political philosophy of rich elites as their own. Bill Moyers, noted journalist and former policy advisor to President Lyndon B. Johnson, epitomized the significance of this ruling, declaring that with it, "the activist reactionary majority of the Supreme Court . . . has opened the floodgates for oligarchs and plutocrats to secretly buy our elections and consolidate their hold on the corporate elite." Moyers decried the huge new influx of money into the political process that will unquestionably be "the dagger directed at the heart of democracy."[64]

The contention of conservative economist Thomas Sowell is representative of conservative ripostes to this study's characterizations of conservative economic policies. Sowell argues that most inequalities of poverty and wealth are not the result of volitional acts or volitional causes such as intentional exploitation and underpayment of workers; nor does he accept that it is the result of policies, legislation, and judicial rulings that are intentionally crafted principally to benefit the rich. Instead, Sowell and similarly thinking political conservatives argue that the overwhelming causation of economic disparities in American society is systemic constraints, that is, the natural by-products of the systemic functioning of market economies.[65] He forcefully indicts non-conservative political thinkers for not taking into account the distinction between volitional causation of income and wealth inequalities and systemic causation of them, charging that these differences are "seldom considered by [liberal?] intellectuals when discussing economies. . . . Yet that distinction has been commonplace among economists for more than two centuries."[66]

What Sowell does not acknowledge (is his blind spot volitional or systemic?) is the great extent to which the wealth disparities in America *are* the intentional result of policies, practices, and laws purposefully crafted to ensure that result. What are we to make of major historical causes like the huge wealth concentrations that resulted from the *volitional* collusion of monopolies and trusts, from *volitional* exploitation of the free labor of enslaved human beings? What of *volitional* price-fixing? *Volitional* union-busting? *Volitional* underpayment of wages to women and people of color? *Volitional* exploitation of farm and migrant workers? Has Sowell or those who think as he does ever read *The Grapes of Wrath* or *The Jungle,* or even heard of the terrible economic abuses they describe? How can one possibly deny that the vast disparities between poverty and wealth that have resulted from economic abuses like these are the direct result of intentional, *volitional* choices made to *systematically value profits over people,* to enrich some by dispossessing others through outright theft of their labor and treasure, or by erecting barriers that deny them full economic freedom, mobility, and opportunity? Yet Sowell asks, "Who did the robber barons rob when they lowered their prices?"[67] apparently never considering the human toll their fortunes cost, the lives, limbs, and families their quest for riches destroyed, or even wondering why they are called "robber barons." Sowell's claim that the causes of America's economic class divide are "overwhelmingly" systemic can only be correct if one accepts that ownership of most of the wealth in America by a tiny fraction of its population is natural and intrinsic to our economic system and that the unconscionable abuses it allows — and sometimes causes — are somehow morally acceptable. But in biblical terms, at least, this is never acceptable.

In the final analysis, then, the emphasis of conservative economic principles is on what best serves the interests of the rich. Whether this is intentional or a matter of purely economic calculation does not matter. Intentional or not, what is clear is that conservative economic principles reflect no evidence of being influenced by biblical moral and ethical imperatives of responsibility for rank-and-file Americans, and certainly not for the disadvantaged and vulnerable. Even the most general observation of U.S. social and economic policies will bear this out. Despite repeated pronouncements of woes upon the upper-class elites by Jesus and the prophetic pronouncements against those who selfishly "join house to house [and] add field to field,"[68] there is nothing in political conservatism's economic philosophy that precludes some Americans from amassing extraordinary wealth while other Americans literally starve. Indeed, many of the acclaimed large fortunes in America, particularly those comprised of "old money," are in no way the result of equal access to the means of wealth formation that is prescribed by biblical ethics; nor can they be attributed to equitable distribution of rights and opportunities. But rather than question the legitimacy of these family fortunes and huge personal concentrations of wealth, the economic policies of political conservatives instead seek to protect them, if not valorize them.

The specific terminology of supply-side economics is no longer part of the rhetoric of political conservatives in the twenty-first century, yet a perusal of any day's news headlines attests that their core principles remain the same: cutting taxes and cutting governmental regulatory protections, both of which disproportionately benefit the rich. They have shown themselves willing to do so even if it puts the common good at risk. At the beginning of the second decade of the twenty-first century, political conservatives are championing the same interests and attacking the same vital policy bulwarks against their quest for unlimited control of America's wealth, much the same as did the wealthy political conservatives of the American Liberty League almost a century ago.

The ideological nature of supply-side economics and its current policy progeny are the same; they have the same genesis and the same continuing impetus to do exactly what Kirk identified as basic to the politically conservative social vision: maintain disparities of poverty and wealth wide enough to differentiate Americans into separate and distinct economic classes. Political conservatives fight tooth and nail against governmental regulations as a matter of course because regulations will make them accountable for their actions. All this makes it very difficult not to conclude, with John Kenneth Galbraith, that "the modern conservative is engaged in one of man's oldest exercises in moral philosophy: that is, the search for a moral justification for selfishness."

REJECTING THE BIBLICAL WHEAT
FOR THE CONSERVATIVE CHAFF

Any who proclaim Christian bona fides while simultaneously professing faith in the economic policies of political conservatism are doubly wrong. Their willingness to maintain a social order of vast disparities of poverty and wealth in America, no matter the basis for their reasoning, is ultimately anti-biblical *and* specifically anti-Christian Gospel. Too many Christians in particular profess to accept Jesus as their Lord and Savior, yet they reject — and in the case of conservative politicians often loudly deride — one of the most crucial dimensions of the salvation offered by his message: salvation from class oppression and exploitation, salvation from grotesque disparities of poverty and wealth, and salvation from the material, physical, and psycho-emotional legacies of systematic and systematically enforced poverty. They simply do not seem to realize, or selfishly do not care, that the economic aspects of their political philosophy cannot be reconciled with the egalitarian Gospel vision of Jesus. Thus while some might be fully sincere, ultimately they are sincerely mistaken.

Thomas Jefferson wrote in the Declaration of Independence, "We hold these truths to be self-evident, that all men are created equal, that they are endowed by their Creator with certain unalienable Rights, that among these are Life, Liberty, and the pursuit of Happiness."

I do not doubt that sincere proponents of political conservatism hold these words dear, as do all Americans of good will. Nevertheless, there is no question that the barriers of class that political conservatives deem to be necessary for a healthy nation stand in the way of all Americans pursuing their "self-evident" rights to the fullest. Moreover, to seek to retain these inequities of wealth and economic mobility when millions of American children go hungry every day is to literally spit upon the egalitarian teachings of the biblical prophets and the good news of Jesus. Maintenance of economic classes in American society, which by definition represent great differences in economic wealth, socio-economic mobility, and quality of life, is such an integral and foundational principle of political conservatism that to renounce gross disparities of poverty and wealth, to decry the abuse and exploitation of the poor by the rich is, in essence, to reject the very premises on which political conservatism is based. This is a hard truth, but it is a biblically based truth. One can reject it, but no one can reject it and legitimately consider oneself a person of true biblical faith.

HOW THE ECONOMIC PHILOSOPHY OF POLITICAL CONSERVATISM GARNERS THE SUPPORT OF THOSE IT EXPLOITS

Given all of this, there remains a looming question. The upward economic mobility of great numbers of Americans is limited or fully frustrated by the economic policies of political conservatism that consistently and inordinately skew toward the interests of the rich and impede upward

income mobility. Yet many of the most ardent supporters of these policies are the working poor of America who can barely make ends meet.
And a plurality of them, if not the majority of them, are self-identified
Christians. Still many of these poor and struggling Americans support
to the death the policies of economic conservatism that not only so
disproportionately work to the disadvantage of themselves and the life
chances of their children, but also thoroughly militate against basic tenets
of their Christianity.[69] This is especially evident in the rise of the Tea
Party phenomenon of 2010.[70] This brings us to our question: Why do
so many Americans support economic policies that both work against
their own interests and violate the tenets of their faith? This is a very
important and complex question that deserves a full and complex treatment.[71] Unfortunately, a full consideration of this question is beyond
the purview of this chapter. However, we can venture some preliminary
observations.

1. One reason average Americans support the economic philosophy
of political conservatism, even as its basic principles consistently militate
against their own interests, has to do with *hegemony, or strategic ideological domination of public political discourse*. Political conservatives have
used their vast resources to dominate political discourse in the United
States by presenting their ideas as the only acceptable "patriotic" norm for
all Americans, regardless of their particular social or economic circumstances. Conservative political organizations have spent untold millions
of dollars to disseminate their ideas at least since the founding of the
American Liberty League and the American Enterprise Alliance, those
early and extremely well-heeled organizations that were committed to
making political conservatism the dominant American political philosophy. The John M. Olin Foundation alone disbursed some $400 million
to conservative causes between 1973 and its disbanding in 2005. Bil-
lionaires like the brothers Nelson B. and William H. Hunt, and the
billionaire corporate scions Richard Mellon Scaife and Joseph Coors, have
funded influential think tanks like the Heritage Foundation, the Man-
hattan Institute, the Center for Strategic and International Studies, the
American Enterprise Institute, and the Hoover Institute; and they have
underwritten pamphlets and books that espouse conservative business
principles while usually demonizing opposing points of view. They have
also sponsored movies and political "documentaries" that serve the same

purpose. Political conservatives control the top-rated radio talk shows and have at their disposal the twenty-four-hour Fox cable "news" network — America's most watched, by the way — that is dedicated to propagating the goals and interests of political conservatism to everyday Americans, during every minute of every day of the year. (I've placed "news" in quotation marks because Fox's parent company, the News Corporation, publicly eschewed all pretense of being an objective, nonpartisan journalistic enterprise with its August 2010 $1 million campaign donation to the Republican Governors Association.) Wealthy political conservatives have sponsored legitimate academic works, like Friedrich von Hayek's *The Road to Serfdom*, but today routinely underwrite numerous journalistic hack jobs comprised of half-truths and outrageous claims disguised as serious scholarship.

An example of this outrageous pseudo-scholarship, Dinesh D'Souza's *The Roots of Obama's Rage*,[72] was released as I completed this book. Consistent with his bitterly racist, ironically titled *The End of Racism*,[73] which called African American culture "barbaric," in his newest project, D'Souza, a 1978 immigrant from India, with at best specious documentation, charges that under Barack Obama the United States is being ruled "according to the dreams of [Obama's father] a Luo tribesman of the 1950s," whom D'Souza calls a "philandering, inebriated African socialist, who raged against the world for denying him the realization of his anti-colonial ambitions."[74] The extent of the ludicrousness and maliciousness of D'Souza's "study" is seen in the observations of a more informed observer. After conducting an exhaustive study of Barack Obama's writings as both an undergraduate and graduate student that included close readings of every article published at the *Harvard Law Review* while Obama was at its helm, Harvard historian James T. Kloppenberg dismisses D'Souza's charges summarily: "Adams and Jefferson were the only anti-colonialists whom Obama has been affected by. He has a profound love of America."[75]

2. In moments of candor, conservative political strategists have admitted that the strategic goal of all these efforts is no less than full *ideological domination of America's politico-economic discourse*. William Baroody, who headed the American Enterprise Institute in the 1950s, while specifically speaking of the strategy to influence public opinion and public policy that his organization waged, nonetheless offered perhaps an inadvertent insight

into the strategy of contemporary conservative think tanks in general: "I make no bones about marketing. . . . We pay as much attention to the dissemination of the product as we do the content. . . . We hire ghost writers for scholars to produce op-ed articles that are sent to the one hundred and one cooperating newspapers — three pieces every two weeks."[76]

The American Enterprise Institute has by no means been alone in this venture. The 2000 edition of the Heritage Foundation's guide to conservative research organizations and lobbyists in Washington listed a full three hundred such organizations in the Washington, D.C., area alone.[77] As a group these politically conservative institutions are extremely well financed. A 2004 report by the National Committee for Responsive Philanthropy listed the 2001 aggregate assets of politically conservative foundation grant makers as being in excess of $7 billion, with some $250 million in grants distributed to conservative causes between 1999 and 2001.[78] As a result of the massive public relations efforts of these organizations to dominate public opinion, politically conservative organizations have successfully — and falsely — characterized their goal of maintaining and widening wealth-based class disparities as serving the best interests of those benefited least by it: America's rank-and-file.

3. Furthermore, because politically conservative philosophy is predicated on the conviction that by virtue of their ownership and control of the bulk of the nation's wealth the richest Americans have the right to decide this nation's economic policies, many conservative politicians have taken an ends-justifies-the-means approach to politics, revealing a willingness *to engage in deceit and intentional falsehoods to advance their interests.* Their amoral ends-focused approach has allowed them to discard core biblical virtues like *emet* (truthfulness) and *chesed* (kindness, civility).[79] Today this strategy can be seen daily in the public rhetoric of many politicians, pundits, and other adherents to political conservatism. One example of this widely employed strategy is the charge that was continually repeated by many political conservatives, including Senator Charles Grassley (R-IA) and ex-vice presidential candidate Sarah Palin, that the Affordable Health Care Act of 2010 contained "death panels" for senior citizens. Although both Grassley and Palin were fully aware that the Act contained no such provision, these and numerous other self-avowed political conservatives continued to repeat this false charge for months, while

omitting any mention of the crucial benefits that the Act offers Americans. In this way, political conservatives have successfully persuaded millions of citizens who would greatly benefit from the Affordable Health Care Act to publicly oppose it and, thus, to actually oppose their own material interests.

4. Conservative politicians have also successfully obscured the reality that their primary political concern is to protect the privileged status claims of America's economic elites by employing the old strategy used by the American Liberty League: *clothing themselves in the rhetoric of patriotism and the rule of law* by equating their vested interest in being able to "enrich themselves at the expense of their fellow men," as Franklin Roosevelt once put it,[80] *with the very concept of freedom itself.* Instead of candidly admitting the threat they felt the New Deal posed to their own control over America's economic wealth, the upper-class elites of Roosevelt's day claimed that the New Deal posed a threat to the principles upon which our government was formulated.[81] A case in point is J. Howard Pew, a co-founder of the Sun Oil Company and a founder of the Pew Charitable Trusts, who strenuously denied that his opposition to the New Deal had anything to do with economic considerations, claiming instead that his motivation was purely idealistic: "My attack on the New Deal has not been prompted by materialistic considerations, but rather as a desire to preserve in America an opportunity for coming generations."[82] It is not a coincidence, however, that Pew and other wealthy political conservatives and the "coming generations" of their own wealthy families stood to receive far, far greater financial benefits than the vast majority of Americans from the economic policies that they advocated in the name of freedom.

This remains a stock strategy in use by upper-class economic elites that is in clear evidence today. For instance, in September 2010 a subsidiary of energy giant Koch Industries, which is owned by the billionaire Koch brothers, contributed at least $1 million to Proposition 23, a November 2010 ballot initiative to suspend California's groundbreaking 2006 global warming law that is designed to significantly decrease greenhouse gas emissions by California industries. Koch Industries, whom the University of Massachusetts at Amherst's Political Economy Research Institute named one of the top ten air polluters in the United States, claims its opposition to Proposition 23 is not occasioned by the negative impact it is expected to have on Koch's profits, but rather is the result of, it claims, Koch's neighborly civic concern that the new measure might negatively impact California's dire unemployment picture. However, what Koch Industries fails to mention is that it stands to gain tens of millions of dollars if it is allowed to ignore the common good and continue to pollute California's atmosphere at its current rate. Indeed, the aforementioned 2004 National Committee for Responsive Philanthropy (NCRP) report reveals the Koch political funding efforts to be manifestly self-serving rather than altruistic or civic minded to any appreciable extent. The NCRP report concludes that Koch Industries contributes funding support only "on issues that impact the profit margin of Koch Industries."[83]

5. Another reason rank-and-file Americans have been seduced to support policies that serve the interests of the rich instead of their own interests is that politically conservative politicians and advocates have successfully *conflated the ethos of political conservatism with the moral conservatism of biblical morality,* thus rhetorically equating the goals and concerns of political conservatism to biblical values and moral merit. We saw this in Part I in the example of the 1930s conservative political organization Spiritual Mobilization, whose sole apparent purpose was to defend laissez-faire economic policies by developing and propagating theological justifications for capitalism, including use of the term "spiritual" in its self-identification.[84] We also saw this in the more successful efforts of the Rev. Jerry Falwell and his colleagues in the late 1970s and 1980s to further the economic policies of political conservatives by condemning regulatory market protections as "Communistic aggression." Yet markets that lack outside controls militate against the interests of rank-and-file Americans by allowing the rich to leverage their wealth without any built-in protections against fraudulent representations, exploitation of workers, or monopolistic, price-fixing practices. Falwell and right-wing religionists past and present have failed to admit that refusing to provide protections for those who are at the mercy of the market activities of the rich and powerful is at obvious variance with the biblical tradition. Whether it is their intention or not, these religious figures seriously mislead those whom they claim they are called to care for by equating biblical faith, with its calls for equitable distributions of wealth and protections and care for the poor and the vulnerable, with political conservatism and its vested interest in unprotected, deregulated markets that give the wealthy full rein to

enhance their wealth by engaging in whatever market actions they can get away with.

6. There is another factor in political conservatism's success in getting the non-rich to support policies that maintain the economic advantages of the wealthy: *exploitation of basic human want and aspiration*. The myth has long been purveyed that unfettered markets and deregulation offer everyone the opportunity to become rich. Many Americans have identified with the class whose perquisites and power they themselves would like to possess. Thus although market controls offer protections against abuse and exploitation, more significant for those with dreams of becoming rich is the possibility that market regulations will also close off opportunities for them to enter the ranks of the wealthy. In this way the ephemeral hopes of those on the lower economic rungs of society that they may someday join the ranks of the wealthy have too often resulted in their active support of policies that perpetuate the same disparities of poverty and wealth that ultimately stymie their chances of true upward mobility.

7. Yet another reason that average Americans support conservative economic policies even to their own detriment is the prevalence of the American myth of heroic individualism.[85] This enduring social myth is a vestige of the social history of the pioneers who settled the American West by virtue of their own individual grit and mettle. This myth holds as its central value the belief that all people must make their own way in the world based on their own merits or inner resources. This means that what each person does or does not accomplish solely depends on his or her individual efforts. With regard to material wealth, this means that whatever wealth anyone gets out of life, no matter how much or how little, is exactly the measure they have earned. Thus the rich deserve to be rich; the poor deserve to be poor.

It is true that those pioneers exhibited extraordinary courage and self-dependence, but it is *not* true that all they had to depend on was their own individual initiative and resolve. The notion of heroic individualism is a *myth* because it ignores the substantial assistance those pioneer settlers received and relied upon from the U.S. Army, the U.S. postal service, from neighborly assistance and interdependence, even from the U.S. government–sponsored trailblazing of the explorers Lewis and Clark. Accepting this historical myth as reality distorts our view of actual economic life and choices today.

Concomitant with this myth is the view that responsibility for each individual's experience of poverty or wealth rests solely on individual strengths or weaknesses. This view is mythical as well because it ignores barriers to success that are completely out of the individual's control, such as unfair and illegal market practices on the part of others; structural obstacles to market entry, both purposeful and incidental; corporate collusion and monopolistic practices; the vagaries of nature and natural disasters; and arbitrary factors like simple luck and simple bad timing. Moreover, it ignores the supports and advantages granted by government — both legal and as the result of cronyism — that have enabled businesses and individuals to amass great wealth, such as limited liability and bankruptcy laws and the Supreme Court's aforementioned 1886 reinterpretation of the Fourteenth Amendment to grant "personhood" protections to the actions of corporations from states' efforts to curtail their activities that were most abusive of the common good.

Related to the American myth of heroic individualism is the concept of social Darwinism discussed in Part I, the meaning of which is best expressed by the British philosopher Herbert Spencer's maxim, "survival of the fittest." Social Darwinist thought holds that the strongest, the smartest, and the "fittest" will rise to the top in every life setting. According to this line of thinking, those who are rich deserve to be rich, in the sense that cream always rises to the top. Thus from this perspective possession of great wealth is a sign of individual merit and favor that makes it the just due of the fittest, while poor Americans are poor either because they have not worked hard enough to garner wealth, or because they are deficient, that is, unfit in some way.

Ultimately both the American myth of heroic individualism and the social Darwinist notion of "survival of the fittest" imply that those who are rich deserve to be rich, with the clear implication that those who are poor deserve to be poor. The effective result of the wide acceptance of these ways of explaining the causes and the reality of the grave disparities between poverty and wealthy in America is that both effectively exculpate those who exercise political and economic power from any responsibility to engage in fair play or to ensure a level economic playing field for all. Those who profess any sort of biblical faith should note that the implications of both the American myth of rugged individualism and the social Darwinist notion of "survival of the fittest" do grievous violence to the most basic of all biblical ethics: care for others, especially the poor and the needy, which is expressed in what Jesus likened to the greatest of all commandments: loving our neighbors as ourselves.

8. There is a further, in some ways a much more crucial reason rank-and-file Americans support the economic policies of political conservatives that favor the rich over their own interests, one that may well take on more significance in the current American political climate than all other reasons. It has to do with *the obfuscation of the very meaning of inequality itself.* To be sure, economic inequality is almost always treated as a simple, uni-dimensional concept or existential condition. In reality, however, from a policy perspective economic inequality can be understood as having two major dimensions: "market inequality" and "post-government" inequality.[86]

Extreme disparities of income and wealth are said to be the result of natural forces, according to the economic philosophy of political conservatism. However, these disparities do not just appear out of nowhere; they occur primarily as the result of market inequality. As the sites of remuneration, markets of exchange — including payment of wages and salaries in the employment marketplace — are where equal and just compensation is awarded. However, these markets are also the sites in which occur exploitation, fraud, underpayment, patently unfair wage schemes, rapacious policies that enrich a few, and outright theft. Therefore, market inequality by its very nature is a refutation of the myth that regulatory protection-free, laissez-faire markets are inherently fair and just to all. That is why the economic policy rhetoric of political conservatives ignores the reality of market inequality and instead obsessively — and exclusively — blames "post-governmental" inequality for the egregious poverty and wealth chasm in America.

The concept of post-government inequality essentially says that the true cause of the severe wealth disparities in America is not the inequality that occurs as the result of excesses, exploitation, or dishonesty in markets of exchange. The rhetoric of political conservatives completely ignores these realities. Instead, they contend that the poverty and day-to-day economic struggles of Americans is the result of governmental "seizures" of people's income and wealth by means of federal taxation, which is then "transferred to" or used to benefit, the undeserving, be they faceless "spend-crazy" government bureaucrats or caricatures of shiftless, undeserving poor people, epitomized by Ronald Reagan's mythical "welfare queens." The grievously misleading nature of charges of post-government inequality is summarized by the well-worn but equally misleading slogan, "the people make while the government takes." What is left out of this misleading equation is that if markets are to function in an orderly and economically beneficial fashion, the government must be there to provide crucial supporting actions and mechanisms to facilitate and ensure their effective functioning. These include measures that enforce legitimate contracts, enforce and define the rights and obligations of both corporations and consumers, determine who has standing to bring legal actions, to define and adjudicate what constitutes an unacceptable conflict of interest, etc.

Moreover, with regard to political conservatism's "the people make and the government takes" mantra, it disingenuously ignores that it is the levying of taxes that enables the government to carry out these important responsibilities that keep the markets functioning.[87] Rather than acknowledging the constructive purpose and intentionality of taxes, many conservative politicians today loudly decry government taxation as if it constitutes a sort of theft, despite the clear mandate given to the Congress to "collect Taxes, Duties, Imposts and Excises" by Article 1, section 8 of the U.S. Constitution. In this way political conservatives in recent years have successfully deflected the people's attention from the market inequality that is the major cause of their economic struggles by constantly railing about inequality that they claim is induced by "oppressive," "unfair," and even "unconstitutional" post-government taxation.

9. These strategies have realized great success in gaining ordinary Americans' support of economic policies that harm their own interests. Yet historically one of their most oft employed — and possibly the most successful — of the strategies of political conservatives for getting Americans to focus on the bugaboo of "post-governmental" inequality has been *to appeal to racial antipathies.* The political rhetoric of President Ronald Reagan is a prime example of this ugly strategy. Indeed, Reagan was probably its most successful practitioner. To be sure, he railed against "big" and "intrusive" government like other conservative politicians who successfully used appeals to post-government causes of inequality to their own advantage. But Reagan also focused on another purported cause of economic inequality in the United States that is consistent with the post-government inequality discursive strategy: demonization of the use of tax revenues for

social safety net programs, specifically "welfare," shorthand for the Aid to Families with Dependent Children Program (AFDC), which gave small amounts of direct financial support to families in need.[88] The program had long weathered criticisms not only of its bureaucratic administration, but also of its basic purposes. Surely some of these criticisms were warranted; some, on the other hand, were just the residue of a philosophical clash with the abiding American myth of rugged individualism and the sink-or-swim sensibilities of social Darwinism. But it was Reagan who upped the ante by conflating race and welfare policy into a major cause of economic inequality in America.

The typical welfare recipient during Reagan's presidency, as is the case today, was a white single mother. Yet Reagan used coded terms like "young bucks" and inner-city "welfare queens" to give the impression to struggling white America that the cause of their economic problems was that the U.S. government was giving their tax dollars to those who, despite the historical reality of their being some of the hardest workers in the nation, had long endured being called shiftless and lazy: those being America's "Negroes," in the parlance of Reagan's day. The particular focus of Reagan's racial animus was black welfare recipients. Knowing it would inflame outrage, Reagan fabricated a "welfare queen" with eighty aliases, thirty addresses, twelve Social Security cards, and a $150,000 tax-free annual income from government coffers. As Reagan knew it would, his malicious fabrication resulted in fever-pitched outrage on the part of white workers, whom his knowing falsehoods easily convinced that the cause of their economic distress was AFDC disbursements to unworthy "others," not the supply-side/trickle-down ideology of Reagan and his cohorts. In this way Ronald Reagan used malicious appeals to racialized anger to keep vast swaths of white Americans resentfully focused on post-government inequality while, in actuality, it was his "trickle-down" policies that so bedeviled their lives with immensely heightened market inequality. As we saw above, under Reagan economic inequality grew at a frightening rate, yet his appeals to racial antipathy greatly deflected the popular gaze from the havoc his economic policies were wreaking on the vast majority of Americans.

This same strategy of obfuscating the realities of market inequality, the greatest cause of the grave and growing economic inequality in America by far, with emotional, even demagogic appeals to racially tinged post-governmental causes of inequality has reared its head again in its attacks on President Barack Obama. Several billionaire businesspersons, including the aforementioned David and Charles Koch, scions of the billion-dollar Koch Industries founded by their father, Fred, an ultra-conservative businessman, are among those who have made substantial financial contributions to the angry, loosely aligned Tea Party political movement.[89]

Like the American Liberty League and its ideological descendents, the Tea Party's rhetoric espouses "freedom," which it identifies with laissez-faire policies and which it defines, at least in part, as a drastic reduction in the size of the federal government; reduction in the size of the national debt; deregulation of financial markets; and the dismantling or privatizing of most programmatic elements of the welfare state, including Social Security. But concomitant with these concerns seems to be an indeterminate yet significant degree of racial resentment of Barack Obama, the first American president of African diasporic descent. That is not to say that the Tea Party is by definition a racist movement; there seems to be no overt racial references in its official public rhetoric or in its publicly accessible literature, with the exception of the blogs of the extreme white supremacist groups that the main Tea Party groups publicly disavow. And Mark Williams, former chairman of the Tea Party Express, was expelled from that organization for making patently racist public statements.[90] Yet the high degree of anger and venom that is directed at Obama by the various Tea Party factions, much of it *ad hominem,* cannot be overlooked. Indeed, it is quite curious that America never saw such vicious displays of anger during the Bush administration, whose economic policies virtually destroyed the American economy and really did put the financial future of the average American in doubt: Bush's policies consumed both the $1.9 billion budget surplus of fiscal 1999 and the $86.4 billion surplus in fiscal 2000 bequeathed to it by the Clinton administration, exploded the national debt to record levels, and brought this nation to the very brink of a financial collapse that rivaled the Great Depression in intensity. Yet neither the duplicitous Bush nor his destructive policies elicited anything even approaching the vitriol heaped upon Obama.

In his review of several recent books about the Tea Party, historian Alan Brinkley observes the Party's complex racial dynamics. He acknowledges that the members of the Tea Party interviewed by the books' authors "rarely expressed bigotry, prejudice, or racism." Yet paradoxically, "many self-identified Tea Partiers . . . detest immigration and fear the prospect of an America in which white people will be a minority." He continues, "Older white men, who seem to constitute the majority of the move- ment, often rally around the cry 'Take Back Our Country.'" He concludes, "There is little doubt as to whom they wish to take the country back from."[91]

In an article reprised in the *Religious Consultation,* an international scholarly journal, Carlos Dew, a white American scholar living in Europe, writes of his chagrin when, while visiting his east Texas hometown, he hears the Obama administration referred to as "the nigger show." His observations are worth quoting at length:

> The veiled racism I sense in the United States today is couched, in public discourse at least, in terms that allow for plausible denia- bility of racist intent. And those who resist any policy initiative from the Obama administration engage in a scorched-earth policy that reminds me of the self-centered white flight, the abandonment of public schools, and the proliferation of private schools, that followed the 1954 *Brown v. Board of Education* decision to desegregate public schools.[92]

Dew further explains that "racists in the United States have learned one valuable lesson since the 1960s: They cannot express their racism directly. In public, they must veil their racial hatred behind policy differences."[93]

Even if Dew and others who see strong racist undertones in the Tea Party's rhetoric are correct, it must be acknowledged that the Party's loud- est *public* complaints are lodged against the high levels of governmental debt and what it considers undue taxation, which for the Tea Party are the real causes of the nation's economic distress and the worsening plight of America's workers, who face a high and possibly rising employment rate coupled with shrinking buying power. Yet the widespread slogan directed at Obama — "Take Back Our Country" — began almost immediately after Obama's inauguration, before he'd had the opportunity to accomplish anything of significance except implementing the TARP (Troubled Asset Relief Program) economic stimulus package — which was passed during the George W. Bush administration. And the policies that the Tea Party so forcefully opposes and seeks to defeat — such as the Health Care Act and Obama's abandoned plan to allow the lapse of the George Bush era tax reduction for family income in excess of $250,000 — actually stand to benefit average Americans in significant and multiple ways, such as, in the case of the tax cut lapse, adding billions of dollars to government coffers that could be used to fund crucial governmental initiatives that serve the common good, such as reduction of the national debt, for one. Instead, the reality is that it is not rank-and-file Americans who stand to benefit from the defeat of these policies, but rich elites and major corporate interests.[94] As Carlos Dew observes, "The very people, like my own rural, working-class family back in east Texas, who stand to gain from the efforts of the Obama administration and the Democratic Congress are, because of their racism, willing to oppose policies that would benefit them the most. Their racism outweighs their self-interest."[95] In all of this, one sees, once again, the specter of disingenuous post-government notions of inequality again trumping the true interests of ordinary Americans.

Moreover, Tea Party supporters' strident calls for smaller government often outweigh their self-interests as well. Unfortunately, few of them have taken the time to consider the full consequences of their political stance. A case in point: when informed that because Social Security is the biggest of all government benefits a drastically federal reduced government could endanger both her Social Security and Medicare benefits, one Tea Party supporter responded, "I didn't look at it from the perspective of losing things that I need. I think I've changed my mind."[96]

It is the confluence and the exploitation of these and other social factors and systematic conscious strategies that has culminated in the majority of Americans supporting the economic principles of political conservatism, despite the fact that they are ultimately anathema to their own economic interests and are counter to the most basic ethics of their biblical faith. In this way the bait-and-switch strategy of political conservatives that keeps the resentments of the non-rich focused on everything but the actual causes of economic inequality continues to serve the stated goal of the economic philosophy of political conservatism: maintenance of the vast and still growing economic class disparities in America.

– 5 –

Do You Know the Jesus
That Martin Knew?

An MLK Birthday Sermon
(Luke 4:16–21)

The Spirit of the Lord is upon me, because he has anointed me to preach good news to the poor. He has sent me to proclaim release to the captives and recovering of sight to the blind, to set at liberty those who are oppressed, to proclaim the acceptable year of the Lord. (Luke 4:18–20)

Several years ago it was my practice to scan the Christian television networks — TBN and especially the Word Network — to see the latest thing preachers were up to in the name of Jesus. I don't watch those networks' offerings any more because I no longer can stomach all the drama and showmanship. But back then I was still able to tough it out. One morning I scanned the Word Network and saw that a certain black female preacher, who calls herself a prophetess, was preaching to an audience of thousands at a huge church conference in Atlanta. I listened for a moment, trying to get a handle on what she was saying. Then it hit me: she was preaching about *the importance of shouting!* I'm not kidding, and I'm not exaggerating. She said, "When you shout, it opens the windows of heaven! When you shout, God will satisfy all your needs!"

I thought, "I know she didn't say that. I must have misunderstood her." But then she looked over at her mother and said, "Mother, these people here must not *have* any problems. Because if somebody told me that all I had to do was shout, and God would take care of all my problems, I'd be shouting all over the place!" The crowd was in pandemonium. Folks were on their feet screaming and swooning and shouting to high heaven.

I sat before the TV stunned and outraged. This was a Christian preacher who claimed to be preaching about Jesus, but what did this have to do with Jesus? Could you imagine Jesus teaching his disciples *how to shout?* "You see, Peter, if you shout, the chief priests and the Pharisees will leave us alone." Or, "If you all shout, maybe the Romans won't crucify me." Or "Blessed are you who shout, for you will get everything you want."

Nowhere in the four Gospels does Jesus say anything that can even remotely be construed as "All you have to do is shout and God will answer all your prayers." Yet as surprised as I was by what I heard, I should not have been, for there are plenty of other things that Christians preach and teach and believe that have nothing to do with who Jesus was, what he taught, what he lived for, or what he died for.

One example of how Jesus' teachings have been distorted almost to the point of being unrecognizable is the so-called prosperity gospel. In effect, this blasphemous abuse of Jesus' words tells those who subscribe to it, "You don't have to care about changing the unjust economic pie in society so all of God's children can have life with abundance; you just focus on getting rich yourself."

But the prosperity gospel is only one example of the shameless distortions of Jesus' teachings being foisted upon unsuspecting believers as truth. There are so many doctrines and practices in churches today that have nothing to do with Jesus that it makes you wonder how anyone could ever teach these things, much less believe them. But, sad to say, the answer is clear: too many preachers and teachers in the church today really do not know Jesus. They have gotten so obsessed with Jesus as a personality, as an object of worship, that they seem no longer to have a clue of what he stood *for* or what he stood *against*. It doesn't matter why; whether it's because they don't know what Jesus told us to do, or they don't want to work up a sweat doing it (it is so much easier being a *pulpit entertainer*), or they are afraid they might lose a dollar if they tell hard truths — whatever the reason, it all ends up the same: from where I sit most preachers do not teach the real Jesus.

So who was this Jesus? When asking this question, it is important to keep in mind that we're not talking about his personality; we're not talking from the perspective of a Jesus personality cult, because Jesus exemplified the height of *im*personality. If anything is clear about him in the Gospels, it is that he was a *God-intoxicated man*. Yes, a God-intoxicated man who was so totally consumed by his commitment to God that he had transcended his own personality. That is why Jesus could say, "When you see the father, you see me." That's why in the Gospels Jesus says virtually nothing about the facts of his own life. That's why only two of the twenty-seven books of the New Testament show even the least interest in the details of Jesus' personal life.

So when we try to answer the question, "Who was Jesus?" we can't look to his personality; we must look at the world transformation project that we call his ministry; we must look to the things he taught and did and modeled.

So who was Jesus, and what did he stand for?

Thankfully, we don't have to look far for the answer. In today's sermonic text which Luke presents to us as the very first sermon of Jesus' ministry (Luke 4:16–21), Jesus himself tells us who he is, what God has anointed him to do, and, by extension, what we who claim to know Jesus must also do if we are to really follow him.

The scripture tells us that Jesus stood up in the worship service and announced boldly and without a hint of compromise: *"The spirit of the Lord is upon me because he has anointed me to proclaim good news to the poor."* He didn't say he was anointed to shout and dance and sing until he made himself and everybody else fall out. No, he said he was anointed to bring good news to the poor. And what is the good news to the poor? That he was declaring the beginning of a ministry and a movement sanctioned by God to dismantle the social, economic, and political structures that made people poor and kept them poor. He didn't come just to bring the charity of food pantries and clothing drives and dropping a few coins into outstretched hands, because charity was already here. Jesus came to bring basic structural change to the unjust modes of distribution of wealth and resources, power and authority that deviled the lives of the many who were desperate and needy.

Then he said, *"He has sent me to proclaim release to the captives,"* that is, those who were unjustly held in captivity, of which there were many in Roman jails and dungeons. Thus Jesus tells us by his own testimony that God sent him to stand against criminal justice systems that care little for justice, that incarcerate the poor for stealing a dollar's worth of bread while turning blind eyes to the rich who start wars solely to enrich their corporate buddies. He is anointed by the spirit, Jesus tells us, to stand against unjust systems that play God by legally executing their brothers and sisters, some of them innocent of every crime, all of them children of God.

Jesus also testifies that God has anointed him *"to proclaim restoration of sight to the blind."* That means not only to those physically blinded by disease and malnutrition and accidents of birth, but also to those blinded by political lies and social lies and religious lies, to those blinded to the evil being done to them by unjust principalities and powers and rulers and politicians in high legislative places, evil done much too often in the name of God. Blindness that would cause them to vote for and proclaim as righteous the political men and women who mislead the poor and vulnerable to oppose policies that are in their own interests — like healthcare for all Americans — yet support policy positions that violate the Gospel in the most basic of ways — like tax policies that favor the rich over the poor.

Then Jesus announced that he was anointed *"to liberate those who are oppressed."* He told everyone assembled to make no mistake about it, that his project was a liberation project. He wasn't talking about just saving souls, whatever that means. He was talking about freeing people who are oppressed, beaten down, crushed underfoot by unjust laws and devious practices because of their ethnicity, or because they are poor, or because of their accents, or their religions, or because they are women, or because they happen to love someone of the same gender. But what he meant by liberation could not have stopped there. He must also have been talking about bringing to heel governments that treat other nations as their dumping grounds and playgrounds, governments that invade other nations in the name of "freedom" just because they can.

And he ends with *"He has sent me to proclaim the acceptable year of the Lord,"* which is almost universally understood by biblical scholars to refer to the year of Jubilee in which all those in bondage are to be freed, all crushing financial debts are to be forgiven, and all lands are to be returned to their rightful family and clan owners. In other words, Jesus announces that he was sent to bring social and economic relations back into a just and fair and loving balance.

When you put it all together, Jesus' inaugural sermon has the ring of a revolutionary manifesto. And that is just as it should be, because that's who Jesus was: a freedom-fighter, a political radical, and the harbinger of a revolution of love who announced to the world that he was anointed by God to change the world, not just spiritually, but economically and politically too. In fact, Jesus' economic and political missions are the very foundation of his spiritual mission, because the only evidence of any-one's spiritual relationship with God is the quality of care and concern and treatment they give to God's other children, especially those who are different.

That is what Jesus said in his clearest spiritual directive: not only to love our Lord our God with all our hearts, minds, and strength, but also to love our neighbors as ourselves, to struggle to build the kind of world in which our neighbors' children can have the same good things in life that we desire for our own children. Love of God is vertical love and love of neighbors is horizontal. To have a cross you have to have both. And it is only at the point at which the vertical and the horizontal modes of love meet that true spirituality can be found. Shouting has nothing to do with it. Preachin' down the house has nothing to do with it. Singing folks into an emotional frenzy has nothing to do with it. True spirituality is our love for and connection to God and our personal thankfulness for our blessings as they are expressed in our love for and our service to God's other children. It doesn't matter if we like them. If we love God, we have to try to love our brothers and sisters no matter what skin they are in, love them in the sense of working for them to have what we want for ourselves. I don't care what this prophetess or that bishop or some preacher or evangelist tells you. By the testimony of the Gospel of Jesus, it is only the nexus of our love for our God and our demonstrated love for our neighbors that is true spirituality. Only *that* is true spirituality and nothing less.

When we put it all together we see that this is the mandate that God gave to Jesus and that Jesus gives to us: to love our neighbors by treating people's needs as holy, by treating everyone as worthy of all unselfish care and protection.

"Well, Doc," I hear you say, "we've been in church all our lives. If this is who the Gospels say Jesus is, why don't we know about it?"

If you don't know it is because some seventeen centuries ago Emperor Constantine of Rome turned the *faith movement* of Jesus into the *official religion* of the same Roman empire that had tortured and executed Jesus for standing against it. Since then those in power in the church and the political regimes with which the church aligned itself have defined Jesus as standing for the very things that he died opposing. Jesus told his disciples that he came *to* serve, not *to be* served. But those who supposedly are the disciples' successors — popes and priests and ministers and preachers — too often claim for themselves not a servant's *role,* but a privileged *status* with which they enrich themselves and which they claim gives them the right to expect, even demand the same privileged status and riches as the very religious establishment that opposed Jesus and hounded him to his death. That's why you see very few ministers today getting their shoes dirty or working up a sweat outside of church. And that's why you see very few ministers struggling to establish God's justice in the world: because if the people knew the true radicality of the Gospel, they wouldn't stand for the entertainment and hyper-emotionalism and performance orientation that today masquerades as the Gospel teachings of Jesus. So tragically, between the legacy of Constantine's imperial distortion of Jesus' message and ministers' widespread dereliction of duty to teach the full radicality of the Gospel, most folks who claim Jesus' name don't really know what he died for or, even more importantly, what he calls us to do.

But we are here today because one person who lived among us really did know Jesus. Not only did he read Jesus' inaugural sermon in Luke 4 like you and me, he understood it, and he took it as seriously as his own heartbeat. In many ways it became his guide. He gave up most of the comforts and everyday pleasures of normal family life and ultimately gave his life's blood, all because he heard the call of Jesus to treat the people's needs as holy.

When he was scarcely out of his teens, Martin Luther King declared, "I believe that standing up for the truth of God is the greatest thing in the world." At the end of his life he still had no interest in earthly accolades. "I just want to do God's will," he said.

And God's will for Martin Luther King, Jr., was to follow Jesus and struggle to bring good news to the poor, to the oppressed, to the dispossessed, the enslaved, the incarcerated, and the victims of every kind of blindness. That is why he stands among the foremost practitioners in modern history of the politics and political activism that Jesus modeled for us.

As great a preacher as he was, though, it was the way Martin Luther King *lived* as a follower of Jesus that is his greatest sermon. Some preach the Luke 4 passage, but Dr. Martin Luther King lived it. That is because

Martin Luther King, Jr., knew Jesus. He knew the Jesus who said, *"The Spirit of the Lord is upon me, because he has anointed me to preach good news to the poor,"* because that same spirit anointed Martin Luther King. He is best known as a civil rights leader, but he was much more than that. When he fought for equal rights, he wasn't concerned just with integrating the *social* order so blacks could sit next to whites at lunch counters. He was more concerned with integrating the *economic* order so all could eat of the fullest fruits of the tree of life. That is what brought him to Memphis on that fateful night: he was there to support poor black garbage haulers who were seeking a fair wage and humane working conditions.

Nor did Martin want equal voting rights just so black folks could participate in a civic ritual. He sought full voting rights because voters can sway governmental policies, and governmental policies go far in determining who will get jobs, who will get economic opportunities, who will get government and corporate contracts; voters can help determine who will get decent housing and protection from economic exploitation and rapacious corporate practices. Toward the end of his life King even critiqued capitalism itself, because capitalism values profits over people and making money over loving our neighbors, and that is condemned by the teachings of Jesus.

And King was the first major American figure to publicly oppose the tragic debacle called the Vietnam War, not only because the war itself was immoral, but also because it squandered resources that could be used to feed and clothe and shelter the many poor folks in this land of plenty. On the last day of his life he was planning the Poor People's Campaign to descend upon the seat of American power to force this nation and its leaders to change its policies and practices from bad news for poor folks, to the good news that the systems and policies and structures and arrangements that have made people poor and kept them poor will finally be transformed with the leaven of neighborly love and Godly justice.

Yes, it is clear that Martin Luther King knew Jesus — *the Jesus who said the Spirit of the Lord had sent him to proclaim release to the captives,* because that same spirit anointed Martin Luther King to stand against the criminalization of young black men and women while they are yet in the womb, to stand against ceremonial executions under the cloak of legality, and to stand against all penal laws and policies that disproportionately penalize the poor. That same spirit anointed King to use all his strength to dismantle the social and political structures that held people captive to belligerent ignorance and to spirit-crushing self-hatred. In the final analysis, it anointed him to dismantle all spiritual strongholds that militated against the love of God and the love of our neighbors.

Yes, Martin Luther King knew Jesus — *the Jesus who said the Spirit of the Lord anointed him to proclaim recovery of sight to the blind,* for that same spirit anointed Martin Luther King to labor day in and day out to remove the blinders of rank selfishness and unjust war and pernicious hatred masquerading as patriotism, even while his own government conspired against him, white racists hated him, many of his fellow ministers attacked him, and even more ignored him. Jesus had transcended the old commandment of an eye for an eye, so Martin said he would too, because anything less would leave all peoples blinded by anger, fear, and vengeance in their hearts, and that was neither "good news" nor love for their neighbor.

Martin Luther King did know Jesus — *the same Jesus who said that the Spirit of the Lord sent him to liberate those who are oppressed,* for the same spirit anointed Martin with the burning quest for the liberation of humanity that was the animating force of his entire adult walk in this world. In Martin's vocabulary, besides "God" and "Love," "Freedom" was the word he used most.

Freedom from segregation, freedom from enforced poverty, freedom from systematic ill-treatment by a government that is supposed to serve us, not crush us.

Freedom from nooses around necks, freedom from bullwhips and hoses, from snarling dogs and little girls bombed dead in churches.

Freedom from being called "boy" when you've long been a man, from being called "gal" and "auntie" when elsewhere you're addressed as "sister" and "mother of the church."

Freedom from second-class facilities and third-rate opportunities.

Freedom from hatred, from hard-heartedness, from every custom, law and policy that distorts the human personality and stands in the way of love. And not just love as a sentiment, but love as an action, the kind of love that Jesus spoke of, the love that must move us to struggle each and every day, each in our own way, to re-create the kind of world in which the children of our neighbors can have every good that we seek for our own.

Martin Luther King knew Jesus. And just as Jesus ended his sermon by proclaiming the acceptable year of the Lord, and by intoning the epoch-shattering declaration, "Today this scripture has been fulfilled in your hearing," so too Martin Luther King said in no uncertain terms that the only acceptable time to make good news a reality is now. No doubt you recall that in "A Letter from a Birmingham Jail," he rejected "the tranquilizing drug of gradualism," which tells us that our promised land is over yonder, while other folk have their freedom and their riches right here on earth. He even titled one of his books *Why We Can't Wait,* so everybody would know that when it comes to freedom, there can only be the present tense.

Through it all, through the beatings, the jailings, the stonings, the weeks at a time away from his loving family, the disappointments, the betrayals, through the assassination of his character straight through to the piercing of his flesh, Martin Luther King carried in his spirit the anointing of the Spirit of God and the call of Jesus to work until his dying breath to treat the people's needs as holy.

Yes, Martin Luther King knew Jesus. But do you know the Jesus that Martin knew?

Everywhere you go today you find people who are very quick to say, "I know Jesus for myself" or "Jesus Christ is my personal savior" or — this is my personal favorite — "I'm saved, sanctified, spirit-filled, and washed in the blood of Jesus."

Some of you today might be quick to offer the same testimonies, whether anyone asks you or not. But I say to you, without apology or compromise, that if you really know Jesus, the Jesus who said the Spirit of the Lord anointed him to bring good news to the poor and liberation to the oppressed, how can you say that that same Spirit and that same anointing says that all *you* have to do is go to church and shout? How can you say that you know Jesus for yourself, yet not lift one finger to make this a nation and a world in which justice rolls down like waters and righteousness like a mighty stream?

I tell you today that if you really know Jesus the way Martin Luther King knew Jesus, then your life will be moved by what Dr. King called "divine dissatisfaction" with the way things are in this world.

I tell you that if you really know Jesus you will stop saying, "We sure had church today!" when what you really mean is that you sure had fun.

I tell you that if you really know Jesus, you'll stop talking about "the *anointing*" to describe people or places or things that have nothing to do with the true spirituality and holiness of liberating the oppressed, but everything to do with an emotional response to overwrought songs and overperformed sermons.

I tell you that if you really know Jesus, then you will stop treating your pastor like some kind of prince or chief priest of the Temple and start evaluating his performance as a shepherd, because if he is truly anointed, he is anointed to serve, not to be served. Martin Luther King never strutted around like a peacock, acting like it's all about him. He never got rich off of the people he was called to serve.

I tell you this, too — listen to me — that if you really know Jesus, you will stop building a personality cult around him that he never asked for, and instead, start doing what he said! After all, he said, "Follow me," not "Praise me."

Well, it's time for me to take my seat now, I know it is, but I am moved by the spirit of Martin Luther King today to tell you one thing more: my own testimony.

I've made many mistakes in my life. I've not always been what I should have been or could have been. I've hurt folks and I've let folks down, and I've spent long and tearful hours lamenting my failings and bemoaning my bad deeds. But now I do declare that I'm not looking back any longer. I'm through regretting the past, because I've made up my mind to do my best to *follow* Jesus. I don't mean praising him or worshiping him, because that he never told us to do. And I'm not talking about spouting the stereotyped, self-justifying slogans and rote responses that pass for holiness in too many of our churches.

What I *am* talking about is struggling today, in this time, in this nation, in this world to follow the teachings of a man sent from God who gave his life teaching and modeling how we are to change the bad news of our world to the good news that we should embody. That means that everyday I'm going to try to be open to the true anointing of God's spirit. Not the fake "anointing" that's hollered and shouted and tossed around like a plaything. I'm talking about the true anointing of the Spirit of the God that calls me to do my best to bring good news to the poor, release to the captives, sight to the blind, and liberation to the oppressed. I declare in the sight of God and every watching witness, that it is not my intention to just be a bearer of his name; it is my hope and my intention to strive with all of my striving to follow his revolutionary path to liberate *this* world, *on earth* as in heaven.

From this day forward, every day when I open my eyes I want to say, "Spirit of the Divine, help me to treat the people's needs as holy.

"Help me to stand fast and to wax faithful, so my children and my grandchildren might have better lives, so every baby has enough to eat, so every child receives enough education to find a rightful place in the world, so every working man and woman can earn a living wage, so every old person can end their days with honor and security from danger and material want. Guide me, and guide us all, to struggle to change this world into God's kingdom of justice as Jesus said we should, so one day, one great getting up morning, all God's children will look around and see that every stronghold, every principality, every unjust structure, and every evil power that ever stood against God's love and God's liberation will be brought low and made plane, so on that day, every man, every woman, and every child, can laugh at the chains that once bound them and will know in every part of their being that the time has finally come to really shout. And on that day their shout will be, 'Free at last, free at last, thank God almighty, we're free at last!'"

– 6 –

A Manifesto
Practicing the Politics of Jesus

THE PRINCIPLES OF JESUS' POLITICS

Today's political landscape is rife with politicians proudly — and loudly — identifying themselves as Christians. Some of these imply — indeed, some even claim — that their political positions are inspired, if not fully guided, by the teachings of Jesus. Yet we have seen that the politics of Jesus are very different from the partisan politics of politicians. Partisan politics are characterized by self-serving deals, unethical compromises, and a thinly veiled selfishness in which all seem to seek only after the good of themselves and those they count as their own, while giving little thought to the well-being of others except as it benefits their personal agendas. Rather than "Love your neighbor as yourself," the mantra of today's political culture seems to be "Love yourself and those who are like you." And "*God's* will be done" has been replaced by "*Our* will be done," with the accompanying claim that our will is God's. Unfortunately, the politics of most politicians "of faith" have proven to be cut from that same cloth. However, the politics of Jesus have little to do with what one calls oneself or the faith one confesses. Jesus' politics is based upon principles, not slogans or self-serving rules. Principles are directions or guides as to how we should live our lives and conduct our affairs. The principles of Jesus' politics are rooted in the most foundational ethics of the Hebrew Bible, especially those that we shall revisit below. The first is *mishpat*, "justice," the establishment or restoration of fair, equitable, and harmonious relationships in society. In its purest form this ethic holds that everyone has the same inalienable right as anyone else to life, liberty, and the pursuit

---

This chapter is excerpted by permission from Obery M. Hendricks, Jr., *The Politics of Jesus: Rediscovering the True Revolutionary Nature of Jesus' Teachings and How They Have Been Corrupted* (Doubleday, 2006).

of happiness and wholeness; the same right of freedom from exploitation and oppression and every form of victimization. *Mishpat* also means "judgment" in the sense of setting in balance — that is, resolving — conflicts in a just and equitable fashion with the full rights of all in mind, be they social, economic, political, or religious.

Then there is *sadiqah,* "righteousness," behavior that faithfully fulfills the responsibilities of relationship, both with God and with humanity. Or to put it another way, *sadiqah*/righteousness is the loving and just fulfillment of our responsibilities to others as the ultimate fulfillment of our responsibility to God.

A third foundational ethic of Jesus' politics is *hesed,* "steadfast love," which underlies his rearticulation of Deuteronomy 6:5 and Leviticus 19:18 in his seminal pronouncement of Matthew 22:37–40: "You shall love your lord your God with all your heart, and with all your soul, and with all your mind.... And ... [y]ou shall love your neighbor as yourself." Jesus considered these to be the greatest of all God's commandments and the epitome of "all the law and the prophets." *Hesed, mishpat,* and *sadiqah* are all implied and reflected in these commandments. These are the base ethics of the politics of Jesus. However, they can be encapsulated in this one animating principle: Treat the people and their needs as holy.

POLITICS AND BIBLICAL LEGALISM

One cannot find specific guidance in the Bible for every detail of social and political life. Moreover, when rules and laws are found that appear to speak to particular situations, the myriad cultural changes and adaptations that have occurred over millennia make it unwise to apply specific biblical mandates uncritically to the complexities of life today. That is where principles come in: they can give guidance and perspective where appropriately applicable instructions are lacking.

The weakness of principles, however, is that it is not always clear how they should be applied in practice. And then there is always the danger of their being reduced to narrow laws that can ultimately contradict the very principles they claim to embody. It is for the very reason that principles are not hard-and-fast laws specifying how and when they should be applied that one must approach them with humility, with sincerity, and, for the followers of Jesus and all people of goodwill, also with love. In contrast, a legalistic attitude that reduces principles to inflexible laws requires no humility, sincerity, love, or even mercy. It requires only a spirit of compulsion. Jesus' reply to the Pharisees' contention that his disciples should go hungry rather than pick a few kernels of wheat on the Sabbath made it clear that this kind of inflexible legalism is misguided. "The Sabbath was made for humanity," he said, and not the other way around. In other words, Jesus' view is that laws are to serve us, not oppress us. That is why in our practice we must always stress the foundational principles of Jesus' politics — justice, righteousness, and steadfast love. Any laws that are not based on these principles are inconsistent with the politics of Jesus. Still, in recent years we have seen such reductionistic legalism employed by a number of fundamentalist Christians, with frightening results.

One example is theologian Kenneth L. Gentry's articulation of what he calls "elements of a theonomic approach to civic order."[1] "Theonomy," which means "God's law," is the belief that every nonceremonial Old Testament law must be obeyed by all of humanity. Whether one agrees with them or not, some of Gentry's theonomic biblical interpretations appear to be reasonably mainstream, such as requiring a moral yardstick for electing public officials, punishing "malicious" lawsuits, and forbidding industrial pollution. Others seem to owe more to capitalism than to Christ, like Gentry's concern to specifically protect the rich from too much taxation. Still others can only be called drastic, such as abolishing prison systems in favor of a system of "just restitution" for noncapital crimes, and mandatory execution for everyone convicted of capital crimes. Women who have abortions or commit adultery or lie about their virginity, blasphemers, children who strike their parents, gay men, and witches are included in Gentry's category of those eligible for capital punishment.[2]

Gary North is an economist who is well known in fundamentalist circles for his extensive efforts to reconcile economic theory with Old Testament passages. This excerpt from his explanation of wealth and poverty as divine reward and punishment is, in effect, also an exposition of "just restitution": "[T]he poor man who steals is eventually caught and sold into bondage under a successful person. His victim receives payment; he receives training; his buyer receives a stream of labor services. If the servant is successful and buys his way out of bondage, he re-enters society as a disciplined man, and presumably a self-disciplined man. He begins to accumulate wealth."[3]

Neither Gentry nor North seems to have any sense of the human suffering such biblical interpretations could cause or the potential of such interpretations to foster real injustice. Gentry simply disregards Jesus' admonitions against those who hoard their own riches while the masses of God's children live in poverty. Worse, he outright ignores the rapidly mounting evidence that numerous innocent Americans have been condemned and executed for crimes they did not commit. And his judgment of abortion as a capital crime is on less-than-firm biblical footing.

For his part, North leaves completely unaddressed the question of what happens to the "servant" if he is not "successful," whatever that means. Nor does he seem to mind that his notion of divine "just restitution" reinstitutes the dastardly practice of state-sanctioned enslavement of human beings, despite the fact that the Jesus North confesses as his personal savior would undoubtedly find such a notion abhorrent and sinful. That is why legalistic interpretations of biblical meaning ultimately must be rejected: because they leave no room for the love, mercy, justice, and grace that undergird the Gospel at every turn. This Jesus pointedly affirmed in Matthew 23:23: "Woe to you, scribes and Pharisees, hypocrites! For you tithe mint, dill, and cummin, and have neglected the weightier matters of the law: justice and mercy and faith. It is these you ought to have practiced without neglecting the others."

The Yardstick of Justice

Rather than taking a literalistic or legalistic approach, the politics of Jesus calls for scrutinizing every political policy and policy proposal by this standard: Is it based upon the command to "love your neighbor as yourself"? That is, does it treat the people and their needs as holy? It is important that this principle not be treated as a law with layers of liturgical and organizational requirements. Rather, it is to be seen as a yardstick that at every point seeks to apply *mishpat*/justice, *sadiqah*/righteousness, and *hesed*/steadfast, continually demonstrated love for our neighbors to every public and private act of consequence. This is the way the politics of Jesus enjoins us to approach every question of politics and social policy.

The definition of "people" is crucial. As it is used here, "people" does not refer to any particular grouping; it means people in general. In the politics of Jesus there can be no seeking advantage for any one group over another, regardless of gender, race, class, creed, or religion. As the biblical witness points out, "there is no perversion of justice with the Lord our God, or partiality" (2 Chronicles 19:7). Jesus himself asks, "[I]f you love those who love you, what rewards do you have?" (Matt. 5:46). Indeed, each of the four Gospels tells us that Jesus ministered to the rich, the poor, women, men, the old, the young, Jew, pagan, the powerful, the powerless. But not only that. He also ministered to those considered to be enemies of the Jews, including Samaritans and Romans. In other words, this devout son of Israel refused to let his love and sense of responsibility to all of humanity be circumscribed by religious chauvinism or by a sense of national loyalty, what we today proudly call "patriotism."

PATRIOTISM AND
THE POLITICS OF JESUS

It is important to discuss patriotism when considering the politics of Jesus because in the strange calculus of American political culture patriotism has come to be virtually equated with Christianity. Love of country is extolled in the same breath as love of God.

That is how patriotism is usually defined: as love of one's country. But patriotism can be destructive as well as constructive. *Constructive* American patriotism, or what James Forbes, the former pastor of the historic Riverside Church in New York City, calls "prophetic patriotism," is the willingness to strive to ensure that this nation is healthy, whole, and secure and is conducting its affairs at home and abroad according to the political doctrines we claim to hold dear. But negative or *destructive* patriotism is more focused on discrediting or destroying those it perceives as opponents of America. In other words, its purview is "us" against "them," "them" being not only foreigners, but also any American who openly disagrees with the official actions of the political leaders of the United States, no matter if the policies espoused by those leaders contradict the politics of Jesus.

Yet good-faith criticism of government policies and practices is squarely in the tradition of the biblical prophets. It is also an underlying component of constructive patriotism. In this sense it is an important principle of the politics of Jesus. It is concerned with political affairs, but it is also concerned with the spiritual and moral health of America. In that it seeks to help the nation become its best and most righteous self, ongoing constructive prophetic oversight of the righteousness of America's deeds is the highest and healthiest form of patriotism. Thus a true patriot will welcome well-intentioned prophetic critiques of the United States government because they will make America more righteous and just. The true patriot will also reject uncritical abdications of our prophetic responsibility, as expressed in such slogans as "America — love it or leave it." Yet in today's political climate, those who engage in prophetic critique to help America be all that it can and should be — at home and abroad — too often are demonized, discredited, and subjected to scurrilous attacks on their character. Their livelihoods are threatened, their integrity is impugned, even their relationship with God is questioned and belittled.

To the degree that patriotism causes division and enmity between any of God's children, it is in opposition to the Gospel. But it is when patriotism seeks to silence prophetic criticism that patriotism becomes more than oppositional; for it is then that it has made an idol of its own beliefs and judgments, no matter how narrow or misguided or unbiblical they might be. Moreover, this blind patriotism is destructive because it values the welfare and even the humanity of some of God's children — that is, Americans, and not all of those, either — over the welfare and humanity of others, particularly those who look and speak and worship differently. Rather than engage in blind patriotism, followers of Jesus should keep in mind the question he posed in the Sermon on the Mount: "Why do you see the speck in your neighbor's eye, but do not notice the log in your own eye? . . . [F]irst take the log out of your own eye, and then you will see clearly to take the speck out of your neighbor's eye" (Matt. 7:3, 5).

Edith Cavell, a British nurse in World War I, was martyred by the Germans for helping Allied solders to escape to neutral Holland. Yet even in the face of those who declared themselves the enemy of all that she held dear, this devout Christian remembered to keep patriotism in Gospel perspective. "Patriotism is not enough," she declared. "I must have no hatred or enmity towards anybody."

In this way, patriotism that is truly guided by the Gospel will confess, like the apostle Peter, "I truly understand that God shows no partiality, but in every nation anyone who fears him and does what is right is acceptable to him" (Acts 10:34–35).

This must be the basis of our patriotism. Not hatred and enmity and the imperial will to exercise power over those who are different from us or who disagree with us. If we must have a patriotic slogan, it should not be some version of "America — love it or leave it." If we truly take seriously the Gospel of Jesus Christ, our patriotism must declare, "America, love your neighbor as yourself." Not only should we sing "God bless America" but, like the pure-hearted Tiny Tim in Charles Dickens's *A Christmas Carol,* we must lovingly pray, "God bless us, every one!" In the final analysis, this means that each day before we pledge allegiance to the flag and the republic for which it stands, we must first recommit our allegiance to the Gospel of Jesus and the justice of God and the love of neighbor it commands. We must remember that the flag doesn't supercede the cross. And if it is the Gospel that is truly the object of our faith and our allegiance, we must thank God for the faithful voices that, despite the derision and even the personal physical harm they risk, nonetheless speak out against every action, policy, and perspective of our leaders and our government that distances us from the politics of Jesus and the kingdom of God.

THE POLITICS OF JESUS AND THE KINGDOM OF GOD

In Luke 4:18–21 Jesus himself says that the good news to the poor and the liberation of the oppressed have been accomplished with the advent of his ministry: "Today this scripture has been fulfilled in your hearing." Yet, long after Jesus' crucifixion, hunger and poverty still persist in every corner of the world, and spirit-crushing oppression reigns over most of humanity. So how have Jesus' life, death, and Gospel teachings fulfilled his promise of economic, social, and political justice in our world?

A major feature of Mark's Gospel is its portrayal of Jesus as always *en te hodo,* "on the way," always moving from village to countryside to village and finally to city, spreading the good news of the kingdom of God to everyone he encountered. Jesus' movement was so incessant that one early-twentieth-century commentator concluded that Jesus suffered from a pathological need to wander! But Jesus' descriptions of the kingdom of God in both the parable of the sower and the parable of the mustard seed (see Mark 4:26–32) as kernels that are to be liberally strewn in every setting and at every opportunity offer a different explanation: Jesus' practice of sowing good news to the poor and oppressed in his every waking moment was an integral part of his strategy to establish God's kingdom of justice, a strategy brought to fruition by his courageous death and the power of his resurrection, both of which affirmed for all time the truth and transformative might of his message when it is rightly understood and practiced. In other words, Jesus' words and deeds set the kingdom in motion. Through his gospel ministry he sowed the seeds of God's kingdom of justice and peace and wholeness and love that we, his followers, must nurture. That was his mission, not to proclaim himself king or to bring immediate, short-term results. His charge was to implant the seeds of God's kingdom of liberation and to give his followers the spiritual food to nourish their growth. Jesus held to his principles without wavering, secure in his knowledge that bearing witness to truth and justice and love for God and neighbor was the only lasting way to establish God's kingdom on earth as in heaven.

Thus, Jesus' model for establishing his politics is for us to nurture his political principles. That means sowing the seeds and the deeds of justice that will grow into the kind of world Jesus seeks for us, not demonizing those who oppose us or forcing our own perspectives on them like we are modern-day Crusaders. Christianity that is truly based upon the teachings of Jesus is a fellowship of faith, and true faith can never be coerced, only lovingly tended. When the seeds of God's kingdom are nourished by deeds of love and justice, gradually they will take root. The deeper their roots, the stronger the stem or trunk, and the higher the plants will grow. The higher their growth, the wider their reach and the greater the fruit they will bear. If lovingly nurtured, they will pervade the fields into which they are introduced, offering peace and shelter to all who need them. This is the only way that the kingdom of God's justice will transform the governments of this world: through the sowing of seeds of truth, love, and mercy by consistent words and consistent deeds.

If Jesus' imagery of the kingdom of God as seeds being sown does not model this strategy clearly enough, he explained it another way, too. In Matthew 13:33 he proclaimed, "The kingdom of heaven is like yeast," which, when introduced in even small measure, can leaven the whole loaf. Or society. Or world.

Thus, if sown lovingly, courageously, and unstintingly, the seeds of God's justice and mercy can change this world to a world of peace and justice and love and righteousness. That clearly seems to have been Jesus' meaning when he proclaimed, "Come to me, all you that are weary and are carrying heavy burdens, and I will give you rest" (Matt. 11:28). R. H. Tawney, the noted British economic historian, educator, and devout Christian, put it this way: "Granted that the Kingdom of God is something more than a Christian social system, we can hardly take the view that it is something less."

FOLLOWERS OF JESUS OR SIMPLY BEARERS OF HIS NAME?

The First Letter of Peter declares, "[I]f any of you suffers as a Christian ... glorify God because you bear this name" (1 Pet. 4:16). Nowadays it seems that many Christians take to heart only the last part of the verse: they simply bear the name. But calling oneself a Christian and actually following Jesus' teachings are not necessarily the same. Consider this statement by a well-known politician:

> The national government will maintain and defend the foundations on which the power of our nation rests. It will offer strong protection to Christianity as the very basis of our collective morality. Today Christians stand at the head of our country. We want to fill our culture again with the Christian spirit. We want to burn out all the recent immoral developments in literature, in the theater, and in the press — in short, we want to burn out the poison of immorality which has entered into our whole life and culture as a result of liberal excess during recent years.[4]

This a clear example of a leader who calls himself a Christian and extols Christianity as the most important force in the nation, but who in actuality is anything but a follower of Jesus. How do we know? The speaker is Adolf Hitler.

Hitler's hypocrisy is sickening. What is frightening about his statement, however, is that it is virtually interchangeable with statements made by any number of self-avowed politicians "of faith" today. And because the statement uses the term "Christian," it would be embraced by many Americans without questioning the speaker's personal integrity or his real agenda, just as it was so easily accepted in Germany.

As followers of Jesus the Messiah we must make a distinction between "Christian" and "follower of Jesus." We must reconsider the faith claims of those in leadership positions. Not just on political grounds but, even more important, on biblical grounds. Christians and all people of goodwill must set aside religious and denominational loyalties, political partisanship, and personal affections to demand truthful and just actions from those leaders who so loudly trumpet Jesus' name. It is our duty. To continue to tolerate misrepresentations of the politics of Jesus is a sin.

When Jesus himself was confronted with the publicly pious leaders who shouted "Lord, Lord" while engaging in traditions and public practices that violated the justice of God, he paraphrased God's lament in Isaiah 29:13, saying, "'This people honors me with their lips, but their hearts are far from me; in vain do they worship me, teaching human precepts as doctrines.'" Then he pronounced his own judgment: "You abandon the commandment of God and hold to human tradition. . . . You have a fine way of rejecting the commandment of God in order to keep your tradition!" (Mark 7:6–9).

If we look honestly and unflinchingly at the political culture in America today, it becomes clear that Jesus' judgment against the religious and political leaders of his day (in reality, they were the same) is also his judgment against the leaders of our day. America's most vocal and self-described politicians "of faith" profess biblical beliefs while consistently acting in ways that contradict biblical justice. Worse, they portray themselves to the American masses as the definitive moral voice of America, the righteous, divinely ordained spokespersons for God to us all. Yet there is little question that if Jesus were walking among us now, he would stand against the political leaders of *our* day — and many of the religious leaders, too — as he stood against them in his own day.

When Jesus was asked, "What must we do to perform the works of God?" He answered, "This is the work of God, that you believe in him whom he has sent" (John 6:28–29). That means much more than simply shouting "Lord, Lord" and proudly bearing Christ's name. It means following him by humbly and sincerely discharging our responsibility to feed the poor, clothe the naked, protect the vulnerable, and dismantle all structures of oppression and exploitation.

The prophetic ministry of Jesus has shown us that to believe in him is to bear witness to the justice of God in every season. Even the evangelist Billy Graham has come to realize this in the unfolding dusk of his days. "If I had my time again," he has said, "I would be stronger on social injustices."

A MANIFESTO

It is in this spirit, the spirit of Jesus the revolutionary, that we who follow him must call upon the religious and political leaders of America to reclaim our biblical mandate to act justly in our nation and in the world.

We call upon our government officials and elected representatives to turn from the greed and imperial ambitions of Caesar to embrace Christ's call for us to care for those in need of care: the weakest, the neediest, those in the twilight of their days.

We call upon the politicians of America to stop the crony capitalism that enriches the few and impoverishes the many.

We call for provision for all Americans of adequate health care, a livable minimum wage, and access to an education that can prepare them to be fruitful in the marketplace and to contribute to the common good of all.

We call upon our political leaders to stop their cynical misuse of religion and "faith" to support exclusionary policies, exploitative policies, policies that deal in killing and death.

We call upon our leaders to serve the justice of God rather than grasping for political power.

We call upon all who claim to be politicians "of faith" to return integrity to America's political culture by embracing the same humility that moved the psalmist to pray, "Search me, O God, and know my heart;/test me and know my thoughts./See if there is any wicked way in me,/and lead me in the way everlasting" (Psalm 139:23–24).

We call upon all who bear the name of Christian to reclaim the holistic spirituality that Jesus taught, not the one-dimensional imitation practiced by many in the Church that frees us from the responsibility to make justice roll down like waters and righteousness like a mighty stream.

Finally, we call upon our politicians to end their ceaseless drive for power and to begin to sincerely serve the needs of those entrusted to their leadership. For the politics of Jesus seeks not possession of worldly power, but to serve the justice of God.

Jesus did not establish a bureaucratic institution, weekly social gatherings, or houses of religious entertainment. He started a movement that demands that rather than spend our time establishing ever more luxurious churches, we must strive to establish God's kingdom of love and justice on earth as in heaven. The Gospel he lived and died for summons us to treat all people and their needs as holy. This means instituting policies that fairly, equitably, and lovingly respond to the suffering and want of all people or, at the very least, of as much of humanity as possible. Yes, *lovingly,* because Jesus' entire Gospel is based on love. But note well that love as it is used here is not mere sentimentality; it is actively working to secure for one's neighbor what one wants for oneself. That is the difference between the politics of Jesus and the politics of politicians: Jesus' way acknowledges God as "our" Father, meaning that all are children of God, and thus the needs of all are holy. It is this standard that separates the politics of Jesus from the politics of politicians.

In the politics of Jesus, then, every policy and policy proposal must be judged by Jesus' yardstick of love and justice. We must ask: Do our social programs treat the people's needs as holy? Do our tax laws? Do our healthcare policies treat as holy all in need of coverage? Do our foreign policies treat all people as children of the same Creator? Or do we treat those outside our borders as children of a lesser god and, therefore, worthy of only inferior chances in life?

Treating the people and their needs as holy should be the perspective of everyone who purports to be a lover of God and humanity, but it must certainly be the perspective of every religious and political leader who claims to follow Jesus. In the politics of Jesus, there can be no "politicians" in the sense of "professional" politicians, whose dedication is to power and self-aggrandizement rather than to principles. There must only be servant leaders, just as the Son of Man came not to *be* served, but *to* serve.

The goal of Jesus' movement, ministry, and politics is a new creation: a political order that truly serves the good of all in equal measure. Those who strive to practice Jesus' politics must always keep that as the focus of our prayers and our compassion, of our love and our most faithful social action. It is not optional; it is required of every follower of Jesus. He declared as much in terms that left no doubt: "Whoever is not with me is against me" (Matt. 12:30). That is to say, if you do not work for, or in some real way support, the establishment of God's kingdom of love and justice, then your silence and inactivity ultimately serve the forces of injustice.

It will not be easy. It seems that every aspect of today's political culture militates against the Gospel's call for truth, honesty, and sincere service in the public square. But this is as Jesus foretold it: "I send you out as sheep in the midst of wolves; . . . you will be dragged before governors and kings for my sake, to bear testimony before them" (Matt. 10:16, 18 [RSV]). This means that in every political setting the true followers of Jesus will be called forth to speak truth to power and to find power in the truth. Even as many strut about proudly wearing their faith like crowns, the true followers of Jesus must hold dear his cross of self-sacrificial love.

All of this requires more than simply bearing his name. These things we must do if at the sunset of our lives we are to be counted among those who truly tried to love our neighbors as ourselves by living the politics of he who died so others might live: Jesus the Messiah, Jesus the lover of humanity, Jesus the political revolutionary.

Notes

Chapter 1:
"I Am the Holy Dope Dealer"

1. Quoted in Alan Light, "Say Amen, Somebody," *Vibe* (October 1997): 92. Franklin's statement is discussed on pp. 35–38 below.

2. Among them are Albert J. Raboteau, *Slave Religion* (Oxford: Oxford University Press, 1978), 56–74; Lawrence W. Levine, *Black Culture and Black Consciousness* (Oxford: Oxford University Press, 1977), 19–29; Wyatt Tee Walker, *Somebody's Calling My Name* (Valley Forge, Pa.: Judson, 1979), 15–36; and Jon Michael Spencer, "The Rhythms of Black Folks," *Ain't Gonna Lay My 'Ligion Down,* ed. Alonzo Johnson and Paul Jersild (Columbia: University of South Carolina Press, 1996), 39–51.

3. It is believed that "Steal Away to Jesus" was among the Spirituals used by Nat Turner to signal his compatriots for battle. See Arthur C. Jones, *Wade in the Water: The Wisdom of the Spirituals* (Maryknoll, N.Y.: Orbis Books, 1993), 44–45.

4. Fannie Lou Hamer was known for rousing her compatriots in the civil rights movement with her passionate, spontaneous eruptions into Spiritual song. See Kay Mills, *This Little Light of Mine: The Life of Fannie Lou Hamer* (New York: Dutton, 1993).

5. Cornel West, *The Cornel West Reader* (New York: Basic Civitas, 1999), 29, 31, reminds us that America is "a civilization that is shaped by 244 years of chattel slavery, enslavement of African people, and 81 years of Jim Crow.... White supremacy cuts through, saturates and permeates every institutional nook and cranny." The de facto system of color privilege that pervades America today is heir to the de jure white supremacy that endured in one form or another from the earliest beginnings of the American republic until the Civil Rights Bill of 1965. Reflective of this reality is the thinly veiled racism that has attended the presidency of the nation's first African American president. See Thomas J. Sugrue, *Not Even Past: Barack Obama and the Burden of Race* (Princeton, N.J.: Princeton University Press, 2010). W. E. B. DuBois offers an extremely insightful analysis of the psycho-social dynamics of white supremacy that remains instructive today. See "The Ways of White Folks," in *Darkwater: Voices From Within the Veil* (New York: Harcourt, Brace and Howe, 1920), 19–52. Also see Roy L. Brooks, *Racial Justice in the Age of Obama* (Princeton, N.J.: Princeton University Press, 2009).

6. As dramatically portrayed in the acclaimed 1989 major motion picture *Glory.*

7. The language of the Spirituals is patriarchal, as is that of the Gospel genre. In this sense both reflect the systematic patriarchy that has always been part of the American social order. Although I advocate inclusive language and recognize its necessity,

221

here I cite all lyrics using their original wordings for the sake of historical accuracy and authenticity.

8. See Abraham Joshua Heschel, *The Prophets* (Peabody, Mass.: Hendrickson, 2009; originally published in 1962).

9. For more about the origins of Spirituals see Robert Darden, *People Get Ready* (New York: Continuum, 2008), 70–72.

10. Ibid., 273–82.

11. Horace Boyer, "A Comparative Analysis of Traditional and Contemporary Gospel Music," in *More Than Dancing: Essays on Afro-American Music and Musicians,* ed. Irene V. Jackson (Westport, Conn.: Greenwood Press, 1985), 85.

12. Darden, *People Get Ready,* 281.

13. In Gospel parlance, the term "quartet" refers generally to a small group of indeterminate number singing in harmony, rather than specifically denoting a group of four members. Thus the term can designate a quintet or even a sextet. The term's emphasis is on function rather than form. See Kip Lornell, *Happy in the Service of the Lord: African-American Sacred Vocal Harmony Quartets in Memphis,* 2nd ed. (Knoxville: University of Tennessee Press, 1995), 49.

14. For a comprehensive treatment of the disparities in financial, human, and social capital between African Americans and Euro-Americans see the exhaustive appendix in Brooks, *Racial Justice.*

15. W. E. B. DuBois, *The Souls of Black Folk* (New York: Vintage Books, 1990; originally published in 1903), 180–90; James Weldon Johnson and J. Rosamond Johnson, *The Books of American Negro Spirituals* (New York: Da Capo Press, 1973; originally published as two separate volumes in 1925 and 1926); LeRoi Jones (Amiri Baraka), *Blues People: Negro Music in White America* (New York: Morrow, 1963); Walker, *Somebody's Calling My Name;* James H. Cone, *The Spirituals and the Blues* (Maryknoll, N.Y.: Orbis Books, 1991); Bernice Johnson Reagon, ed., *We'll Understand It Better By and By: Pioneering African American Gospel Composers* (Washington, D.C.: Smithsonian, 1992). Also see the important essays in Bernard Katz, ed., *The Social Implications of Early Negro Music in the United States* (New York: Arno Press, 1969).

16. Walker, *Somebody's Calling My Name,* 43.

17. In biblical criticism the German term *Sitz im Leben* can be roughly translated as "life situation" or "setting in life," which is how we render the notion throughout this book. In other words, every text has a context that helps to shape its meaning.

18. See Terry Eagleton, *Ideology* (London: Verso, 1991), 19–196. Also see Michel Foucault, *Power/Knowledge,* ed. Colin Gordon (New York: Pantheon, 1980), 195.

19. See Margaret Wetherell and Jonathan Potter, *Mapping the Language of Racism: Discourse and the Legitimation of Exploitation* (New York: Columbia University Press, 1992), 85; and Fredric Jameson, *The Political Unconscious: Narrative as a Socially Symbolic Act* (Ithaca, N.Y.: Cornell University Press, 1981), 84.

20. See James C. Scott, *Domination and the Arts of Resistance* (New Haven, Conn.: Yale University Press, 1990), ix–16.

21. Frederick Douglass, *The Life and Times of Frederick Douglass* (New York: Collier, [1885] 1962), 99.

22. Mikhail Bahktin, *The Dialogic Imagination: Four Essays,* ed. Michael Holquist (Austin: University of Texas Press, 1981), 352.

23. Gwendolin Sims Warren, *Ev'ry Time I Feel the Spirit* (New York: Henry Holt, 1997), 16.

24. Quoted in Raboteau, *Slave Religion,* 249

25. Ibid., 248.

26. See Scott, *Domination,* 108–53.

27. See Antonio Gramsci, *Selections from the Prison Notebooks* (New York: International, 1971), 5–23; and Joseph Femia, *Gramsci's Political Thought: Hegemony, Consciousness, and the Revolutionary Process* (Oxford: Clarendon, 1987), 44–45.

28. Theophus Smith, *Conjuring Culture: Biblical Formations of Black America* (New York: Oxford: University Press, 1994), 62–68. Cf. Werner Sollors, *Beyond Ethnicity: Consent and Descent in American Culture* (New York: Oxford University Press, 1986).

29. Smith, *Conjuring Culture,* 7.

30. Raboteau, *Slave Religion,* 311.

31. Wendel Phillips Whalum, "Black Hymnody," *Review and Expositor* 70, no. 3 (Summer 1973): 342.

32. A moral economy is a constellation of ethics and values that guides and drives social relations in a particular social group. See James C. Scott, *The Moral Economy of the Peasant: Rebellion and Subsistence in Southeast Asia* (New Haven, Conn.: Yale University Press, 1976).

33. For alienation, see Karl Marx, *Economic and Philosophic Manuscripts of 1844* (Buffalo, N.Y.: Prometheus Books, 1988), 69–84. For a succinct treatment see Tom Bottomore, ed., *A Dictionary of Marxist Thought,* 2nd ed. (Cambridge: Basil Blackwell, 1991), 11–17.

34. B. B. King, *Blues All around Me: The Autobiography of B. B. King* (New York: Avon, 1996), 57. The extreme importance of agrarian labor to the self-definition of the smallholder is reflected in greater depth in the testimony of the eponymous African American peasant activist in Theodore Rosengarten, *All God's Dangers: The Life of Nate Shaw* (New York: Knopf, 1975).

35. Quoted in Isabel Wilkerson, *The Warmth of Other Suns* (New York: Random House, 2010), 97.

36. Ibid.

37. DuBois, *Souls of Black Folk,* 188.

38. David Walker, *Appeal in Four Articles* (Salem, N.H.: Ayer, 1989; originally published in 1829), 80.

39. Quoted in Anthony Heilbut, *The Gospel Sound,* rev. ed. (New York: Limelight, 1997), 27. This has proved to be an important resource, particularly for the study of the culture of Gospel music.

40. Ibid., 35.

41. Mahalia Jackson, *Movin' On Up* (New York: Hawthorne, 1966), 72.

42. Heilbut, *Gospel Sound,* 7.

43. Levine, *Black Culture,* 175.

44. Horace Clarence Boyer, "Charles Albert Tindley: Progenitor of African American Gospel Music," in Reagon, *We'll Understand It Better*, 53.

45. For an exploration of the meanings and modes of expression of apocalyptic, see John J. Collins, *The Apocalyptic Imagination* (New York: Crossroad, 1989).

46. Reverend Charles Walker, "Lucie E. Campbell Williams: A Cultural Biography," in Reagon, *Understand It Better*, 129–30.

47. This kind of moral judgment is reflected, for instance, in the unyielding refusal of the insurrectionist Denmark Vesey to include "house n[egroes]" among his co-conspirators. See David Robertson, *Denmark Vesey* (New York: Knopf, 1999), 70.

48. Quoted in Heilbut, *Gospel Sound*, 17.

49. Quoted in ibid., 35.

50. See Phillips Verner Bradford and Harvey Blume, *Ota Benga: The Pygmy in the Zoo* (New York: St. Martin's Press, 1992).

51. Heilbut, *Gospel Sound*, 35.

52. Luvenia A. George, "Lucie E. Campbell: Her Nurturing and Expansion of Gospel Music in the National Baptist Convention, U.S.A., Inc.," in Reagon, *We'll Understand It Better*, 116–17.

53. Michael Eric Dyson, *Between God and Gangsta Rap* (New York: Oxford, 1996), 60–61. Here Dyson uses "Cook," the original spelling of the singer's name before it was changed for show business purposes.

54. Lornell, *Happy in the Service of the Lord*, 141.

55. Ibid., 143.

56. Reagon, "Herbert Brewster: Rememberings," *We'll Understand It Better*, 201.

57. Heilbut, *Gospel Sound*, 17.

58. See note 33 above.

59. Quoted in George F. Will, review of Robert Kanigel, *The One Best Way: Frederick Winslow Taylor and the Enigma of Efficiency* in the *New York Times Sunday Book Review*, June 15, 1997.

60. Ibid.

61. Karl Evanzz, *The Messenger: The Rise and Fall of Elijah Muhammad* (New York: Pantheon, 1999), 55.

62. Melvin I. Urofsky, *Louis D. Brandeis* (New York: Pantheon, 2009), 61.

63. Heilbut, *Gospel Sound*, 17.

64. See note 13.

65. George, "Campbell," in Reagon, *We'll Understand It Better*, 126.

66. Quoted in Heilbut, *Gospel Sound*, 49.

67. Ibid., 121.

68. Ibid., 48.

69. In some of her recordings Tharpe sounds eerily reminiscent of the seminal Depression-era Delta bluesman Robert Johnson, particularly in her classically bluesy "Nobody's Fault but Mine." Interestingly, this song mentions neither God nor Jesus, although it does mention prayer. For comparison, consider "Robert Johnson: The Complete Recordings" (Columbia/Legacy C2K 64916). For further information on Johnson, an important figure in black music in his own right, see, in addition to the

accompanying liner notes, Robert Guralnick, *Searching for Robert Johnson* (New York: Plume/Penguin, 1989). Also see Gayle F. Wald, *Shout, Sister, Shout: The Untold Story of Rock-and-Roll Trailblazer Sister Rosetta Tharpe* (New York: Beacon, 2007).

70. Heilbut, *Gospel Sound,* 105.

71. Ibid., 145.

72. Heilbut, *Gospel Sound,* 116.

73. Thomas A. Dorsey, "Ministry of Music in the Church," ed. Kenneth Morris, *Improving the Music in the Church* (Chicago: Martin and Morris, 1949), 42.

74. Heilbut, *Gospel Sound,* 104.

75. Ibid., 117.

76. Aretha Franklin, *Aretha: From These Roots* (New York: Villard, 1999), 220.

77. "Bobby Jones Gospel" first aired on January 27, 1980.

78. Quoted in Warren, *Ev'ry Time,* 270.

79. Karl Marx and Friedrich Engels, *On Religion* (New York: Schocken Books, 1964), 42.

80. Frank Breeden quoted in Janelle Carter, "Rocking the Flock: More Churches Using Professional Musicians," *Dayton Daily News,* September 4, 1999.

81. Kirk Franklin, *Church Boy: My Music and My Life* (Nashville: Word Publishing, 1998), 21.

82. See Light, "Say Amen, Somebody."

83. Ibid.

84. Kirk Franklin, *The Blueprint* (New York: Gotham, 2010).

Chapter 2:
The Grapes of Wrath and the True Vine

1. See Herodotus, *The Landmark Herodotus,* ed. Robert B. Strassler (New York: Anchor, 2007).

2. My emphasis. All references are from Thucydides, *History of the Peloponnesian War,* trans. Rex Warner (New York: Penguin, 1972), 47.

3. Ibid., 48.

4. Quoted in G. E. M. de Ste. Croix, *The Origins of the Peloponnesian War* (Ithaca, N.Y., Cornell University Press, 1972), 33.

5. Ibid., 122.

6. Ibid.

7. Thucydides, *The Peloponnesian War,* 1.138.3.

8. John Dominic Crossan takes another view. He argues that because of Nazareth's proximity to the Hellenized city of Sepphoris, "the village or hamlet of Nazareth, while certainly off the beaten track, was not very far off a well beaten track." See John Dominic Crossan, *The Historical Jesus: The Life of a Mediterranean Jewish Peasant* (San Francisco: HarperSanFrancisco, 1991), 15–19.

9. In his discussion of the Great Fire of Rome in 64 C.E. Tacitus (c. 56–c. 114), using the Latinized Greek translation of "messiah," writes of a "Chrestus" who "suffered the extreme penalty" (*Annals,* 15.44). Suetonius (69–140 C.E.) mentions a "Chrestus" who instigated disturbances that resulted in the expulsion of Jews from

Rome (*Lives of the Twelve Caesars*). In a letter to the Emperor Trajan about 112 C.E.,
Pliny the Younger (c. 61–c. 112), the provincial governor of Pontus and Bithynia,
explains how to deal with Christians — those who refused to worship the emperor and
worshiped "Christus" instead (*Letters* 10.96–97). Two disputed passages in Josephus'
Antiquities of the Jews mention Jesus by name. In 18.3.3 (known as the *Testimonium
Flavianum*) he calls Jesus "the Christ"; and he mentions Jesus in his brief discussion
of James, whom he identifies as "the brother of Jesus, who was called the Christ"
(20.9.1). Since Origen's time doubt has been cast on the authenticity of the first
Josephan passage. Most scholars accord some degree of authenticity to the second.

10. Gayatri Spivak and Ranajit Guha, eds., *Subaltern Studies* (Oxford: Oxford
University Press, 1988), 35.

11. Bruce J. Malina, *The New Testament World: Insights from Cultural Anthropology* (Louisville: Westminster John Knox, 1981) and *Christian Origins and Cultural
Anthropology* (Louisville: Westminster John Knox, 1986).

12. Fernando Belo, *A Materialist Reading of the Gospel of Mark* (Maryknoll, N.Y.:
Orbis Books, 1981).

13. Michel Clevenot, *Materialist Approaches to the Bible* (Maryknoll, N.Y.: Orbis
Books, 1985).

14. Ched Myers, *Binding the Strong Man* (Maryknoll, N.Y.: Orbis Books, 1984).

15. Itumeleng J. Mosala, *Biblical Hermeneutics and Black Theology in South Africa*
(Grand Rapids, Mich.: Eerdmans, 1989).

16. Gerd Theissen, *Sociology of Early Palestinian Christianity* (Philadelphia: Fortress, 1978).

17. Richard A. Horsley, *Sociology and the Jesus Movement* (New York: Crossroad,
1989).

18. John Dominic Crossan, *The Historical Jesus* (San Francisco: HarperSan-
Francisco, 1991).

19. John P. Meier, *A Marginal Jew: Rethinking the Historical Jesus* (New York:
Doubleday, 1991).

20. Kenneth E. Bailey, *Poet and Peasant* (Grand Rapids, Mich.: Eerdmans, 1976)
and *Through Peasant Eyes* (Grand Rapids, Mich.: Eerdmans, 1980).

21. Norman Gottwald and Richard A. Horsley, eds,. *The Bible and Liberation:
Political and Social Hermeneutics* (Maryknoll, N.Y.: Orbis Books, 1993).

22. Janice Capel Anderson and Stephen D. Moore, eds., *Mark and Method: New
Approaches in Biblical Studies* (Minneapolis: Fortress, 2006).

23. Erich Auerbach, *Mimesis: the Representation of Reality in Western Literature*,
trans. Willard R. Trask (Princeton, N.J.: Princeton University Press, 1953), 42.

24. Ibid., 47.

25. See Richard A. Horsley, *The Liberation of Christmas* (Eugene, Ore.: Wipf &
Stock, 2006; originally published in 1993), 101–6.

26. Luke 6:20; Matt. 5:14; 25:45.

27. Robert Redfield, *Peasant Society and Culture* (Chicago: University of Chicago
Press, 1960), 41–42.

28. James C. Scott, "Protest and Profanation: Agrarian Revolt and the Little Tradition," *Theory and Society* 2 (1977): 211.

29. Richard A. Horsley, "Ethics and Exegesis: 'Love Your Enemies' and the Doctrine of Non-Violence," *Journal of the American Academy of Religion* 54 (1986): 23, my emphasis.

30. Micah's status as an outsider to the corridors of elite priestly power is reflected in: (1) the fact that the addressees of his prophetic oracles are the rulers of Israel, to whose discursive practices he vociferously objects with the fervor of an opponent, not the corrective sensibilities of a colleague (e.g., Micah 3:1) and (2) his designation as "the Morashite" (Micah 1:1), which, by identifying him with a small village, specifically situates him outside the ministrations of the power center of Jerusalem. For alternative opinions of Micah's social status, see Francis I. Anderson and David Noel Freedman, *Micah*, Anchor Bible Series (New York: Doubleday, 2000), 108–10.

31. See Martin Goodman, *The Ruling Class of Judea* (Cambridge: Cambridge University Press, 1987), 57–58.

32. Josephus, *The Jewish War*, 2.427.

33. Richard A. Horsley, *Bandits Prophets, and Messiahs: Popular Movements in the Time of Jesus* (San Francisco: Harper & Row, 1988), 190–243.

34. See Mosala, *Biblical Hermeneutics, 118–22.*

35. See Frantz Fanon, *The Wretched of the Earth,* trans. Constance Farrington (New York: Grove, 1963), 249–310.

36. In July 2010 Glen Beck devoted an entire segment of his Fox News Network program to an ill-informed attack on black liberation theology and its founder, Dr. James Cone, the Charles Augustus Briggs Distinguished Professor of Systematic Theology at Union Theological Seminary in New York City.

37. Here I exercise my author's prerogative to refuse to dignify this silly book—and the whole silly genre it represents—by citing its full title. I think this is a judgment that is appropriate and that should be exercised whenever one is faced with foolishness masquerading as journalism or scholarship that seeks only to mislead and destroy.

38. Ernesto Cardenal, *The Gospel in Solentiname,* vol. 1, trans. Donald D. Walsh (Maryknoll, N.Y.: Orbis Books, 2000; originally published separately in 1976).

39. Ibid., xi.

40. James C. Scott, *The Moral Economy of the Peasant* (New Haven, Conn.: Yale University Press, 1976), 157–92.

41. See note 8 above.

42. This term comes from Judith Fetterley's classic work of feminist reader-response criticism, *The Resisting Reader: A Feminist Approach to American Fiction* (Bloomington: Indiana University Press, 1978).

43. Teodore Shanin, *Peasant and Peasant Societies* (New York: Penguin, 1971), 14–15

44. See Jonathan Walton, *Watch This!* (New York: New York University Press, 2009); and Sarah Posner, *God's Profits* (LaVergne, Tenn.: Polipoint, 2008).

45. For instance, see A. N. Sherwin-White's classic, *Roman Society and Roman Law in the New Testament* (Oxford: Oxford University Press, 1963), 139.

46. For this reading see William Herzog, *Parables as Subversive Speech* (Philadelphia: Westminster John Knox, 1994), 79–97; and my *The Politics of Jesus* (New York: Doubleday, 2006), 133–44.

47. See Ched Myers, *Binding the Strong Man* (Maryknoll, N.Y.: Orbis Books, 1984), 320–23; and Hendricks, *Politics of Jesus,* 121–22.

48. See Hendricks, *Politics of Jesus,* 101–12.

49. Douglas Oakman, *Jesus and the Economic Questions of His Day* (Lewiston, N.Y.: Edwin Mellen 1986), 57–62.

50. Cited in Louise Schottroff and Wolfgang Stegemann, *Jesus and the Hope of the Poor,* trans. Matthew J. O'Connell (Maryknoll, N.Y.: Orbis Books, 1986), 41. See A. Ben-David, *Talmudische Okonomie* (Hildesheim: George Olms, 1974).

51. R. H. Tawney, *Land and Labor in China* (Boston: Beacon, 1966; originally published in 1932), 77.

52. Salo Wittmayer Baron, *A Social and Religious History of the Jews,* rev. ed., vol. 1 (New York: Columbia University Press, 1958), 279–80.

53. E. P. Sanders, *Judaism: Practice and Belief, 63 B.C.E.–66 C.E.* (London: SCM, 1992), 149.

54. See Emil Schurer, *The History of the Jewish People in the Time of Jesus Christ,* rev. ed. (Edinburgh: T.&T. Clark, 1973), 257–74.

55. See Jacob Neusner, *Judaism in the Beginning of Christianity* (Philadelphia: Augsburg Fortress, 1984), 22.

56. See Gerd Theissen, *The Shadow of the Galilean* (Philadelphia: Fortress, 1987), 68–69, 204, n.8

57. See Horsley, *Bandits, Prophets, and Messiahs,* 48–87.

58. See G. E. M. de Ste. Croix, *The Class Struggle in the Ancient Greek World: From the Archaic Age to the Arab Conquests* (Ithaca, N.Y.: Cornell University Press, 1981), 18.

59. James C. Scott, *Domination and the Arts of Resistance* (New Haven, Conn.: Yale University Press, 1990), 158.

60. Roland de Vaux, *Ancient Israel: Its Life and Institutions,* trans. John McHugh (New York: McGraw-Hill, 1961), 328. However Ezekiel 5:5 does call Jerusalem "the center of the nations" and Ezekiel 38:12 calls Jerusalem the "navel" (Hebrew, *tabbur*) of the earth. But numerous biblical texts either reject or bring into question the notion of the Jerusalem Temple as the center of earth and the rightful center of humanity's reverence and obedience. Those texts include 1 Samuel 7:5–7, Jeremiah 35:2ff., and Acts 7:48. Some scholars also include Psalms 40, 50, and 51. See Paul Hanson, *The Dawn of Apocalyptic* (Philadelphia: Fortress, 1979), 169.

61. See the Mishnaic tractate *Kelim* 1:6–9.

62. Geza Vermes, *Jesus the Jew* (Philadelphia: Fortress, 1981), 52–53.

63. See W. F. Albright, *The Archaeology of Palestine* (Baltimore: Penguin, 1961), 244. Also Vermes, *Jesus the Jew,* 53–54; 190–91; 261, n. 144.

64. See Alfred Edersheim, *The Life and Times of Jesus the Messiah* (Grand Rapids, Mich.: Eerdmans, 1971), 225–26.

65. These sentiments occur in at least two tractates or chapters of the Babylonian Talmud: *Megillat* (24b) and *Erubin* (63b).

66. Quoted in Aharon Oppenheimer, *The 'Am Ha-Aretz,* trans. I. H. Levine (Leiden: E. J. Brill, 1977), 76.

67. L. E. Elliott-Binns, *Galilean Christianity* (London: SCM, 1956), 26.

68. See Richard A. Horsley, *Galilee: History, Politics, People* (Valley Forge, Pa.: Trinity Press International, 1995), 144–46.

69. Quoted from the Jerusalem Talmud tractate *Shabbat* (15d) in Vermes, *Jesus the Jew,* 57.

70. Mishnah tractate *Aboth* (2:5).

71. Quoted in Oppenheimer, *The 'Am Ha-Aretz,* 173.

72. Ibid., 176.

73. Ibid.

74. Ibid., 170.

75. Sean Freyne, *Galilee from Alexander the Great to Hadrian 323 B.C.E. to 135 C.E.* (Edinburgh: T.&T. Clark, 1980), 199.

76. Pierre Bourdieu, *Theory of an Outline of Practice,* trans. Richard Nice (Cambridge: Cambridge University Press, 1977), 18.

77. See Goodman, *The Ruling Class of Judea,* 51–75, N.B. 57.

78. *Life of Josephus,* 63, 80.

79. *Antiquities of the Jews* 20: 205, 207.

80. *The Jewish War* 6:300–310.

81. Although we have seen that the biblical vine imagery can represent both Israel in general and the priests in particular, Jesus would necessarily have intended to contrast himself with the Jerusalem priesthood. It would have made no sense for him to contrast himself with all of Israel.

82. Ramsay MacMullen, "Peasants during the Principate," *Aufsteig und Niedergang der Romischen Welt II* 1 (1974): 257.

83. For a classic treatment of the genres of the New Testament writings in relation to their Greco-Roman environment, see David Aune, *The New Testament in Its Literary Environment* (Philadelphia: Westminster, 1987).

84. In anthropology and other fields, a thick description of a human behavior is one that explains not just the behavior itself, but its context as well, such that the behavior becomes meaningful to an outsider. See Clifford Geertz, "Thick Description: Toward an Interpretive Theory of Culture," *The Interpretation of Cultures: Selected Essays* (New York: Basic Books, 1973), 3–30.

85. John Steinbeck, *The Grapes of Wrath* (New York: Penguin, 2006; originally published in 1939), xxvi. All citations are from the 2006 Penguin Classics edition.

86. Ibid., xxxi.

87. Ibid., xxxiii.

88. Ibid., xxxi.

89. Ibid., xl.

90. For an extended exploration of the peasant class affinities of the writer of the Gospel of John, see Obery M. Hendricks, Jr., "A Discourse of Domination: A

Socio-rhetorical Study of the Use of Ioudaios in the Fourth Gospel" (unpublished doctoral dissertation, the Department of Religion, Princeton University).

91. Ibid., 190.

92. Timothy Egan, *The Worst Hard Time* (New York: Houghton Mifflin, 2006), 235. The glaring capitalization is in the original.

93. Steinbeck, *Grapes of Wrath*, 221.

94. Freyne, *Galilee from Alexander the Great to Hadrian*.

95. Steinbeck, *Grapes of Wrath*, 307.

96. Ibid., 288.

97. See James C. Scott, *The Moral Economy of the Peasant: Rebellion and Subsistence in Southeast Asia* (New Haven, Conn.: Yale University Press, 1976), 157–92.

98. Ibid., 81.

99. See Hendricks, *Politics of Jesus*, 132–44.

Chapter 3:
A Camel through the Eye of a Needle (Part 1)

1. Stephen Mansfield, *The Faith of George W. Bush* (New York: Tarcher/Penguin, 2003), 109.

2. Arnon Regular, *Haaretz.com*, June 24, 2003.

3. "Bush Quietly Meets with Amish Here," *Lancaster New Era*, July 16, 2004.

4. Quoted in "DeLay Targets Legal System in Schiavo Case," Associated Press, March 31, 2005. Apparently DeLay soon came to doubt that conservative partisans' actions in the Schiavo case really did have God's seal of approval. After the release of a poll showing that the grand gestures and pronouncements of DeLay and his conservative colleagues were not profiting them politically, their righteously indignant voices suddenly fell silent. DeLay resigned from Congress in 2005 after being indicted for criminal charges, including money laundering for the purpose of funding several 2003 Texas GOP congressional candidates. He was convicted of money laundering and conspiracy to commit money laundering by a Texas jury in November 2010, and in January 2011 he was sentenced to three years in prison.

5. Lisa Miller, "How Sarah Palin Is Reshaping the Religious Right," *Newsweek*, June 11, 2010.

6. Bruce Lincoln, *Holy Terrors* (Chicago: University of Chicago Press, 2002), 20. Also see Kevin Phillips, *Wealth and Democracy* (New York: Basic Books, 2002), 205–8. In a related development, Chris Hedges, *American Fascists* (New York: Free Press, 2008), 13–20, describes a process he calls "logocide," in which the "old definitions of words are replaced by new ones.... Code words of the old belief system are deconstructed and assigned diametrically opposed meanings." Thus liberty, for instance, is not about political freedom, for Christian right-wingers, but about obedience to right-wing Christian interpretations of the Bible.

7. This bias is explored at length by John Isbister, *Capitalism and Justice* (West Hartford, Conn.: Kumarian Press, 2001). For an evangelical Christian perspective that reaches different albeit questionable conclusions, see Craig M. Gay, *With Liberty and Justice for Whom? The Recent Evangelical Debate over Capitalism* (Vancouver: Regent

College Publishing, 2000) and Wayne Grudem, *Politics According to the Bible* (Grand Rapids, Mich.: Zondervan, 2010), 301–4.

8. The term "laissez faire" was coined by the Physiocrats, eighteenth-century French economists who believed that the wealth of nations was derived solely from the value of land, whether used for agriculture or developed for other uses. It differed from earlier schools of economic thought, particularly the prevalent Mercantilists, who focused on the rulers' wealth, specifically rulers' accumulation of gold, and on the balance of trade, as the basis of economic activity.

9. Jeffrey Tucker, "Are Antitrust Laws Immoral?" *Journal of Markets and Morality* (Spring 1998): 75–82

10. See Kim Phillips-Fein, *Invisible Hands: The Business Crusade against the New Deal* (New York: W. W. Norton, 2009), 73. Fifield was also a virulent racist who called voices protesting the Daughters of the American Revolution's race-based exclusion of the African American operatic contralto Marion Anderson from Constitution Hall, "an abomination unto the Lord." This is a fascinating study of the history of political conservatism in the twentieth century.

11. Falwell was a major player in conservative political circles. In a 2005 interview he bragged about the influence of the Council for National Policy that he co-founded with Tim LaHaye, co-author of the best-selling apocalyptic *Left Behind* novels: "Ronald Reagan, both George Bushes . . . you name it. There's nobody who hasn't been here. . . . We often call the White House and Karl Rove while we are meeting. Everyone takes our calls." Quoted in Craig Unger, "American Rapture," *Vanity Fair,* December 2005. Also see Obery M. Hendricks, Jr., *The Politics of Jesus: Rediscovering the True Revolutionary Nature of Jesus' Teachings and How They Have Been Corrupted* (New York: Doubleday, 2006), 250.

12. Quoted in Phillips-Fein, *Invisible Hands,* 229.

13. Grudem, *Politics According to the Bible,* esp. 274–309. Grudem's engagement of politics and economic issues is wide ranging. Unfortunately, his use of the Bible is flat-footed and completely lacking in the degree of crucial cultural and anthropological nuance and contextualization needed for his work to be fully credible.

14. See Jill Lepore, "The Commandments," *New Yorker,* January 17, 2011.

15. Cheney refused to divulge any information about the proceedings of those meetings, including the names of attendees, even when ordered to by the U.S. Congress. To this day not one bit of information from those meetings has ever been released. See Michael Weisskopf and Adam Zagorin, "Getting the Ear of Dick Cheney," *Time.com,* February 3, 2002.

16. According to Josh Israel et al., "John Boehner: A Pro-Business Agenda," *The Center for Public Integrity,* June 9, 2010, "Boehner's career has been marked by aggressive support of business interests. He has backed the U.S. Chamber of Commerce's position 93 percent of the time through his Congressional career. The AFL-CIO says he voted against their interests on every vote he cast in 2008 and 2009, and, as of 2008, backed the labor coalition just 5 percent of the time over his career."

17. Brian Montopoli, "Darrell Issa Asks Businesses Which Regulations Should Be Killed," *cbsnews.com,* January 4, 2011.

18. David Callahan, *Fortunes of Change* (New York: Wiley, 2010), 43.

19. Quoted in ibid., 44.

20. Phillips, *Wealth and Democracy.*

21. See my *The Politics of Jesus,* 256–62, for a brief survey of the often out-rageous charges and scurrilous misinformation leveled at politically liberal policies, policymakers, and supporters.

22. "Letter of George Washington to the Roman Catholics of the United States, 1789," in *The Letters of George Washington,* vol. 12, ed. Jared Sparks (Boston: American Stationers Company, 1837), 178.

23. Robert Kuttner, "The Poverty of Neoliberalism," *American Prospect,* June 23, 1990.

24. For a fuller treatment of these issues see Alan Wolfe, *The Future of Liberalism* (New York: Knopf, 2009), 3–29.

25. Lionel Trilling, *The Liberal Imagination* (New York: New York Reviews Books, 2008; orig. 1950), xvi.

26. Russell Kirk, *The Conservative Mind* (New York: Henry C. Regnery, 1953).

27. Lee Edwards, "The Origins of the Modern American Conservative Move-ment," November 21, 2003, Heritage Lecture no. 811.

28. Lee Edwards, "Old School Ties," *Chronicle of Higher Education,* May 5, 2004.

29. See the book jacket of Kirk, *The Conservative Mind,* 7th ed.

30. In a 1963 article Kilpatrick submitted to the *Saturday Evening Post* entitled, "The Hell He Is Equal" (which, to its credit, the *Post* refused to print), he wrote, the "Negro race, as a race, is in fact an inferior race."

31. Quoted in Richard Goldstein, "James J. Kilpatrick, Conservative Voice in Print and on TV, Dies at 89," *New York Times,* August 16, 2010.

32. See the book jacket of Kirk, *The Conservative Mind,* 7th edition.

33. See Kirk, *The Conservative Mind,* 8–9.

34. John W. Dean, *Conservatives without Conscience* (New York: Viking, 2006), 7.

35. See Dan Gilgoff, *The Jesus Machine* (New York: St. Martin's Press, 2007).

36. Jacqueline L. Salmon, "Most Americans Believe in Higher Power, Poll Finds," *Washington Post,* June 24, 2008.

37. Indeed, historically conservatives have shown themselves perfectly willing to eschew gradual change and proceed with all due speed when it serves their interests. For example, conservative politicians of the 104th Congress called their 1994 "Contract with America" political plan "a revolution," and proceeded to implement it with all the urgency and haste that are typically associated with revolutionary intentions. Newt Gingrich, then Speaker of the House of Representatives, even said of himself and his fellow political conservatives, "We are the new revolutionaries."

38. Class is a slippery concept that is given to multiple meanings, from strictly material and economic considerations to stratified gradational social sensibilities. My understanding of class in this essay is a basic one. A class is a large group of people who occupy a similar economic position in society based on economic factors, such as income and wealth, and political factors, including their relation to power and author-ity and the degree to which they are able to have their material interests and concerns

acknowledged and addressed within the society's governmental structure. There are a number of social and cultural factors that could be included in my definition, ranging from gender to cultural authority to occupation to chronological age, but in this essay I specifically focus on economic and political criteria to keep from veering into a cul-de-sac of cultural anthropological questions, as well as to keep our gaze upon the economic nature of our subject. For the complexity and the fluidity of class as a concept, see Stanley Aronowitz, *How Class Works* (New Haven, Conn.: Yale University Press, 2003).

39. Kirk, *The Conservative Mind,* 8.

40. Egalitarianism can refer to (1) a political doctrine that holds that all people should be treated as equals and have in common the same political, economic, social, and civil rights; and to (2) a social philosophy advocating the leveling of economic inequalities among people. In this essay I exclusively refer to the political sense. See Lane Kenworthy, *Egalitarian Capitalism* (New York: Russell Sage Foundation, 2004), 1–4. Also see "Egalitarianism," *Stanford Encyclopedia of Philosophy.* See online *http://plato.stanford.edu/entries/egalitarianism/.*

41. Friedrich von Hayek, *The Road to Serfdom* (Chicago: University of Chicago Press, 2007; originally published in 1941).

42. See Steven Horwitz, "Say's Law of Markets: An Austrian Appreciation," *Two Hundred Years of Say's Law,* ed. Steven Kates (Westhampton, Mass.: Edward Elgar Publishing, 2003), 82–98.

43. Jean-Baptiste Say, *A Treatise on Political Economy* (New Brunswick, N.J.: Transaction Publishers, 2001; 1855), chapter 15.

44. See Jennifer Burns, *Goddess of the Market* (Oxford: Oxford University Press, 2009).

45. The following discussion is based upon Phillips-Fein, *Invisible Hands.*

46. Louis Hartz authored the acclaimed study of political liberalism, *The Liberal Tradition in America* (New York: Harcourt, Brace, 1955)

47. See Howard Zinn, *A People's History of the United States* (San Francisco: HarperCollins, 2003; originally published in 1980), 354–55.

48. See Philip Yale Nicolson, *Labor's Story in the United States* (Philadelphia: Temple University Press, 2004), 108–10, 163–64.

49. Phillips-Fein, *Invisible Hands,* 6.

50. George McGovern, *The Essential America* (New York: Simon and Schuster, 2004), 95.

51. Phillips, *Wealth and Democracy,* 220.

52. See H. W. Brands, *Traitor to His Class: The Privileged Life and Radical Presidency of Franklin Delano Roosevelt* (New York: Anchor, 2009).

53. Phillips, *Wealth and Democracy,* 220.

54. Quoted in James MacGregor Burns and Susan Dunn, *The Three Roosevelts* (New York: Grove Press, 2001), 126, 309.

55. Phillips-Fein, *Invisible Hand,* 20.

56. Ibid., 12.

57. Ibid.

58. The germane portion of Exodus 34:7 reads, "visiting the iniquity of the parents upon the children and the children's children, to the third and fourth generation."

59. Joseph Cummins, *Anything for a Vote* (Philadelphia: Quirk, 2007), 185.

60. "Koch Industries and Network of Republican Donors Plan Ahead," *New York Times,* October 20, 2010.

61. Ibid.

62. Newt Gingrich, *To Save America: Stopping Obama's Secular-Socialist Machine* (Washington, D.C.: Regnery, 2010), 42.

63. The propagandistic nature of Gingrich's treatment of the subject is also highlighted by his failure to acknowledge that socialism is not necessarily totalitarian. In fact, there are forms of socialism that are democratic, that is, they are ruled not by totalitarian regimes but by the democratic voting process. Examples are Nordic nations like Norway, Sweden, Finland, and Denmark, which are all democratically ruled and have median incomes close to the median income of the United States, yet all feature socialized welfare services. Denmark has a wide-reaching welfare system, which broadly redistributes wealth by ensuring that all Danes receive tax-funded socialized healthcare and unemployment insurance. Great Britain, our closest democratic ally, even has the Social Democratic Party as a major officially recognized political party. Incidentally, Norway, Sweden, Finland, and Denmark were found to have the happiest populations in a 2010 *Fortune* magazine survey. See *www.forbes.com/2010/07/14/world-happiest-countries-lifestyle-realestate-gallup-table.html.*

64. See Roger Lowenstein, "A Question of Numbers," *New York Times Magazine,* January 16, 2005; Jonathan Oberlander, *The Political Life of Medicare* (Chicago: University of Chicago Press, 2003); on Ronald Reagan, see Will Bunch, *Tear Down This Myth* (New York: Free Press, 2009), 59–61.

65. Archie Brown, *The Rise and Fall of Communism* (New York: HarperCollins, 2009). Brown goes beyond the writings of Karl Marx about the communistic workers' utopia he envisioned — which was for Marx not the means but the ultimate end of a long process of social change and political and economic reorientation — to also explore the various attempts to institute "Marxist" communism, most of which Marx himself probably would not recognize as being inspired by him.

66. Ibid., 105–14.

67. "GOP Rep: Pilgrims Knew 'Unbiblical' Socialism 'Wasn't Going to Work,'" *Huffington Post,* November 25, 2010; see online *http://thinkprogress.org/2010/11/25/todd-akin-pilgrims-socialism/.*

68. Michael Newman, *Socialism: A Very Short Introduction* (Oxford: Oxford University Press, 2005), 1–15.

69. Peter Irons, *A People's History of the Supreme Court* (New York: Penguin, 1999), 238.

70. John Maynard Keynes, *The General Theory of Employment, Interest and Money* (New York: Palgrave Macmillan, 2007; originally published in 1936).

71. Fredrich von Hayek, *The Road to Serfdom* (Chicago: University of Chicago Press, 2007; originally published in 1941).

72. Hayek's later works include *Individualism and Economic Order* (Chicago: University of Chicago Press, 1948); *The Constitution of Liberty* (Chicago: University of Chicago Press, 1960); *Law, Legislation and Liberty* (Chicago: University of Chicago Press, 1973–79, 3 vols.); *The Fatal Conceit: The Errors of Socialism* (Chicago: University of Chicago Press, 1988; the content of the book was heavily influenced by William Warren Bartley). The books that preceded *The Road to Serfdom* (Chicago: University of Chicago Press, 1944) include *Monetary Theory and the Trade Cycle* (London: Jonathan Cape, 1933); *Prices and Production* (London, G. Routledge & Sons 1931); *Profits, Interest and Investment: And Other Essays on the Theory of Industrial Fluctuations* (London: Routledge, 1939).

73. Quoted at *www.glennbeck.com/content/articles/article/198/41653/*.

74. Jennifer Schuessler, "Hayek: The Back Story," *New York Times,* July 9, 2010.

75. Ibid.

76. Paul Samuelson, "A Few Remembrances of Friedrich von Hayek (1899–1992)," *Journal of Economic Behavior and Organization* 69 (2009): 1–4.

77. The biblical concept of the kingdom of God is based upon the Hebrew notion of *malkuth shamayim* ("sole sovereignty of the heavens," i.e., of God). It is both a religious and a political principle. It is religious in that it is a fundamental statement of the uncompromising monotheistic faith of Israel (see Deut. 6:4). It is political in that with monotheism comes the recognition that no form of human domination or exploitation is to be recognized as legitimate. In the New Testament, the kingdom of God (*basileia tou theou*, Greek) as a political principle appears in bold relief in several instances, most notably in the Lord's Prayer (Matt. 6:10; cf. Luke 11:2). See my *Politics of Jesus,* 19–23.

78. Quoted in John Dominic Crossan, *The Historical Jesus* (New York: Harper, 1991), 278.

79. See Bernard Brandon Scott, *Hear Then the Parable* (Philadelphia: Fortress, 1989), 380.

80. This meaning of the phrase is attested in Matthew 6:26: "Look at the birds of the air; they neither sow nor reap nor gather into barns."

81. To be landless in an agrarian setting is, with few exceptions, to be poor.

82. For a basic survey of the ways distributive justice is understood and applied see Michael Sandel, *Justice* (New York: FSG, 2009). For more in-depth treatment, see John Rawls, *A Theory of Justice* (Cambridge, Mass.: Belnap, 2006; originally published in 1971); Amartya Sen, *The Idea of Justice* (Cambridge, Mass.: Belnap, 2009); Nicolas Wolterstorff, *Justice* (Princeton, N.J.: Princeton University Press, 2008); and Michael Waltzer, *Spheres of Justice* (New York: Basic Books, 1983). A challenge to distributive justice as a fully effective category for social inquiry is offered by Iris Marion Young, *Justice and the Politics of Difference* (Princeton, N.J.: Princeton University Press, 1990).

83. However, Rawls was a devout Christian in his early life. This can be seen in his 1942 senior undergraduate thesis at Princeton University, "A Brief Inquiry into the Meaning of Sin and Faith," which was rediscovered in 2006 by Eric Gregory, a professor in the religion department at Princeton, in that institution's archives, where it had languished since Rawls's graduation. See John Rawls et al., *A Brief Inquiry into*

the Meaning of Sin and Faith: With "On My Religion" (Cambridge, Mass.: Harvard University Press, 2010). Also see Eric Gregory, "Before the Original Position: The Neo-Orthodox Theology of the Young John Rawls," *Journal of Religious Ethics* 35, no. 2 (2007): 179–206.

84. John Rawls, *A Theory of Justice* (Cambridge, Mass.: Belnap, 2006; originally published in 1971). The political journalist Howard Fineman offers this lucid laymen's summary of *A Theory of Justice:* "The essence of his vision was simple enough: that the best government was one that distributed liberty and wealth equally with greatest efficiency, providing 'fair equality of opportunity' for all, especially for the disadvantaged. It was okay, in other words, to distribute benefits unequally if the poorest and weakest benefited disproportionately. Any society could be judged — should only be judged — by how well it treated the most vulnerable of its members." See Howard Fineman, The *Thirteen American Arguments* (New York: Random House, 2008), 93.

85. See Sharon Ringe, *Jesus, Liberation, and the Biblical Jubilee* (Philadelphia: Fortress, 1985), 36–45; and John Howard Yoder, *The Politics of Jesus* (Grand Rapids, Mich.: Eerdmans, 1972), 34–77.

86. David A. Fiensy, *The Social History of Palestine in the Herodian Period* (Lewiston, N.Y.: Mellen, 1991), 8–9; emphasis added. The classic treatment of the Jubilee is Robert North, S.J., *Sociology of the Biblical Jubilee* (Rome: Pontifical Biblical Institute, 1954). Also see John S. Bergsma, *The Jubilee from Leviticus to Qumran* (Leiden: Brill, 2007) and Eric Nelson, *The Hebrew Republic* (Cambridge: Harvard University, 2010), 64–87.

87. In the West those who have taken the economic teachings of Jesus seriously range from Thomas Aquinas (1225–74), one of the most influential of all Christian thinkers, and his principal commentator, Cardinal Tommaso Cajetan (1469–1534), to the fifteenth century Hutterite Anabaptists and certain later Anabaptist offshoots, to Walter Rauschenbusch (1861–1918) and the Social Gospel movement in early twentieth-century America. A contemporary example is Habitat for Humanity International, a Christian organization founded in 1967, which builds affordable housing for those in need while charging no interest on its mortgage loans. Its official website calls its mortgage policy, "the economics of Jesus," which it describes as "people act[ing] in response to human need, giving what they have without seeking profit or interest."

88. See Bruce J. Malina, *The New Testament World: Insights from Cultural Anthropology* (Louisville: Westminster John Knox, 2001), 89–90.

89. Aristotle, *Politics* III, 9 1256b, Loeb Classic Library.

90. George M. Foster, "Peasant Society and the Image of Limited Good," *American Anthropologist* 67, no. 2 (1965): 293–315.

91. They were *virtually* powerless, but not completely so. See James C. Scott's discussions of subtle and hidden forms of resistance in his seminal texts, *Weapons of the Weak* (New Haven, Conn.: Yale University Press, 1987) and *Domination and the Arts of Resistance* (New Haven, Conn.: Yale University Press, 1992).

92. Bruce J. Malina, *The Social Gospel of Jesus* (Minneapolis: Fortress, 2001), 106–7.

93. Quoted in ibid, 106.

94. Ibid.

95. Ibid., 167–68. Also see Halvor Moxnes, *The Economy of the Kingdom* (Philadelphia: Fortress, 1988), 75–98.

96. James, the brother of Jesus, was a real historical personage. Josephus mentions him in *Antiquities of the Jews,* 20:9. However, there is no historical evidence to support the claim that the author of this letter is the same James. James (*Ya'aqov,* Hebrew; *Iakobos,* Greek), was a popular name in first-century Israel.

97. See the discussion of linguistic collocation in Malina, *Social Gospel,* 98–100.

98. Ibid., 99.

99. A. N. Sherwin-White, *Roman Society and Roman Law in the New Testament* (Oxford: Oxford University Press, 1963), 139.

100. See Richard A. Horsley, *Jesus and the Spiral of Violence* (San Francisco: Harper, 1987); and Douglas E. Oakman, *Jesus and the Economic Questions of His Day* (Lewiston: Maine: Edwin Mellen, 1986). Also see the wide-ranging Marxist analysis of issues of class, poverty, and wealth in late antiquity in de Ste. Croix, *The Class Struggle.*

101. *The Life of Flavius Josephus,* 1f; *Antiquities of the Jews,* 16.187.

102. Harold Hoehner, *Herod Antipas* (Cambridge: Cambridge University Press, 1972), 52–53. Also see Oakman, *Jesus,* 70.

103. Wealth was so concentrated that every first-century mansion that has been excavated in the Judean environs is located in Jerusalem. Outside of Jerusalem none has been found within twenty-five miles, and then with nothing approaching Jerusalem's concentration. Many of those are seasonal residences. See Goodman, *Ruling Class,* 55.

104. B. Golomb and Y. Kedar, "Ancient Agriculture in the Galilee Mountains," *Israel Exploration Journal* (1971): 138, place the average acreage of an enclosed field in Galilee at about four acres. Martin Goodman, *State and Society in Roman Galilee, A.D. 132–212* (Totowa, N.J.: Rowman & Allanheld, 1983), 35, extrapolates a figure of 2.5 hectares (6.175 acres) from a survey of farm sizes in first-century Western Samaria. He also notes a text quoted by Eusebius that asserts that two kinsmen of Jesus possessed 4.78 hectares (11.78 acres) for two families.

105. Fiensy, *Social History,* 24.

106. Ibid., 23.

107. For instance Mark 12:1–10; Matt. 20:1–16; and Luke 9:9–18.

108. See Goodman, *Ruling Class,* 57.

109. Fiensy, *Social History.* 78–79.

110. Goodman, *Ruling Class,* 55.

111. See Joachim Jeremias, *Jerusalem in the Time of Jesus* (Philadelphia: Fortress, 1962), 92–99.

112. See Gerhard E. Lenski, *Power and Privilege* (Chapel Hill: University of North Carolina Press, 1984), 283.

113. See Gerd Theissen, *The Shadow of the Galilean* (Philadelphia: Fortress, 1987), 68–69; 204 n8.

114. See Lev. 19:13; Deut. 24:51f; Job 7:1f, 14:6; Mal. 3:4; Sir. 34:27.

238

115. Felix Gryglewicz, "The Gospel of Worked Workers," *Catholic Biblical Quarterly* 19 (1957): 191.

116. Fiensy, *Social History,* 89.

117. David Mealand, *Poverty and Expectation in the Gospels* (London: SPCK, 1980), 6.

118. See in the Mishnah Peah 5:6 and Maas. 2:7–8.

119. See Schottroff and Stegemann, *Jesus and the Hope of the Poor,* 41; Fiensy, *Social History,* 88–89; Oakman, *Jesus,* 57–60.

120. John Kenneth Galbraith, *The Affluent Society* (New York: Houghton Mifflin, 1958), 1–2.

121. These include the excoriations of the priests and their scribe and Pharisee retainers in Matthew 23 and numerous instances in the Gospel of John. Jesus' *ego eimi* sayings (Greek for "*I* am") in John's Gospel consistently characterize Jesus as replacing the major religious rituals and institutions of Israel, including the hereditary priesthood. For example, as we saw in chapter 2, in John 15:1–4 Jesus declares that he is the "true vine" who has made "clean" or "pure" (*kathoros,* Greek) those in his hearing, which is an unmistakable usurpation of the priests' defining function of restoring supplicants to ritual purity through the medium of ritual sacrifice, thus thoroughly delegitimating their authority.

122. Representative passages include Matt. 19:21–24; Luke 1:51–52; 12:15–21; 18:24.

123. Warren Carter, *Matthew and the Margins* (Maryknoll, N.Y.: Orbis Books, 2001), 263.

124. See Exod. 20, Deut. 5, and Josh. 24.

125. The Law Codes consist of three different biblical passages: the Book of the Covenant (Exod. 20:22 to 23:33), which is the oldest of the codes, having originated while Israel was still a confederacy governed by a council; the Deuteronomic Code (Deut. 12–16), which was codified about 772 B.C.; and the Holiness Code (Lev. 17–26), which originated sometime before or immediately after the conquest of Jerusalem by the Babylonians in 587 B.C.

126. Abraham Joshua Heschel, *The Prophets* (Peabody, Mass.: Hendrickson, 2009; originally published in 1962).

127. Quoted in ibid., 167.

128. Ibid.

129. Leslie J. Hoppe, *Being Poor: A Biblical Study* (Wilmington, Del.: Michael Glazier, 1987), 87.

130. Parenthetically, for his part Jesus went further than the teachings of the Hebrew Bible in his echoing of the Old Testament prescriptions for social and economic equity: in his narrated practices and pronouncements he makes no distinction between the rights of women and men. In fact, some scholars have argued that the Jesus movement actually fostered alternative, non-patriarchal familial arrangements. See Elisabeth Schüssler Fiorenza, *In Memory of Her: A Feminist Reconstruction of Christian Origins* (New York: Crossroad, 1983).

Chapter 4:
A Camel through the Eye of a Needle (Part II)

1. Emmanuel Saez, "Striking It Richer: The Evolution of Top Incomes in the United States" (updated with 2007 estimates), August 5, 2009, *http://elsa.berkeley.edu /~saez/saez-UStopincomes-2007.pdf.*

2. Jacob S. Hacker and Paul Pierson, *Winner-Take-All Politics* (New York: Simon & Schuster, 2010), 15–17.

3. The simple designation "upper class," meaning the upper quintile of earners, will not suffice because one can live well on several hundred thousand dollars of income, but that does not represent inordinate economic power. Moreover, the incomes of most members of the upper class or top income quintile are consumed by lifestyles and living expenses, with most of their accumulated wealth concentrated in their primary residences.

4. This is explored in fascinating detail in David Callahan, *Fortunes of Change: The Rise of the Liberal Rich and the Making of America* (Hoboken, N.J.: Wiley, 2010).

5. Urban Institute–Brookings Institution Tax Center Policy, "The Tax Policy Briefing Book: A Citizen's Guide for the 2008 Election and Beyond," 15. See online *www.taxpolicycenter.org/briefing-book/background/bush-tax-cuts/ignore.cfm.*

6. Milton Friedman and Anna Jacobson Scwartz, *Monetary History of the United States, 1867–1960* (Princeton, N.J.: Princeton University Press, 1971).

7. Paul Krugman, "Who Was Milton Friedman?" *New York Review of Books,* February 15, 2007.

8. Quoted in Paul Krugman, "Glorifying the Gilded Age," *New York Times,* February 20, 2009. Norton Garfinkle, *The American Dream vs. the Gospel of Wealth* (New Haven, Conn.: Yale University Press, 2006), 54, in an assessment that is probably much closer to the historical record, describes the Gilded Age magnates that Friedman apotheosizes as "crude, allegedly self-made railroad magnates who absorbed millions in government loans and then exacted monopoly-like control over the communities that grew up along their rail lines."

9. Quoted in Michael Hirsh, *Capital Offense* (New York: Wiley, 2010), 30.

10. Krugman, "Who Was Milton Friedman?"

11. Jean-Baptiste Say, *A Treatise on Political Economy* (New Brunswick, N.J.: Transaction Publishers, 2001 [1855]), chap. 15.

12. Political conservatives derive the vaunted notion of an "invisible hand" that guides markets with an almost mystical efficiency, thus legitimating their laissez faire principles, from Adam Smith's 1776 classic in economic thought, *An Inquiry into the Nature and Causes of the Wealth of Nations.* However, in the one million or so words Smith published in his lifetime, the phrase "invisible hand" appears only three times, and none of those occurrences have anything to do with free markets. Nor does the term "laissez faire" appear in his work. In fact, Smith's writings indicate that he was by no means a doctrinaire laissez faire free marketer. In *The Wealth of Nations* he approves restraints on trade, export subsidies and restrictions, compulsory qualifications for craftsmen, and limits on interest rates. As Nobel economist Joseph Stiglitz puts it, "the reason Adam Smith's invisible hand had often seemed invisible was that it was

not there." Joseph E. Stiglitz, "Learning How the Economy Really Works," *Harvard Business Review Agenda* (2011): 25.

13. Walter Heller, *New Dimensions of Political Economy* (New York: Norton, 1966), 9.

14. Lawrence Summers was riffing on this headline when he declared after Milton Friedman's death, "We are all Friedmanites now."

15. Jude Wanniski, "The Mundell-Laffer Hypothesis — A New View of the World Economy," *Public Interest* (Spring 1975): 49.

16. Arthur B. Laffer, *The End of Prosperity* (New York: Simon and Schuster, 2008), 32.

17. Quoted in D. M. Giangreco and Kathryn Moore, eds., *Dear Harry... Truman's Mailroom, 1945–1953* (Mechanicsburg, Pa.: Stackpole, 1999), 6.

18. Sean Wilentz, *The Age of Reagan* (New York: Harper, 2008), 146–47.

19. George Gilder, *Wealth and Poverty* (New York: Basic Books, 1981), 63.

20. Quoted in William Grieder, "The Education of David Stockman," *Atlantic* (December 1981): 27.

21. John Kenneth Galbraith, *The Affluent Society* (New York: Houghton Mifflin, 1958), 68.

22. Laffer, *The End of Prosperity,* 40.

23. James K. Galbraith, *The Predator State* (New York: Free Press, 2008), 27.

24. See Sheila Collins, *Let Them Eat Ketchup!* (New York: Monthly Review, 1996), 112.

25. See Robert S. McIntyre and Robert Folen, Citizens for Tax Justice, *Corporate Income Taxes in the Reagan Years: A Study of Three Years of Legalized Tax Avoidance* (Washington, D.C.: Citizens for Tax Justice, 1984).

26. Hacker and Pierson, *Winner-Take-All Politics,* 16.

27. Ibid., 16–17.

28. Ibid., 3; emphasis added.

29. N. Gregory Mankiw, *Macroeconomics,* 3rd ed. (New York: Worth, 1997).

30. See Paul R. Krugman, *Peddling Prosperity: Economic Sense and Nonsense in the Age of Diminished Expectations* (New York: W. W. Norton, 1994), 115–17.

31. That is why, according to Nobel laureate economist Paul Krugman, "Supply-side doctrine, which claimed without evidence that tax cuts would pay for themselves, never got any traction in the world of professional economic research, even among conservatives." See Paul Krugman, *Conscience of a Liberal* (New York: W. W. Norton, 2007), 119. For a defense of supply-side principles by one of its architects, see Laffer, *The End of Prosperity.* For perhaps the most comprehensive scholarly treatment in support of supply-side economics, see Brian Domitrovic, *Econoclasts* (Wilmington, Del.: ISI, 2009).

32. Quoted in Sidney Blumenthal, *The Rise of the Counter-Establishment* (New York: Harper & Row, 1988), 195.

33. Ibid., 171.

34. Jude Wanniski, "There Went Out a Decree from Caesar," *Wall Street Journal,* November 9, 1981.

35. Irving Kristol, "American Conservatism, 1965–1995," *Public Interest* (Fall 1995): 80–96.

36. Jude Wanniski, *The Way the World Works,* 4th ed. (Washington, D.C.: Regnery, 1998), xv;. emphasis added. Wanniski's messianic assessment of his role is revealed in his use of the New Testament term "good news." Wanniski's book should not be judged by this hubris alone, however. Actually it is a serious study. The conservative political commentator Robert D. Novak hailed it as "one of the most influential pieces of political writing of the post–World War II era." The noted economist Arthur Laffer called it "the best book on economics ever written." It has not been taken seriously outside the circle of Wanniski's supply-side partisans, however.

37. See Howard Zinn, *Passionate Declarations: Essays on War and Justice* (New York: Harper, 2003), 149.

38. Quoted in Krugman, *Conscience of a Liberal,* 105.

39. "Reagan Raps Press on Botulism Quote," *Los Angeles Times,* March 14, 1974.

40. See "Backtalk: Hey Jude," *Mother Jones,* February 1997.

41. George F. Will, "The Cultural Contradictions of Conservatism," American Enterprise Institute for Public Policy, public address, December 6, 1995.

42. Steven Greenhouse, "Union Membership Up Sharply in 2008, Report Says," *New York Times,* January 29, 2009.

43. The consistency of this conservative approach is seen in the June 2011 proposal of ex-Minnesota governor and major conservative presidential candidate Tim Pawlenty to slash corporate tax rates from 35 percent to 15 percent — more than half — and to abolish all taxes on dividends, investments, capital gains and estates, all of which benefit the richest Americans in vast disproportion.

44. Janny Scott and David Leonhardt, "Class in America: Shadowy Lines That Still Divide," *New York Times,* May 15, 2005.

45. Thomas Sowell, *Intellectuals and Society* (New York: Basic Books, 2009), 36–41.

46. Hacker and Pierson, *Winner-Take-All Politics,* 29.

47. Ibid., 28–29.

48. For instance, see Michael W. Cox and Richard Alm, *Myths of Rich and Poor* (New York: Basic Books, 2000).

49. Economic Policy Institute, "The State of Working America, 2006/2007," 1, executive summary.

50. The data that follow are from Ross Gregory Douthat, *Privilege: Harvard and the Education of the Ruling Class* (New York: Hyperion, 2004), 50–51.

51. Callahan, *Fortunes of Change,* 24.

52. The report, "Trends in College Spending 1998–2008," is discussed in Sam Dillon, "Share of College Spending for Recreation is Rising," *New York Times,* July 8, 2010.

53. David Cay Johnston, "Most Taxpayers Get Little Help from Latest Bush Tax Plan," *New York Times,* April 8, 2001.

54. Howard Gleckman, "Death, Taxes and George W. Bush," *Bloomberg Businessweek,* February 8, 2006.

55. Public Citizen's Congress Watch, *Spending Millions to Save Billions: The Campaign of the Super Wealthy to Kill the Estate Tax* (April 2006): 11–14.

56. Ibid., 8.

57. Ibid., 25.

58. Paul Sullivan, "Estate Tax Will Return Next Year, but Few Will Pay It," *New York Times,* December 17, 2010.

59. Howard Zinn, *A People's History of the United States* (New York: Harper, 2003), 261.

60. See Marvin D. Felt and Marvin J. Holosko, *Health and Poverty* (Binghamton, N.Y.: Haworth Press, 1997), 49–64; J. D. Kasper, "Effects of Poverty and Family Stress over Three Decades on the Functional Status of Older African American Women," *Journals of Gerontology,* Series B, Psychological Sciences and Social Sciences, 63, no. 4 (July 2008): S201–S210; and Kevin Drum, "Poverty and Stress," *Mother Jones,* April 5, 2009.

61. Quoted in Janny Scott, "Life at the Top in America Isn't Just Better, It's Longer," *New York Times,* May 16, 2005.

62. Quoted in Cass R. Sunstein, *The Second Bill of Rights: FDR's Unfinished Revolution and Why We Need It More Than Ever* (New York: Basic Books, 2004), 13. Also see my *The Politics of Jesus* (New York: Doubleday, 2006), 306–7.

63. See Richard Wolffe, *Revival* (New York: Crown, 2010), 9–25.

64. "Democracy for Sale," *The Nation,* November 1, 2010.

65. Sowell, *Intellectuals and Society,* 50.

66. Ibid.

67. Ibid., 35.

68. Isaiah 5:8.

69. According to Robert D. Putnam and David. E. Campbell, *American Grace* (New York: Simon & Schuster, 2010), 379–73, "Roughly 70 percent of highly religious evangelical Protestants and Mormons identify as Republicans, with highly religious mainline Protestants right behind at 62 percent."

70. For a journalist's view of the Tea Party phenomenon, see Kate Zernicke, *Boiling Mad: Inside Tea Party America* (New York: Times Books, 2010). For a relatively sophisticated insider's perspective, see John M. O'Hara, *A New American Tea Party* (New York: Wiley, 2010).

71. Such a treatment would include an exploration of various approaches to the role and meaning of hegemony and discourse, including the works of such seminal thinkers as Antonio Gramsci on the bifurcation of hegemony into the cultural and political spheres in *Prison Notebooks* (New York: International Publishers, 1971), and the examination of the Ideological State Apparatus in Louis Althusser, *For Marx* (New York: Pantheon, 1959). Also worthy of consideration is Michel Foucault's notion of the discursive manufacture of a subject whose "acceptance" of interests and definitions of discourses of power exceeds even consent, as it is articulated in texts including *Power/Knowledge* (New York: Pantheon, 1980). Not to be overlooked are the signal insights of the cognitive scientist George Lakoff in works including *Thinking Points* (New York: FSG, 2006) and *The Political Mind* (New York: Penguin, 2009). For an

extended non-academic treatment of this question, see Thomas Frank, *What's the Matter with Kansas? How Conservatives Won the Heart of America* (New York: Metropolitan, 2004).

72. Dinesh D'Souza, *The Roots of Obama's Rage* (Washington, D.C.: Regnery, 2010).

73. Dinesh D'Souza, *The End of Racism* (New York: Free Press, 1995).

74. D'Souza, *The Roots of Obama's Rage*, 198.

75. See "James T. Kloppenberg Discusses His Reading Obama," *New York Times,* October 28, 2010.

76. Quoted in David Ricci, *The Transformation of American Politics* (New Haven, Conn.: Yale University Press, 1993), 171.

77. National Committee for Responsive Philanthropy, *Moving a Public Policy Agenda,* July 1997, 20.

78. See Jeff Krehely, et al., *Axis of Ideology: Conservative Foundations and Public Policy* (Washington, D.C.: National Committee for Responsive Philosophy, 2004), 20–21.

79. For instance, legitimate, if idealized political rulership is suggested by Isaiah 16:5: "then a throne shall be established in civility [*chesed*] in the tent of David, and on it shall sit in truth [*emet*] a ruler who seeks justice [*mishpat*] and seeks to do what's right [*sadiqah*]." And see the admonition for those in power that is pronounced by Zechariah 8:16: "Render [*'emet*] truth and peaceful [or perfect] justice [*mishpat*] in your gates." See Moshe Weinfeld, *Social Justice in Ancient Israel and in the Ancient Near East* (Jerusalem: Magnes Press, 1995), 25–74.

80. Quoted in Kim Phillips-Fein, *Invisible Hands: The Business Crusade against the New Deal* (New York: W. W. Norton, 2009), 11.

81. Ibid., 10.

82. Ibid., 71.

83. See Krehely, *Axis of Ideology,* 40.

84. Phillips-Fein, *Invisible Hands,* 73.

85. For a rigorous treatment of the role the ideal of heroic individualism plays in the perpetuation of social and economic inequality in American life, see William M. Epstein, *Democracy without Decency* (University Park, Pa.: Penn State University Press, 2009).

86. Basic definitions of these concepts are offered by Jacob Hacker and Paul Pierson, *Winner-Take-All Politics* (New York: Simon and Schuster, 2010), 54–55; and Krugman, *Conscience of a Liberal,* 251–56.

87. Ibid., 55. Hacker and Pierson base their observations on the insights of Karl Polanyi, *The Great Transformation* (Boston: Beacon Press, 1944).

88. This program was replaced in 1996 by Temporary Assistance to Needy Children (TANC), the Clinton administration's controversial "end of welfare as we know it," which, parenthetically, Senator Edward Kennedy characterized as "legislative child abuse."

89. Andrew Gold, "The Billionaire Party," *New York Magazine,* August 2, 2010, and Jane Mayer, "Covert Operations," *New Yorker,* August 30, 2010.

90. See Matt DeLong, "Tea Party Leader Expelled over Slavery Letter," *Washington Post,* July 18, 2010.

91. Alan Brinkley, "Anatomy of an Uprising," *New York Times Book Review,* October 10, 2010.

92. Carlos Dew, "The Nigger Show," *Religious Consultation* (December 2010).

93. Ibid. For a discussion of the nuances of the racial discourse of the Tea Party, see Paul Street and Anthony DiMaggio, *Crashing the Tea Party* (Boulder, Colo.: Paradigm, 2011), 75–99.

94. See Drew Armstrong, "Insurers Gave U.S. Chamber $86 Million Used to Oppose Obama's Health Law," *Bloomberg,* November 17, 2010.

95. Also see the interesting analysis of this in Frank, *What's the Matter with Kansas?* esp. 157–78.

96. Quoted in Kate Zernike, *Boiling Mad* (New York: Times Books, 2010), 8.

Chapter 6:
A Manifesto: Practicing the Politics of Jesus

1. See Kenneth L. Gentry, *God's Law in the Modern World* (Phillipsburg, N.J.: Presbyterian and Reformed, 1993).

2. John Suggs, "One Nation under God," *Mother Jones* (December 2005).

3. Gary North, "The Covenantal Wealth of Nations," *Biblical Economics Today* 21, no. 2 (February–March 1999).

4. Adolf Hitler, *My New Order: The Speeches of Adolf Hitler,* vol. 1 (New York: Reynal & Hitchcock, 1941), 871–72.

Index

Proposition 23 (California), 185–86
prosbul, 54–55
prosperity gospel, xv, 63–64, 196
Proverbs, book of, bourgeois didactic
  character of, 138
psalms, reflecting opposition to economic
  classism, 137
Public Interest, 161

Raboteau, Albert, 10, 11
racial antipathy, appeal to, 190–93
Rand, Ayn, 103
Rauschenbusch, Walter, 236n87
Rawls, John, 120
Reagan, Ronald, 93, 110, 146, 150, 159,
  190–91
  demonizing society's poorest, 154
  disdain of, for the poor, 162–63
  economic policies of, designed to serve
    the rich, 157–58
  as first supply-side president, 155
  policies of, adding to U.S. economic
    inequality, 165
Reaganomics, 146, 155, 157–58. *See also*
  supply-side economics
Reagon, Bernice Johnson, 7
reciprocity, 85–86
Redfield, Robert, 52
regulation, opposition to, 164–65
regulatory loopholes, 177
regulatory protections, divinely
  mandated, 137
religious leaders, claiming a status role,
  200
religious right
  controlling U.S. political discourse,
    xv–xvi
  lacking thoughtful analysis, 100
  shamelessly interpreting the Bible,
    xv–xvi
Republican Governors Association, 183
Republicans, 94–95
resistance
  discursive formation of, 7–8
  expressed in coded language, 8–10
resistance discourse, 7–8
resistance sensibilities, 37–38
resistant reading, 60–62
rich
  Jesus' concept of, 126–28
  in Jesus' setting, 128–30
riches, accumulation of, 124–25

right-wing politicians, controlling U.S.
  political discourse, xv–xvi
Rise and Fall of Communism, The
  (Brown), 110
Road to Serfdom, The (Hayek), 102–3,
  113–14, 183
robber barons, Friedman's praise of, 149
Robertson, Pat, 100
Rogers, Will, 156
Roosevelt, Eleanor, 81
Roosevelt, Franklin D., 81, 93, 104,
  106–8, 163–64, 175, 185
Roots of Obama's Rage, The (D'Souza),
  183

Sabbath, as weekly enactment of radical
  equality, 134–35
sabbatical year, 54–55, 134
sadiqah, 208, 210
Samuelson, Paul, 114, 148–49
Sanders, E. P., 65
Say, Jean-Baptiste, 102–3, 151
Say's Law, 102–3, 150, 151–52, 155–56
Scaife, Richard Mellon, 182
Schiavo, Terry, 89–90
Schlesinger, Arthur, 153
Schumer, Charles, 95
Schwartz, Anna Jacobson, 148
Scott, James C., 11, 52, 67
Shanin, Teodore, 63
Sherwin-White, A. N., 128
Sinclair, Upton, 78
Single Path, The (Fifield), 93
slaves
  agrarian labor of, offering sense of
    possibility, 13
  eschatological hopes of, 14–15
  freeing of, biblical mandate for, 134
  redefining biblical events, 11–12
Smallwood, Richard, 38–39
Smith, Adam, 150, 151, 239–40n12
Smith, Theophus, 11
social Darwinism, 188–89
social history, "new" approach to, 47
socialism, origins of, 111–12
social marginalization, in first-century
  Israel, 66–67
Social Security, conservative attacks on,
  109–10
soloists, in Gospel music, 29–30
Solow, Robert, 160
Soul Stirrers, 23–24, 30
Soul Train, 31